More Praise for *Smart but Stuck*

"*Smart but Stuck* will help you get unstuck! Drawing upon a lifetime of clinical experience, Tom Brown once again strikes gold in this practical, authoritative, and, above all, helpful book. No matter where you are in your journey to success, if you have ADHD this book will help to speed you on your way. I could not recommend it more highly."
—**Edward (Ned) Hallowell, M.D.,** author, *Driven to Distraction* and *Delivered from Distraction*

"This is an exceptionally important book for those coping with ADHD and family members who care about them. It addresses a much overlooked component of the disorder—the importance of emotions. Clearly written, rich in detail, and full of helpful advice, this book will be beneficial to anyone with ADHD and to those who struggle to live with, understand, and help them."
—**Russell A. Barkley, Ph.D.,** clinical professor, psychiatry and pediatrics, Medical University of South Carolina; author, *Taking Charge of ADHD* and *Taking Charge of Adult ADHD*

"This book, reflecting Dr. Brown's 35 years of clinical practice combined with the latest findings from affective neuroscience, is a must-read for anyone who is interested in ADHD."
—**James J. Gross, Ph.D.,** professor, psychology, Stanford University; editor, *Handbook of Emotion Regulation*

"Dr. Brown introduces a forgotten piece in the life of those suffering from ADHD: the role of emotions. He provides an integrative and easy-to-understand view of how executive functioning impairments interact with emotional control in ADHD. He also offers thoughtful strategies to minimize the impact of these impairments."
—**Luis Augusto Rohde, M.D., Ph.D.,** president, World Federation of ADHD; professor, psychiatry, Federal University of Rio Grande do Sul, Brazil

"These engaging vignettes vividly bring to life emotional difficulties that, even for very intelligent teens and adults, can lead to frustration and failure in efforts to overcome their deficits in attention, organization, and motivation. Here Tom Brown combines a reader-friendly summary of relevant research with his clinical expertise in helping people with ADHD to get on track to success."

— **Mina K. Dulcan, M.D.,** professor of psychiatry, behavioral sciences and pediatrics, Ann & Robert H. Lurie Children's Hospital of Chicago and Northwestern University Feinberg School of Medicine

smart but stuck

emotions in teens and adults with ADHD

thomas e. brown, ph.d.

JB JOSSEY-BASS™

A Wiley Brand

Cover design by Jeff Puda
Cover image © PM Images | Getty

Published by Jossey-Bass
A Wiley Brand
One Montgomery Street, Suite 1200, San Francisco, CA 94104-4594—www.josseybass.com

Jossey-Bass books and products are available through most bookstores. To contact Jossey-Bass directly call our Customer Care Department within the U.S. at 800-956-7739, outside the U.S. at 317-572-3986, or fax 317-572-4002.

Wiley publishes in a variety of print and electronic formats and by print-on-demand. Some material included with standard print versions of this book may not be included in e-books or in print-on-demand. If this book refers to media such as a CD or DVD that is not included in the version you purchased, you may download this material at http://booksupport.wiley.com. For more information about Wiley products, visit www.wiley.com.

Library of Congress Cataloging-in-Publication Data has been applied for and is on file with the Library of Congress.

ISBN 978-1-118-27928-1 (cloth); ISBN 978-1-118-41975-5 (ebk); ISBN 978-1-118-42176-5 (ebk)

Printed in the United States of America
FIRST EDITION
HB Printing   10 9 8 7 6 5 4 3 2 1

contents

A new understanding of ADHD and emotions; why emotions can be so troubling in the lives of those with ADHD; how the ADHD brain processes emotions differently; the influences of temperament and experiences on emotions and motivations.

"I'm in a great university where I want to do well, but I just can't get myself motivated to do the work. I did really well in high school; now my grades have tanked. I've been spending too much time hanging out with my girlfriend and smoking weed. I've tried some ADHD medicines, but they make me too jittery."
—20-year-old university student

"My parents always taught me that I have an obligation to behave and achieve in ways that would not bring shame on my family. When I failed out of college, they helped me prepare to try again. I wanted very much to do it, but on that critical day when I was supposed to start the last two courses I needed to get readmitted, I was too afraid to walk in the classroom door."
—22-year-old university student

the author

Thomas E. Brown, Ph.D., is a clinical psychologist, assistant clinical professor of psychiatry at Yale University School of Medicine, and associate director of the Yale Clinic for Attention and Related Disorders. His award-winning book *Attention Deficit Disorder: The Unfocused Mind in Children and Adults* (Yale University Press, 2005) has been published in seven languages. He developed the Brown Attention Deficit Disorder Scales (PsychCorp/Pearson) and has published numerous articles in professional journals. His past books include *ADHD Comorbidities: Handbook of ADHD Complications in Children and Adults* (American Psychiatric Press, 2009) and *A New Understanding of ADHD in Children and Adults: Executive Function Impairments* (Routledge, 2013). To learn more, go to www.drthomasebrown.com.

acknowledgments

Impetus for this book was sparked in a conversation I had several years ago with my son, Dave, while we were hiking a small mountain called Sleeping Giant. He asked what I considered to be the biggest missing piece in the current understanding of ADHD. My answer was "the importance of emotions." After I explained what I meant, Dave insisted: "You've got to make that your next book, and you have to explain it with real-life stories of patients so people will catch on!" Dave read and offered helpful comments on my initial draft of each chapter. I am deeply grateful for his nudging encouragement and love.

My administrative assistant, Lisa Dziuba, and my research assistant, Ryan Kennedy, have both contributed by assisting with countless details of organizing, checking, and preparing the manuscript as well as by helping me remain organized throughout the process of working on this project while I was also attending each day to a full schedule of caring for patients.

I am grateful also for the continuing love and support of Bobbie, my beloved wife, the light of my life. Thanks too to Liza, Abel, Nancy, Noah, and Simone, for their love, enthusiasm, and encouragement, which enrich my life.

Strong encouragement and much helpful guidance to render this book more readable have been provided generously by Margie McAneny, my editor at Jossey-Bass/Wiley. Thanks also to

Tracy Gallagher for her assistance with permissions, Pat Stacey for additional helpful edits and suggestions, Michele Jones for her very careful copyediting, and Joanne Clapp Fullagar for thoughtfully guiding the book through production.

Above all, I am deeply grateful to my patients—the children, adolescents, and adults who have trusted me with exploring their stories and have helped me learn of the subtle complexities of ADHD and the multiple intertwined and often conflicted emotions that can get any of us stuck—and can keep all of us going.

Thomas E. Brown
January 2014

introduction

All information processing is emotional . . . emotion is the energy level
that drives, organizes, amplifies and attenuates cognitive activity.
—KENNETH DODGE, NEUROSCIENTIST

Although the scientific understanding of ADHD has changed
dramatically over the past decade, most people affected by this
disorder—and many who diagnose and treat them—have not yet
had the opportunity to gain a clear, up-to-date understanding of this
complex condition. As you'll read in the chapters that follow, ADHD is
not a simple problem of misbehavior, lack of willpower, or inability to
focus attention. In this collection of true stories about extremely bright
teenagers and adults, you'll find multiple examples of the ways that
ADHD can cause even very intelligent individuals to experience chronic
frustration and failure, which gets them "stuck" in their schooling or
work and many other aspects of daily life. Fortunately, in most cases it's
possible for a person with ADHD to get unstuck, and in these pages
you'll find numerous examples showing how effective treatment has
helped those suffering from ADHD to get back on track.

> NOTE: Throughout this book, the term *ADHD* is used to refer
> to the disorder currently understood as Attention Deficit/Hyper-
> activity Disorder (ADHD) and/or Attention Deficit Disorder (ADD).

1

Clinical and neuroscience research has revealed that ADHD is essentially a complex set of dynamically interacting impairments of the brain's management system, otherwise known as its "executive functions." These functions involve a number of critical operations of the brain, including the abilities to

- Get organized and get started on tasks
- Focus on tasks and shift focus from one task to another when needed
- Regulate sleep and alertness, sustain effort, and process information efficiently
- Manage frustration and modulate emotions
- Utilize working memory and access recall
- Monitor and self-regulate action

Everyone has trouble with these functions from time to time, but people with ADHD have much more difficulty with them than do their same-age peers. (I offer more detailed descriptions of these various executive functions in Chapter One.)

○ the missing link: emotions

Despite progress made in ADHD research, one element has been lacking in most current descriptions of the disorder: the critical role played by emotions in every one of the executive functions. This book describes that missing piece. In 1996, neuroscientist Joseph LeDoux published *The Emotional Brain*, a book highlighting evidence of the central importance of emotion in the brain's cognitive functioning. He emphasized that emotions — mostly unconscious emotions — are powerful and critically important motivators of human thought and actions.[1] This understanding of the essential role of emotion in all aspects of human behavior has not yet been integrated into current thinking about ADHD.

We must recognize the critical role of emotions, both positive and negative, in initiating and prioritizing tasks, sustaining or shifting interest and effort, holding thoughts in active memory, and choosing to engage in or avoid a task or situation.

To fully understand the role of emotions in ADHD, we must not only recognize that those with the disorder often have a hard time managing how they express their emotions but also acknowledge the critical role that emotions, both positive and negative, play in the executive functions: initiating and prioritizing tasks, sustaining or shifting interest and effort, holding thoughts in active memory, choosing to engage in or avoid a task or situation. As was observed by neuroscientist Kenneth Dodge, "All information processing is emotional . . . emotion is the energy level that drives, organizes, amplifies and attenuates cognitive activity."[2]

Emotions — sometimes conscious, more often unconscious — serve to motivate cognitive activity that shapes a person's experience and action. For those with ADHD, chronic problems with recognizing and responding to various emotions tend to be a primary factor in their difficulties with managing daily life.

The stories in this book highlight the role that various emotions, positive and negative, played in the struggles of some of my patients with ADHD. Some readers of these stories might think, "Oh, this is a person with ADHD and several other disorders — anxiety, depression, or OCD. Their emotional struggles are just part of those additional disorders, not ADHD." My response is that ADHD is not one silo of cognitive problems with another silo of emotional difficulties beside it. Problems with responding to and managing emotions are intimately, dynamically, and inextricably involved in ADHD.

Problems with responding to and managing emotions are intimately, dynamically, and inextricably involved in ADHD.

o   learning from patients and research

I am a clinical psychologist. For more than thirty-five years, I have spent most of my working hours talking with and listening to children, adolescents, and adults, most seeking help for problems related to ADHD. Many also have had additional difficulties with other problems involving emotions, learning, or behavior. My primary source of learning about ADHD has been the countless conversations with these patients — young and old alike — who shared with me ongoing stories of their struggles to recognize and overcome their attention impairments and to extricate themselves from feeling stuck in patterns of demoralizing frustration and failure. The stories in this book are based on my notes from conversations with some of these patients. All have been modified to protect the privacy of those involved, but the essential details of all are true.

Recently expanding research in neuroscience, psychology, and psychiatry has helped explain many puzzling facts reported by patients with ADHD, such as how they can focus and work energetically on a few favored activities, but simply can't get started or sustain enough effort for other activities that they know are important and want to do. In these pages, true stories of patients are intermingled with accessible explanations of research that will help you better understand each patient's struggles and the fuller nature of the relationship between ADHD and emotions.

One of my special interests over the years has been adolescents and adults who are especially bright. They have taught me that being smart is no protection from attention impairments. Not only is it possible for people with a high IQ to suffer from ADHD, but it's likely that they'll suffer longer without adequate support or treatment because the people in their lives assume, quite mistakenly, that anyone who is really smart can't suffer from ADHD.

Not only is it possible for people with a high IQ to suffer from ADHD, but it's likely that they'll suffer longer without adequate support or treatment because the people in their lives assume, quite mistakenly, that anyone who is really smart can't suffer from ADHD.

The patients I write about in this book are all extremely bright. They scored within the top 9 percent of the population on IQ tests, but they were stuck. They sought treatment because they were unable to get themselves out of chronically unproductive, self-defeating patterns of emotions, thought, and action. They felt trapped in their daily dealings with their education, their job, their relationships with others, or a combination of these. Their stories illustrate the persistent difficulties those with ADHD have in managing themselves and their emotions. Some are stories of amazing successes and impressive accomplishments; others are tales of ongoing frustration and tragic disappointment. Most are a mixed bag. Yet each story illuminates the complex role that emotions play in ADHD.

○ what you'll find in this book

Chapter One describes this new understanding of ADHD, drawing on the latest research findings by clinicians, researchers, and neuroscientists. Chapters Two through Twelve offer stories of real teenagers and adults with ADHD, highlighting their particular struggles with the disorder, with their emotions, and with related problems in their family or various other contexts. The final chapter summarizes some of the ways that emotions affect the life experiences of those with ADHD and what can be offered to appropriately support and treat those affected.

The stories that follow illustrate the limitations of diagnostic "pigeonholes." The individuals you'll read about in these pages can't be neatly categorized under one or several diagnoses. Each person is a unique and complex combination of interacting strengths and difficulties in each of the shifting contexts in which he or she lives. There is great diversity among people with ADHD as well as in the varied settings in which they encounter daily life.

In telling stories of these adolescents and adults, I have also shared some of my own reactions and challenges as I tried to provide the help they sought from me. Many of the stories are success stories. I share the resources and strategies that contributed to these successes. Several stories also illustrate the significant obstacles and struggles that some people with ADHD may experience.

Stories in this book also illustrate what we currently know about how ADHD changes—sometimes for the better, sometimes for the worse—as a person progresses into the increasing challenges of adolescence and adulthood. Each story describes medications and other treatments provided to these individuals to help in alleviating their ADHD impairments.

In none of these cases were medications alone sufficient to resolve the complex difficulties. For each of these patients, therapeutic success also depended on a therapeutic relationship with many therapeutic conversations. These were essential for assessing and understanding the nature and emotional complexities of his or her difficulties. The therapeutic relationship also was the vehicle for close collaboration to develop effective treatments, help the patient to make necessary changes in environment and lifestyle, repair damaged self-esteem, and work through the frustrations, stresses, and puzzlement that inevitably arise in interactions among patients, their family members, and their doctors.

The emotional conflicts and struggles these patients experience aren't unique to those with ADHD—nor are they unique to those who are exceptionally intelligent. You will probably recognize emotional pressures, conflicts, and struggles that aren't so different from your own or from those of your family and friends.

Throughout this book, I've tried to illustrate not only the weaknesses and struggles of those with ADHD and their families but also their impressive strengths and diverse talents. There is much to respect and admire in each of the people described in these pages.

1

ADHD and the emotional brain

Emotions, and struggles with and between various emotions, play a central role in the daily life of all children, adolescents, and adults. Emotions guide what we notice and what we ignore, what we focus on intently and what we carefully avoid. Conflicting emotions can cause us to disrupt engagement with a task we want to accomplish, or lead us repeatedly to do what we consciously intend never to do again. In many ways — sometimes recognized, sometimes not, subtly and powerfully — we are pushed and pulled by our emotions. Yet we also exercise some control over them: we try to distract ourselves from uncomfortable emotions; we choose how much we want our emotions to show in our words or actions; we talk to ourselves to try to tone down or jack up how noticeable our emotions are to others and to ourselves. We manage and are managed by the complexity of our emotions.

In my work as a clinical psychologist, I've seen that emotional struggles play an especially large role in the daily life of people with attention deficit disorders. The same chronic impairments that interfere with other aspects of their cognitive functioning also tend to interfere with their ability to manage and be adequately guided by their emotions. People with ADHD often suffer chronic difficulties in responding to and sustaining emotions that motivate them for important tasks.

Most people with ADHD experience the same frustrations, fears, sadness, pride, shame, excitement, and so on that spontaneously arise in everyone else in various situations. What is different is the chronic difficulty most people with this disorder experience in managing and responding to their emotions, particularly in the many situations where emotions are mixed and conflicting. As noted earlier, stories in this book illustrate the fact that being very smart does not prevent a person from struggling with these emotional problems, nor does it prevent having ADHD.

This book highlights the idea that emotions are linked to the brain. Often people think of emotion as distinct from the brain, as being "from the heart" or "in the gut," but these are metaphors that serve simply to suggest that emotions come from the depth of the person. The actual source of emotions is the brain.

The difficulties that people with ADHD have with emotions are similar to the problems they often have in prioritizing tasks, shifting focus, and utilizing working memory. While cleaning a room, they may get interested in some photos they pick up, soon becoming completely diverted from the job they had begun. While searching for some specific information online, they may notice a web page that draws them off the search they started and into a protracted investigation of something totally unrelated, derailing their original task. They may abandon a task they find boring, overlooking the fact that adequate and timely completion of this task is essential to gaining something they really want, and that failure to complete the task will inevitably bite them with a painful payback.

> People with ADHD report that momentary emotion often gobbles up all the space in their head, as a computer virus can gobble up all the space on a hard drive, crowding out other important feelings and thoughts.

In a similar way, many people with ADHD tend to get quickly flooded with frustration, enthusiasm, anger, affection, worry, boredom, discouragement, or other emotions, not keeping in mind and responding to related emotions also important to them. They may vent their momentary anger on a friend or family member with hurtful intensity that does not take into account that this is a person whom they love and do not want to hurt. People with ADHD report that momentary emotion often gobbles up all the space in their head, as a computer virus can gobble up all the space on a hard drive, crowding out other important feelings and thoughts.

○ "attentional bias"

Many with ADHD also report that they tend to have a lot of difficulty with *attentional bias*. They tend to be particularly alert and quick to notice any comments or actions that fit with the emotions that preoccupy them, often without paying much attention to the context or to other information that might provide a useful different view. Some seem to be constantly alert for signs of things to worry about; others are excessively alert for any signs of potential frustration or discouragement. They become too easily immersed in one especially salient emotion and tend to have chronic problems in shifting their focus to keep in mind other aspects of the situation that might call for a very different response. For example, someone hearing just a slight uncertainty in a coworker's reaction to a suggestion may interpret this as stubborn disapproval and quickly start arguing for his or her idea without listening adequately to understand the coworker's actual response. Attentional bias may fuel feelings of depression, anxiety, or argumentativeness or cause the person to lose interest in a particular goal.[1]

Watching Basketball Through a Telescope

For those with ADHD, life can be like trying to watch a basketball game through a telescope, which allows them to see only a small fragment of the action at any specific time. Sometimes that telescope stays too long on one part of the court, missing out completely on important events occurring elsewhere at the same time. At other times, the telescope may randomly flit from one

> bit of action to another, losing track of where the ball is and what various players are in a position to do. To follow what is going on in a basketball game, a person needs to be able to watch the whole court, noting movements of the ball and rapidly shifting positions of the players as they present multiple risks and opportunities in the game.

o the unacknowledged role of emotions in ADHD

Current diagnostic criteria for ADHD include no mention of problems with emotions, but those who live with this disorder and those who care for them know very well that problems with experiencing and managing emotions—interest, comfort, desire, anxiety, frustration, worry, disappointment, hurt, excitement, anger, pride, sadness, and shame, in various blends and sequences—play a critical role in their daily difficulties. Sometimes people with ADHD are unable to manage expression of these emotions; at other times, they have trouble experiencing and clearly recognizing emotions in themselves that can guide them in social interactions and fuel behaviors important for achieving longer-term goals.

Researchers have recently been challenging the omission of problems with emotional regulation in current diagnostic criteria for ADHD. For example, a team of European researchers studied more than a thousand children with ADHD and found that almost 75 percent demonstrated significantly more intense and frequent problems with low frustration tolerance, irritability, hot temper, sadness, and sudden mood shifts than non-ADHD children of the same age.[2]

A longitudinal study of over a hundred hyperactive children and a matched comparison group followed into young adulthood showed that those whose ADHD persisted into adulthood continued to have significantly more difficulties with low frustration tolerance, impatience, irritability, hot temper, and emotional excitability than the comparison group.

Such mood problems tend to persist into adulthood for many people with ADHD. A longitudinal study of over a hundred hyperactive children and a matched comparison group followed into young adulthood showed that those whose ADHD persisted into adulthood continued to have significantly more difficulties with low frustration tolerance, impatience, irritability, hot temper, and emotional excitability than the comparison group. Another study demonstrated that deficient self-regulation of these negative feelings is found in a subgroup of adults with ADHD, and also that this type of emotional dysregulation tends to occur with greater frequency among siblings of those affected adults.[3]

These recent studies have explored the role of emotions in ADHD, but most dealt exclusively with the combined type of ADHD, excluding those without hyperactive symptoms. Also, these studies have been focused primarily on difficulties in controlling negative emotions such as irritability and anger; they have neglected the role of emotions that are central to positive motivations, such as interest, enthusiasm, desire, pride, and pleasure. These studies also have not adequately explored anxiety, discouragement, stress, and hopelessness, which often compromise a person's motivation to act.

In a comprehensive review article, Russell Barkley, a leading researcher, has argued that "deficient emotional self-regulation" should be included in diagnostic criteria for ADHD and considered a core component of the disorder, though only for the combined subtype. His emphasis is on insufficient control of more negative, disruptive emotions:

ADHD creates a state in which the normal emotion-generating properties of the limbic system, and particularly the anger, frustration, and aggression-generating properties of the amygdala, are inadequately regulated by higher cortical functions. (p. 10)[4]

○ the problem of ignition and motivation

Thus far, researchers and clinicians have focused too much on how people with ADHD demonstrate problems in *putting the brakes* on expression of emotions. There hasn't been sufficient attention given to the emotional problems with *ignition* — chronic difficulties with getting started on necessary tasks and staying motivated to finish what needs to be done.

An important clue to understanding these problems with ignition in ADHD can be found in the most puzzling and frustrating fact about children, adolescents, and adults with attention deficit disorders: their symptoms are not consistent. A person's ADHD symptoms vary considerably from one situation to another, depending on the task or context in which he or she is operating and on the incentives involved. Despite their chronic problems with organizing themselves, getting started on tasks, and staying focused, all people with ADHD have a few activities in which they have no such problems. If you watch them while they engage in those activities, you would swear that they have no problem with attention at all.[5]

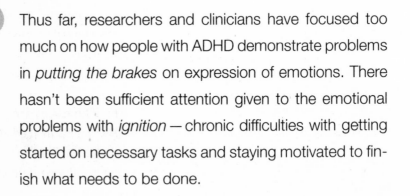

Thus far, researchers and clinicians have focused too much on how people with ADHD demonstrate problems in *putting the brakes* on expression of emotions. There hasn't been sufficient attention given to the emotional problems with *ignition* — chronic difficulties with getting started on necessary tasks and staying motivated to finish what needs to be done.

Typically each person with ADHD, young or old, is able to focus very well for a few activities in which he or she has strong personal interest. This might be playing a sport or video games, drawing or painting, repairing a car, playing music, or using Facebook. Yet for virtually all other activities and tasks, people with ADHD have extreme difficulty in achieving and maintaining focus, with the possible exception of situations where they expect a very immediate unpleasant consequence if they don't attend to the task at hand. If you ask a person with ADHD why he can focus for this and not for that, he will usually respond along the following lines:

> I focus well on things that interest me, but if it's not something that really interests me, I just can't keep my focus. If I'm really freaked that something very unpleasant is going to happen quickly unless I take care of this right here, right now, that may help me focus for a while. But unless it feels like there is a gun to my head, I really have to be interested.

Because they can focus well on tasks that interest them, yet often focus very poorly or inconsistently on almost anything else, people with ADHD are often accused of lacking willpower. ADHD clearly looks like a problem with willpower, but it is not. One patient called his chronic difficulty with attaining and sustaining focus "erectile dysfunction of the mind." He said,

> If the task is something that really interests me, I can get "up" for it and I can perform. But if it's not a task that "turns me on," I can't get up for it, and I can't perform. Doesn't matter how much I say to myself, "I need to, I ought to, I should." I can't make it happen. It's just not a willpower kind of thing.

○ immediate or delayed "payoffs" in the ADHD brain

Underlying this "can focus for this, but not for that" problem is an important problem with emotion in ADHD: difficulty in mobilizing and sustaining interest for activities that don't offer an immediate "payoff" of pleasure or relief. Most of us may not think of interest as an emotion, but it is in fact a critically important positive emotion. "Passionate interest" represents an intense level of sustained emotional engagement with a task or person, but interest occurs in varying degrees and with varying levels of persistence. Interest reflects the degree of a person's motivation and emotional engagement with a task or relationship. Psychologists

James Gross and Ross Thompson have emphasized that "emotions not only make us feel something, they make us feel like *doing* something."[6]

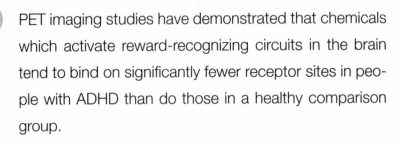

PET imaging studies have demonstrated that chemicals which activate reward-recognizing circuits in the brain tend to bind on significantly fewer receptor sites in people with ADHD than do those in a healthy comparison group.

Emotions motivate action—action to engage or action to avoid. Many people with untreated or inadequately treated ADHD can readily mobilize interest only for activities offering very immediate gratification; they tend to have severe difficulty in activating and sustaining effort for tasks that offer rewards only over the longer term.

Problems of activating and sustaining motivation and effort for necessary tasks—lack of sufficient interest—may have to do with how people with ADHD are "wired": they may be less sensitive to potential rewards, as opposed to immediately available rewards, than are others of the same age.

PET imaging studies have demonstrated that chemicals which activate reward-recognizing circuits in the brain tend to bind on significantly fewer receptor sites in people with ADHD than do those in a healthy comparison group.[7] These and other imaging studies may help explain why people with ADHD tend to be less able than their peers to anticipate pleasure or register satisfaction with tasks for which the payoff is delayed. An important effect is that often they have great difficulty in activating themselves to get started on tasks that are not especially interesting to them and in sustaining motivation to complete tasks for which the rewards are not imminently available. I discuss implications of this research in Chapter Two.

Problems in activating and sustaining interest (focus) and effort for tasks are two of the multiple cognitive functions included in the complex syndrome currently identified as ADHD. As I noted in the Introduction, this disorder is no longer seen as simply a problem of young children who misbehave. In fact, misbehavior is something of a red herring in the mystery of ADHD and has eclipsed the truly debilitating aspects of the disability as it often progresses to young adulthood and into middle age, bringing heartbreaking suffering, internal turmoil, and frustration in actualizing life goals. It is in fact now clear that many people with ADHD have never had significant behavioral problems, and even for those who did have such difficulties, problems with misbehavior usually tended to be among the least of their troubles. The primary problem for most individuals with ADHD, especially as they enter adolescence and adulthood, is a wide range of cognitive impairments in the management system of the brain. All of these impairments are linked to various problems with emotion.

○ emotions, ADHD, and executive functions

Neuroscience is quickly changing our understanding of the neurological underpinnings of psychological phenomena. Nowhere is this research more salient than in the study of ADHD, where we need better to understand how brain functions are intimately tied to emotional experiences, feelings, and decision-making processes. Here I offer a brief review of the model of executive functions (EFs) impaired in ADHD, as well as a model for how emotional processing has a special relationship to these brain functions.

understanding executive functions

In 2005, I published the book *Attention Deficit Disorder: The Unfocused Mind in Children and Adults*. Eight years later, I updated it with *A New Understanding of ADHD in Children and Adults: Executive Function Impairments*.[8] In those books, I described six clusters of chronic difficulties experienced by most people with ADHD. I explained how these six clusters together constitute a description of problems in the brain's management system, its executive functions. Building on my own research and the work of others, I have suggested the new working definition of ADHD shown here:

A New Working Definition of ADHD

ADHD =

- a complex syndrome of
- developmental impairments of executive functions,
- the self-management system of the brain,
- a system of mostly unconscious operations.
- These impairments are situationally-specific,
- chronic, and significantly interfere with functioning in many aspects of the person's daily life.

Source: T. E. Brown, 2013, *A New Understanding of ADHD in Children and Adults,* New York: Routledge.

In those earlier books, I also highlighted the puzzling question of why those with ADHD tend to have chronic EF problems in most areas of daily life, yet have almost no difficulty in effectively deploying these same functions in a few specific activities. This book explains how problems with emotion underlie this ability of people with ADHD to focus on some tasks very intently while also being chronically unable to focus on many other tasks that they know are important.

Among the six clusters of this model, illustrated in Figure 1.1, there is one that includes problems in managing frustration and modulating emotions. This book is not focused only on that one aspect of EF; it is not only about emotion management. It is about the multiple and subtle ways in which problems with emotion underlie chronic difficulties in all six clusters of EF: problems of emotion in prioritizing and getting started on tasks, in holding focus and shifting focus appropriately, in regulating alertness and sustaining effort, and in utilizing working memory—all this in addition to problems with managing frustration and emotional expression and experience.

building blocks of the executive functions

The model in Figure 1.1 provides a way to think about the variety of cognitive functions that make up the executive functions of each

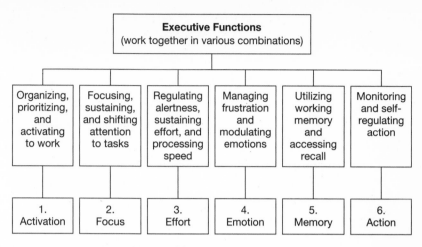

Figure 1.1   Executive Functions Impaired in ADHD
Source: From *Attention Deficit Disorder: The Unfocused Mind in Children and Adults* (p. 22), by T. E. Brown, 2005, New Haven, CT: Yale University Press. Reprinted with permission.

person's brain. The six boxes are not unitary variables like height, weight, or blood pressure — all one thing of which you can have more or less. Rather, each of these boxes represents a cluster of related cognitive functions. For most tasks that require self-management, several, if not all, of these six clusters of cognitive functions interact dynamically to do the task. Usually they operate so quickly that they are automatic, faster than lightning, not dependent on step-by-step conscious thought. The following list describes these six clusters in more detail:

1. **ACTIVATION**: organizing tasks and materials, estimating time, prioritizing tasks, and getting started on work tasks. Patients with ADHD describe chronic difficulty with excessive procrastination. Often they will put off getting started on a task, even a task they recognize as very important to them, until the very last minute. It is as though they cannot get themselves started until the point where they perceive the task as an acute emergency.
2. **FOCUS**: focusing, sustaining focus, and shifting focus to tasks. Some people with ADHD describe their difficulty in sustaining focus as similar to trying to listen to the car radio when you drive

too far away from the station and the signal begins fading in and out: you get some of it and lose some of it. They say they are distracted easily not only by things that are going on around them but also by thoughts in their own minds. In addition, focusing on reading poses difficulties for many. They can generally understand the words as they read, but often have to read the material over and over again to fully grasp and remember the meaning.

3. **EFFORT**: regulating alertness, sustaining effort, and working with adequate processing speed. Many with ADHD report that they can perform short-term projects well, but have much more difficulty with sustained effort over longer periods of time. They also find it difficult to complete tasks on time, especially when required to do expository writing. Many also experience chronic difficulty regulating sleep and alertness. Often they stay up too late because they can't shut their head off. Once asleep, they often sleep like dead people and have a big problem getting up in the morning.

4. **EMOTION**: managing frustration and modulating emotions. Although the most current version of the manual used for psychiatric diagnosis does not recognize any symptoms related to the management of emotion as an aspect of ADHD, many with this disorder describe chronic difficulties managing frustration, anger, worry, disappointment, desire, and other emotions. They speak as though these emotions, when experienced, take over their thinking the way that a computer virus invades a computer, making it impossible for them to attend to anything else. They find it very difficult to get the emotion into perspective, to put it to the back of their mind, and to get on with what they need to do.

5. **MEMORY**: utilizing working memory and accessing recall. Very often, people with ADHD will report that they have adequate or exceptional memory for things that happened long ago, but great difficulty in being able to remember where they just put something, what someone just said to them, or what they were about to say. They may describe difficulty holding one or several things "online" while attending to other tasks. In addition, people with ADHD

often complain that they cannot retrieve from memory information they have learned when they need it.

6. **ACTION**: monitoring and regulating self-action. Many people with ADHD, even those without problems of hyperactive behavior, report chronic problems in regulating their actions. They often are too impulsive in what they say or do and in the way they think, jumping too quickly to inaccurate conclusions. People with ADHD also report problems in monitoring the context in which they are interacting. They fail to notice when other people are puzzled, hurt, or annoyed by what they have just said or done and thus fail to modify their behavior in response to specific circumstances. Often they also report chronic difficulty in regulating the pace of their actions, in slowing themselves down or speeding up as needed for specific tasks.

In looking at this model, keep in mind that the capacity of any person to use these executive functions depends on a developmental process that starts in very early childhood and is not fully completed until the late teen years or early twenties. In other words, these cognitive functions mature and come online only gradually over the long course of development from early childhood to early adulthood.

The brain infrastructure needed for these executive functions is very slow to develop. The abilities to organize and start tasks on your own, sustain focus on a task, regulate your alertness and capacity to keep one thing in mind while doing something else—all these abilities and other EFs develop only in very rudimentary form during early childhood. For all humans, it takes almost two decades of gradual development for EFs to reach their mature capacity.

ADHD is essentially a developmental delay or ongoing impairment of these six clusters of EFs. Later in this chapter, I describe our current understanding of causes of ADHD; for additional information about how ADHD impairments appear in various forms at different ages, please refer to my two earlier books.

o a critically important hub in the brain

The amygdala, a small region deep inside the brain, is the primary locus of the rapid initial processing of anything perceived, thought about, or imagined. This critically important hub links with almost every other region of the cerebral cortex to facilitate instantaneous emotional assessment—positive and negative—of current perceptions, thoughts, or imaginings. These assessments are then very rapidly communicated to various sections of the brain via the amygdala's output of a variety of neurotransmitter chemicals and hormones that quickly stimulate responses within the brain and throughout the body.[9]

Figure 1.2 illustrates the density of connections between the primate amygdala and other regions of the cerebral cortex. The amygdala, one of the emotional centers of the brain, is like a transit station through which massive amounts of processing take place.

The amygdala, shown in the center of the diagram, is directly linked to sixty of sixty-eight regions of the cortex, including many involved in reasoning and high-level decision making. No other area of brain is so fully and directly connected with the rest of the cortex. Within this matrix of brain connections, emotional reactions are assigned and adjusted moment by moment. There, in an instant, initial appraisals are made of how potentially appealing or dangerous that specific perception or thought seems to be for that person in that moment. These initial assessments may or may not be reconsidered and may or may not be followed by responsive actions, depending on how other areas of brain respond to the amygdala's initial assessment.

Two primary sources shape the brain's appraisal of what we see, hear, or think: instincts, and memories derived from past experiences. Instinctual reactions include quick withdrawal from perceptions associated with danger—for example, blinking and trying to get out of the way when a large, fast-moving object moves closely toward one's face, spitting out foods that smell or taste rotten. Likewise, we feel instinctively drawn toward people or activities that seem to promise comfort or pleasure.

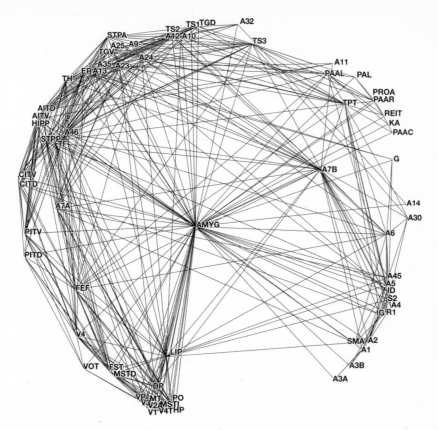

Figure 1.2   Schematic Graph Showing the Complex and Widespread Output
Connections Between the Amygdala and Most Other Areas of the Cortex
Source: Figure 9 from "Analysis of Connectivity: Neural Systems in the
Cerebral Cortex," by M. P. Young, J. W. Scannell, G.A.P.C. Burns, and
C. Blakemore, 1994, *Reviews in the Neurosciences, 5*, p. 243. Reprinted with
permission from Walter de Gruyter GmbH.

With amazing speed, the brain also accesses emotional centers that
store and process memories, which have embedded emotions (see the
later discussion of memory and emotions). It links whatever the person
has seen, heard, thought, or imagined to relevant instincts or to memories that provide clues from past experiences. These memories weight
the perception or thought with some degree of emotional significance,
and the brain directs or redirects attention accordingly.

o "hot" and "cool" executive function

Links between EF and emotions are complex. Some researchers have proposed that EF might be categorized along a dimension of emotional intensity; they differentiate between "hot" EF for dealing with tasks involving relatively strong emotional involvement, and "cool" EF for dealing with more abstract, less emotionally charged tasks.[10] Others have suggested that hyperactive/impulsive ADHD symptoms involve more impairments of hot EF, whereas the inattention symptoms of ADHD involve more impairments of cool EF.[11] Still others have argued that both hot and cool EF usually work in integrated ways. Stories in this book illustrate the complex and dynamic ways in which hot and cool aspects of EF interact in individuals with ADHD, regardless of subtype.

o it's all about context: situational influences

What causes "hot" intense involvement or "cool" disinterested involvement in any given task is not the task itself but how the person perceives the task — which includes his or her emotions related to the task — in any particular moment. One university student may be intensely engaged in trying to complete a term paper long before the deadline set by the professor; another student in the same course may feel only weak interest or not even care about getting the paper in on time.

These emotions can change readily. The student who usually works hard to get every paper in on time may suddenly not care at all about the paper while he is upset because his girlfriend has just broken up with him and is now dating someone else. The student whose interest in completing papers on time is usually just lukewarm may quickly intensify interest and work hard to get a specific paper in before the deadline if he learns that timely submission may make the difference between passing or failing the course and possibly losing eligibility to continue playing on the school football team. Depending on changes in a person's situation and viewpoint, any given task may suddenly appear far more hot or cold, or he or she may vacillate between extremes of emotional interest.

Emotions don't exist as independent abstract entities; they are always embedded in perceptions, thoughts, sensations, images, or imaginings as assessed by a given individual in a particular context at a particular moment in time. Sometimes an emotion is attached to a category of people or perceptions—for example, a special affection or dislike for people of a specific race, ethnic background, or appearance, or a persistent interest in or discomfort with particular erotic images or behaviors. But often even these generalized emotions can be traced back to specific experiences or events. It is true that some people manifest a more limited range of emotions, seeming to specialize in expressions of irritability, guilt, longing, pride, and so on; these are their more salient emotions, the ones most readily elicited and expressed. But most often a wide variety of emotions are attached to or embedded in the details of particular thoughts, sensations, perceptions, or imaginings.

Please note, however, that EF capacities are not primary determinants of emotional experience for people with ADHD or for anyone else. Emotions arise from biological processes that emerge in the temperament in infancy; these are gradually shaped by development and modified by countless life experiences. From his research with infants followed into adolescence, developmental psychologist Jerome Kagan has described and emphasized how

> each child is born with a profile of temperamental biases . . . that creates initial tendencies to be vocal or quiet, vigilant or relaxed, irritable or smiling, and energetic or lethargic with regard to particular events or situations. Parental behaviors, sibling rivalries, friendships, teacher attitudes, emotional identifications with family, ethnic class, religious or national categories, and even the size of the community during the childhood years combine with a host of chance events to sustain, or more often to alter, the relative strength and exact form of the traits the early biases produced.[12]

Emotional responses arising within each person, shaped by that person's inborn temperament and modified by his or her ongoing life experiences, are often referred to as the "bottom-up" aspect of emotional experience. This book presents examples of people who vary widely in the bottom-up flow of temperament into their experience. Some, by nature, tend to be much more anxious; others are more quick to give up in discouragement. However, in these stories, I will emphasize the "top-down" aspect of emotional experience for people with ADHD: their ability or lack of ability to utilize their EF capacities to recognize, modulate, and respond to the complexities of their emotional experience. These top-down processes can guide, shape, and alter the way people perceive and react to situations.[13]

○ the profound importance of memory

To understand the role of emotions in ADHD, it is essential to appreciate the intimate connection between emotions and memory. The brain's emotional reactions are guided by our personal memories linked to what we are seeing, hearing, thinking about, or imagining. Just as a search engine like Google can instantly pull up from the Internet a vast array of sites associated with a few key words, so the brain can far more quickly, in fractions of a second, select specific fragments and clusters of memories associated with any given perception, thought, or imagining, each memory carrying its own "charge" of associated emotion. Some memories derive directly from actual experiences in our remote or recent past that may seem relevant; other memories may emerge less directly from stories we've heard or movies we've seen or from recall of what happened to others whom we have observed in an apparently comparable situation. Some memories carry a "charge" of fear or shame; others are charged with desire and attraction; many are complicated by multiple layers and blends of emotion.

Without any conscious thought, in just milliseconds, the brain automatically appraises incoming perceptions, thoughts, or imaginings and generates reactions—to jump back or move forward, to pursue or to ignore. Often this initial appraisal leads to no significant reaction; the particular stimulus simply does not seem interesting or important in the moment. In some circumstances, the incoming perception primes us to generate more intensive or sustained reactions, which may arouse conscious awareness, thoughts, and associated memories.

Regardless of the source, within those milliseconds, the brain does its calculus and yields emotionally loaded reactions to signal further approach and engagement. This process of calculating weights of emotion attached to relevant memories is the amazing mechanism by which the brain assigns valence, positive or negative value, and relative importance to every passing perception and thought. These instantaneous, automated emotional reactions, strong or relatively weak, are the basis on which the brain allocates attention to specific perceptions, thoughts, actions, or situations, and ignores others.[14]

Some emotions are readily recognizable, intense and clear; more often they are subtle and blended, jumbled and conflicting, layered and sequential. Some are brief and transient; others are recurrent or long persisting, but they are all generated by the brain and embedded in our perceptions and thoughts.

Each trace of memory is charged with one or, more often, multiple emotions that may vary in intensity from insignificant to overwhelming. Sometimes these emotions are linked specifically to the initial content of the memory trace — for example, a pleasurable or embarrassing or frightening situation. For other memories, associated emotions may be added later — for example, delayed pride, guilt, or resentment over a past thought or experience. It is the emotional charge attached to our countless strings of associated memories that provides what the neuroscientist Dodge described as "the energy level that drives, amplifies and attenuates cognitive activity."[15] We depend on working memory to pull up the relevant information and associated emotions to help us size up situations and to guide us in coping with the countless tasks and interactions of daily life. Understanding of these processes is complicated, however, by the fact that emotions do not operate only at the level of consciousness. In fact, most emotional activity goes on outside our conscious awareness.

○ the role of unconscious emotions

Many people think of emotions as involving only conscious feelings, limited to sensations of sadness, anger, pleasure, worry, and so on that a person is fully aware of and generally able to identify. Neuroscience research has shown that conscious feelings are only the tip of the massive iceberg of emotion that operates within each person to motivate executive functions.

emotions at various levels of consciousness

Much of emotional processing goes on outside of our awareness, and the less conscious emotions are often subtle, contradictory, and complex. Emotions involved in activities or relationships are often difficult to assess because they operate on multiple levels of consciousness. Often a person consciously thinks of a particular task as quite important, honestly believing that she wants to give it immediate attention and full effort, yet she does not act accordingly. She may continue to procrastinate, busying herself with work on other tasks that are not as urgent, or repeatedly interrupting work on the seemingly important task and actually making little progress at all. Or she may actively seek out distractions by initiating contact with friends, surfing the Internet, getting high, or going to sleep. Such contradictions make sense only when we realize that emotions often are not fully conscious and often are conflicting. We may be powerfully influenced by emotions we don't even know we have. For those with ADHD who are seriously stuck, talk therapy is often essential to unraveling their emotions and helping them move toward recovery.

Neuroscientist Antonio Damasio was describing these unconscious influences of emotions on EF when he wrote that

> the emotional signal can operate entirely under the radar of consciousness. It can produce alterations in working memory, attention and reasoning so that the decision-making process is biased toward selecting the action most likely to lead to the best possible outcome, given prior experience. The individual may not ever be cognizant of this covert operation.[16]

Another neuroscientist, Joseph LeDoux, argued that

> many of the things we do, including the appraisal of the emotional significance of events in our lives and the expression of emotional behaviors in response to those appraisals, do not depend on consciousness, or even on processes that we necessarily have conscious access to.[17]

Social psychologists have demonstrated that much of our behavior is shaped or primed in a given situation by situational factors that we don't consciously recognize. These situational factors may stir up, accentuate, or diminish various emotions without our being at all aware of their influence. One study showed that university students who completed a short writing task unscrambling sentences that included words referring indirectly to rudeness were significantly more quick to interrupt an experimenter when kept waiting for a long time to hand in their survey forms after completion than were other students whose task forms had had a similar number of words related not to rudeness but to politeness. It appeared that even indirect references to rudeness or politeness activated thoughts and emotions that primed students to act more politely or more rudely when frustrated.[18]

automaticity, not repression

These influences tend to be unconscious, not in the psychoanalytic sense of repression, but in the more modern sense of "automaticity," which refers to rapid activation of attitudes, emotions, or behaviors that emerge in that specific context without any conscious thought to direct them.[19]

Sometimes decisions are more conscious and may depend largely on the interpersonal situation. My wife and I were once on a transatlantic flight during which the flight attendants prepared freshly baked chocolate chip cookies. I was dieting to lose some weight, and my wife tended to serve as the food police to remind me of what I should not eat. The cookies smelled delicious as they were being baked, and my wife was asleep beside me as the flight attendant came down the aisle to serve them. If my wife had been awake, I certainly would have declined the delicious cookie and felt proud of my self-restraint. However, she was asleep, and I wanted the cookie. After briefly struggling with the decision, I accepted from the flight attendant not only a cookie for myself but also one for my sleeping wife. I then promptly ate both of them and hastily returned the plate to the galley to dispose of the evidence. Often what we do depends heavily on who is with us and what they are doing!

Psychoanalytic clinicians emphasize the multiple levels of emotion that we may experience simultaneously, only some of which may be in our awareness at any given moment.[20] You might feel strong dislike for a new friend of your old friend, making critical remarks about that new friend's interests, appearance, or abilities, realizing only much later that the intensity of your dislike was fueled by jealousy or worry that this new friend might bring the loss of your own closeness to the old friend. At yet another level, your hostile feelings about the newcomer might also mask feelings of attraction to the new friend. It is not unusual for your feelings about a person or task to be contradictory or shifting between extremes, particularly in close relationships.

> Having conflicting or unrecognized emotions about certain people or tasks isn't unusual for anyone, with or without ADHD. But *managing* these complicated emotions and the tasks and relationships they affect is considerably harder for those with ADHD.

The same contradictory emotions may be true in your reactions to a task. You may want very much to work hard on a term paper to earn a good grade, yet this does not rule out the possibility that you may also feel like not putting out much effort for the paper because the teacher who assigned it has been unhelpful or because your parents have been too persistent in reminding you about the importance of doing well on it or because you expect your classmates to hand in papers that will be much better.

Having conflicting or unrecognized emotions about certain people or tasks isn't unusual for anyone, with or without ADHD. However, as illustrated in the stories in this book, *managing* these complicated emotions and the tasks and relationships they affect is considerably harder for those with ADHD than for most others of the same age.

o how do ADHD impairments of the brain affect processing of emotions?

Sometimes the working memory impairments of ADHD allow a momentary emotion to become too strong; the person is flooded with one emotion and unable to attend to other emotions, facts, and memories relevant to that immediate situation.

There are two primary ways in which emotions play a critical role in the chronic difficulties of people with ADHD. Both are related to working memory impairments—the person's limited capacity to keep in mind and use multiple bits of emotion-laden information at the same time. Sometimes the working memory impairments of ADHD allow a momentary emotion to become too strong; the person is flooded with one emotion and unable to attend to other emotions, facts, and memories relevant to that immediate situation. At other times, the working memory impairments of ADHD leave the person with insufficient sensitivity to the importance of a particular emotion because he or she hasn't kept other relevant information sufficiently in mind or factored it into his or her assessment of the situation. To understand how and why these problems with emotions become more complicated in persons with ADHD, it is necessary to begin with a brief review of what is now known about the problems of the brain that contribute to the impairments of ADHD.

o structural and chemical brain impairments that underlie ADHD

Over recent years, research in neuroscience has demonstrated four aspects of brain development and functioning that tend to be different in people with ADHD compared to most others of the same age.

These involve impairments in brain connectivity and in coordination of brain rhythms, delays in brain maturation, and differences in the dynamics of brain chemistry. For those with ADHD, any or all of these may be involved in their impairments of executive functions and in the related complexities of emotions.

impaired brain connectivity

The networks that carry information related to emotion and other aspects of brain functioning tend to be somewhat more limited in individuals with ADHD compared to most others. Years ago, most scientists thought that impairments of ADHD were due primarily to problems within specific regions of the brain, particularly the prefrontal cortex. New technologies, however, have shown that some of the impairments of people with ADHD may be more related to networks of fibers that support interactive communication between various regions of the brain.[21]

One type of communication between brain regions occurs via connections referred to as "white matter." Dense networks of these fibers, most buried deep in the brain, rapidly carry messages from one area of the brain to the other. Some are very short, less than an inch; other fibers extend considerably longer. The total volume of white matter in the brain is huge. If all the white matter fibers in the brain of a twenty-year-old male were laid end to end, they would stretch over 109,000 miles (176,000 kilometers).[22]

Imaging studies have shown abnormalities in the structure of white matter in brains of children, adolescents, and adults with ADHD; such abnormalities may explain some of the difficulties these individuals have — for example, with keeping one thing in mind while doing something else.[23] One study has shown that methylphenidate, a medication used to treat ADHD, can normalize the connectivity limitations in the motivation and reward networks of children with ADHD when they are performing some assigned tasks.[24]

impairments in coordination of brain rhythms

One of the important ways in which the brain coordinates and synchronizes activities essential to emotional regulation, attention, and memory is through dynamic shifts in the rate and rhythms of oscillations in groups of nerve cells. Recent research has shown that when the mature brain isn't busy with specific tasks, it doesn't shut down; it shifts into a default pattern of relatively slow oscillations that become coordinated across a network of regions within the brain. In this mode, the conscious mind tends to wander, without specific focus, while less conscious aspects of the brain activate in ways that organize and integrate information. When we are faced with a task requiring more attention, this default mind-wandering mode is supposed to be turned down or off. Otherwise, we tend to be less alert; we slow down in responding, intermittently space out, and tend to make more mistakes.[25]

Imaging studies have shown that people with ADHD tend to have more problematic connections between those regions of the brain that support coordinating functions of the default network. Studies have also demonstrated that people with ADHD, compared to peers, tend to have more difficulty in turning down or shutting off the default mode in order to attend to specific tasks that require more active attention.[26] Some studies have also demonstrated that stimulant medication used for ADHD significantly improved the ability of children and adolescents with ADHD to suppress the default mode so that they could more adequately pay attention to assigned tasks.[27]

delays in brain maturation

Sometimes EF impairments experienced by those with ADHD are simply delays in development. The cognitive functions we all depend on to manage our emotions and activities in daily life aren't fully developed in childhood; these executive functions are among the slowest developing aspects of the human brain. The brain infrastructure on which EF depends develops very gradually, not reaching mature functioning capacity until late adolescence or early adulthood.

There are many ways in which EF can become impaired — trauma or diseases, for example — but those types of impairment usually occur in people who have had normal EF development and then lose it as a result of damage to brain tissue. ADHD is now understood as a *developmental* impairment of EF whereby the neural networks in the brain that support EF simply do not unfold and "come online" at the time they usually appear in most others of the same age.

An imaging study compared a sample of over two hundred children diagnosed with ADHD and a matched comparison group, conducting repeated brain scans over childhood and adolescence. The study reported that, on average, those with ADHD were about three to five years later than most age mates in reaching maturity of brain networks that support EF. Other structures of the brains of those with ADHD seem to develop at the same rate as most others in the same age group.[28]

This delay causes many with ADHD to function during childhood and adolescence with significantly less maturity in tasks involving EF, and with less ability to manage associated emotions, than do most others of the same age. For many, though not all, with ADHD, this development may catch up later, perhaps in early adulthood. The problem, of course, is that during those years of developmental immaturity of the EFs — critical years of education and preparation for adult life — the person can suffer considerable damage to his or her learning, relationships, and self-esteem. People who experience this delay in the development of these important self-management functions often suffer significant long-term consequences, as do those individuals with ADHD whose EF capacity seems never to develop fully.

brain chemistry dynamics

ADHD is not related only to developmental anomalies in structures and connections of the brain. Another critically important aspect of the EF impairments of ADHD has to do with the dynamics of neurotransmitter chemicals manufactured in the brain. These chemicals facilitate communication within and between networks of neurons, the wiring of the brain. There is considerable evidence that ADHD impairments result from inadequate release and reloading of two critical neurotransmitter chemicals.[29] Often people say that ADHD is a problem with the "balance" of chemicals in the brain. This makes it sound as though there is a problem with the ratio of one chemical to another in the fluid that is within and around the brain, as though the problem of ADHD were simply like having too much or too little salt in a soup.

In fact, the problem in the brain of a person with ADHD is not a global imbalance of chemicals; it is a problem with the release and reloading of two specific chemicals at the infinitesimal junctions of tiny neurons within complex networks. To help compensate for impairments of EF that characterize ADHD, medication treatments are often, though not always, helpful. There is a large body of research demonstrating effectiveness of stimulant and some nonstimulant medications for alleviating recognized symptoms of ADHD.[30]

Recently, researchers have begun to expand research to assess the impact of these medications on the broader range of EF symptoms implicated in ADHD. Experimental studies have shown that stimulant medication can improve the ability of children with ADHD to utilize working memory and to work for delayed rewards.[31] Self-report data have shown that patients with ADHD report significant improvement in a wide range of EF impairments, including emotional regulation, when receiving medication treatment for ADHD, though few studies of medication treatments for ADHD directly address their impact on emotional expression or on the various ways in which emotions affect EF.[32] Imaging studies employing fMRI have shown that stimulant medication can "normalize" activation and functional connectivity in attention and motivation networks in children with ADHD; these are suggestive, but more research is needed to sort out the impact of these treatments on the emotional aspects of EF.[33]

A recent study using electroencephalograms showed that as an alternative or supplement to medication treatment, reward incentives can also activate and normalize brain activity patterns while motivating improved task performance by children with ADHD. To have this beneficial effect, however, the reward incentive needed to be salient and administered promptly on the spot.[34] A previous study showed that both money incentives and stimulant medication can improve task performance of children with ADHD on a long, boring task, though the medication had more potent and sustained effects.[35] These studies and others suggest that for people with ADHD, both medication and immediately available incentives, including social rewards, are likely to support improved performance on EF tasks, many of which are substantially affected by emotional factors.[36]

○ additional psychiatric difficulties

ADHD is rarely the only significant problem for those who have it. Many who suffer from ADHD also have learning disorders or other psychiatric impairments that emerge in adolescence or adulthood, if not before. I have written two books and edited another that describe how these additional impairments often are severe enough to qualify for diagnosis as one or more co-occurring disorders, including a sleep disorder, anxiety disorder, mood disorder, specific learning disorder, obsessive-compulsive disorder, substance use disorder, disorders on the autism spectrum, or some combination of these. Most of these co-occurring disorders also involve specific bottom-up and top-down problems with managing emotions.[37]

All the individuals described in this book have had to struggle with a complicated mix of such interacting challenges. In most cases, adequate treatment involved interventions not only for their ADHD impairments but also for their co-occurring disorders.

○ common problems with emotions in people with ADHD

The stories upcoming in this book offer many examples of conscious and unconscious emotions shaping attitudes and behavior. The next sections describe some of these processes as they occurred in the experiences of these teens and adults who were stuck due to their ADHD.

extreme reactions

An adolescent with ADHD may become flooded with emotion, enraged when his parent refuses him use of the car for a gathering with friends that the teen considers very important. Many teenagers in this situation might persistently argue, loudly complain, swear, and become sullen, but most would not escalate into throwing things, pushing or hitting the parent, or punching a hole in a wall. A teen without ADHD might momentarily consider such extreme responses, but usually would inhibit them because he is able to keep in mind, despite the momentary intensity of anger, that this is a parent whom he loves and upon whom he depends.

Moreover, most teens would probably be able to maintain awareness that those more extreme reactions would be likely to bring harsher punishments. As the typical teenager sizes up such a situation, his working memory will usually factor these other expectations and emotions into his moment-by-moment calculations—with little or no conscious thought—allowing him to maintain a reasonable perspective to appraise the immediate situation in a broader context, modulate his anger, and regulate his behavior.

In coming chapters, you will see examples of this flooding with one emotion that crowds out other relevant facts and emotional priorities—for example, in Martin's immersion in embarrassment that led to his continuing refusal to approach and talk with the professor he had disappointed (Chapter Four), and in Karen's consuming fear of disappointing her parents, which caused her protracted avoidance of telling them directly about her inability to begin the course she needed to be readmitted to her university (Chapter Three).

ignoring emotional information: the importance of working memory

The opposite extreme can be seen in the situation of an adult with ADHD whose alarm clock goes off early in the morning, announcing the need to get up and prepare to leave for work. The initial response of the person may be to awaken briefly and push the snooze button to get a few more minutes of sleep. Perhaps she was up late the night before laboring on a project she had brought home from work or had been engaged in a long argument with a family member or friend. In any case, when the alarm goes off for the second time, she turns the clock off fully, rolls over, and returns to a deep and protracted sleep, uninterrupted by any alarm and without having in mind a recent warning from her supervisor that she had been coming late to work too often and might be jeopardizing her job if the pattern continues. At the moment when she was awake and turning off the clock, her impaired working memory did not protect her by bringing up recall of that warning from the supervisor. Her past experience and awareness of fear of losing her job was not strong enough to help her overcome her strong wish of the moment to get more sleep.

As you'll see in Chapter Eight, Steve's working memory failed him repeatedly when he did not keep in mind his supervisor's warning about coming late to work. Each day, he became immersed in responding to emails or repeatedly listening to a particular CD, ignoring the passage of the time he needed to get to work when expected, totally losing track of the importance of his supervisor's warning. Similarly, as you'll read in Chapter Twelve, James's working memory did not sufficiently maintain his awareness of his urgent desire to work on and complete the term papers that threatened his status in his college. Whenever he approached his computer, he remembered only the games that offered him a reliable way to reduce his stress by allowing him to immerse himself in the pleasures of fantasy violence. Both of these are examples of living too much in the immediate moment and not keeping sufficiently in mind relevant memories of the past and relevant goals for the future.

Working memory is important not only for helping us remember to lock the door when we leave the house or for holding in mind a telephone number while we are dialing. Working memory is also the brain's search engine. It automatically pulls up relevant memories, with their related emotional weightings, to help us decide moment by moment how we will prioritize our conflicting wishes and their accompanying emotions in countless situations of daily life. When working adequately, it helps us make informed decisions about what we will do and when we will do it. For many with ADHD, however, working memory often does not work adequately to keep them aware of the emotional weightings that are important in much of their decision making in daily life.

Working memory brings into play, consciously and/or unconsciously, the emotional energy needed to help us

- Organize and activate for tasks
- Sustain focus and shift focus when needed
- Regulate alertness and sustain effort for tasks
- Guide top-down control to modulate emotional responses
- Encode and access information learned
- Monitor and self-regulate our actions

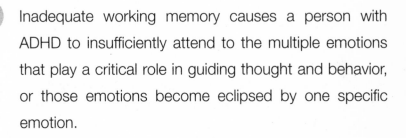

Inadequate working memory causes a person with ADHD to insufficiently attend to the multiple emotions that play a critical role in guiding thought and behavior, or those emotions become eclipsed by one specific emotion.

Chronic impairment of working memory was a primary factor in the difficulties that caused the individuals described in this book to become stuck. As noted earlier in the chapter, inadequate working memory causes a person with ADHD to insufficiently attend to the multiple emotions that play a critical role in guiding thought and behavior, or those emotions become eclipsed by one specific emotion in a way that doesn't adequately take other relevant emotion-connected thoughts into account.

The coming chapters offer examples of how we need to keep in mind many shifting priorities, attending to the emotional weighting—the current personal importance—of multiple factors as well as the relative importance of each over the longer term of hours, days, or more. We depend on working memory to help us keep in mind the bigger picture—the larger context of the moments in daily life—and the variety of emotions that are relevant to our decision making.

When James was engaged in playing video games, he skillfully noticed action on many parts of the screen, assessing and responding to multiple potential threats and opportunities for his avatar. Yet he was not able to keep in mind the urgency he had felt earlier that evening about completing an essay due in class the next day. When Eric

(Chapter Two) suddenly noticed that he was late in leaving to meet his friends, he quickly jumped into his car and drove much too fast on an icy road, thinking only of his not wanting to keep them waiting, and not keeping in mind the risks of speeding on ice until his car slid off the road into a ditch.

Psychologists often measure working memory simply by asking the patient to listen to a string of digits and then to repeat those numbers in reversed order. Many people with ADHD are unable to do this task when the number of digits in each string gets beyond three or four. However, this digit-span test does not assess the far more important function of working memory that I've discussed here: the capacity to keep in mind the relative importance — the immediate and longer-term emotional significance — of various tasks, actions, risks, and opportunities that require attention throughout daily life.

family stresses

Stories in this book also illustrate the multiple ways in which ADHD tends to create chronic stress not only for people with ADHD but also for their families. Sometimes stress is due to conflict between family members. For example, siblings of a child with ADHD often live with chronic frustration, guilt, worry, and anger about their recurrent daily hassles with their brother or sister. Sometimes they harbor resentment over how much attention and privileged status their brother or sister with ADHD seems to receive too often.[38]

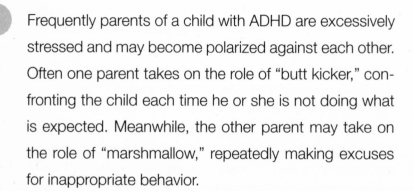

Frequently parents of a child with ADHD are excessively stressed and may become polarized against each other. Often one parent takes on the role of "butt kicker," confronting the child each time he or she is not doing what is expected. Meanwhile, the other parent may take on the role of "marshmallow," repeatedly making excuses for inappropriate behavior.

Frequently parents of a child with ADHD are excessively stressed and may become polarized against each other, repeatedly arguing about how best to react to and deal with their child or children with ADHD. Often one parent takes on the role of "butt kicker," confronting the child each time he or she is not doing what is expected. Meanwhile, the other parent may take on the role of "marshmallow," repeatedly making excuses for inappropriate behavior or offering support and encouragement to that child while trying to arrange for others to modify their expectations and behavior to accommodate the apparent needs or wishes of the child with ADHD.

To adequately understand and effectively treat the individual with ADHD, we also need to understand the context of the family in which that individual lived or lives, and the chronic dynamics and stresses each family member may be coping with and responding to. Most of the stories in this book show how the identified patient created and reacted to stresses in their families, and they illustrate the complexity of the emotional interactions and interpersonal dynamics of people with ADHD.

chronic stress and the burden of the "willpower assumption"

One recurrent factor that complicated the emotions of these very bright individuals was the ongoing discrepancy between what was expected of them by their parents, grandparents, and teachers and even themselves and their frequent failure to achieve the expected success. Most of these patients had struggled since early childhood with continuing conflict between their picture of themselves as exceptionally bright and talented and their view of themselves as disappointing failures, unable to "deliver the goods" expected of them. Some had been very successful in their childhood, earning high grades and strong praise during the elementary school years, then gradually lost status and self-esteem due to increasing evidence of their difficulty in coping with the escalating demands of middle school, high school, and postsecondary schooling.

Every one of the patients whose story appears in this book suffered from being confronted repeatedly with the stark contrast between their impressive abilities, effort, and achievement in a few specific activities where they felt strong personal interest and their very inconsistent effort and weak achievement in many other activities that were clearly important for their longer-term future. Typically their parents, teachers, and others who recognized their strong potential and wanted to help them fulfill it would urge, cajole, and pressure them to exercise "willpower" to show the same strength, effort, and success in those other domains that could significantly improve their future options in life. Most often, those with ADHD joined in criticizing themselves for continuing failure to "just make myself do it." Both the well-intentioned critics and the guilt-ridden criticized shared the erroneous assumption that symptoms of ADHD could be overcome with sufficient determination and continuing exercise of presumably available willpower.

Except for genetic influences, the family does not cause a person to develop ADHD. However, family members can severely exacerbate the difficulties of someone with ADHD if they do not adequately understand the true nature of the disorder and if they tend to punish that individual with harsh and repeated criticism based on the erroneous assumption that ADHD impairments can be overcome simply by willpower. Such criticism is readily internalized, and the resulting shame, resentment, frustration, and self-loathing tend to echo endlessly in the memory of the person with ADHD. Even if they recognize this, those who live or work with a person who has significant ADHD impairments often feel extremely frustrated as they repeatedly encounter chronic lateness, poor planning, excessive forgetfulness, frequent lying, and recurrent disappointment from unfulfilled promises. It's not easy for them to hold back their criticism.

It's very difficult for most people to understand how any individual can be very focused on certain tasks or can mobilize themselves to complete a task effectively under the last-minute pressure of an imminent deadline and yet be unable to force themselves to deploy these same abilities in an appropriate and timely way, especially for tasks that are obviously important. Most do not understand that when a person is faced with a task in which he has strong and immediate personal interest, either because he really enjoys it or because he fears that not doing the task will quickly bring some very unpleasant consequence, the chemistry of the brain is instantly altered to mobilize. And most don't know that this alteration of brain chemistry is not under voluntary control. ADHD clearly appears to be a problem of willpower failure, but it is actually a problem with the interacting dynamics of emotion, working memory, and the chemistry of the brain.

blaming the victim

Failure to understand this basic fact about ADHD — that it appears to be a lack of willpower, when it is not — commonly leads to a blaming of the victim. This manifests both in self-blaming by those with ADHD and in the many subtle or not-so-subtle reactions of family members, teachers, friends, or employers.

When we don't understand the cause of a problem, we tend to assume that the resultant misfortune is somehow the fault of the affected person. In the early 1800s, a massive epidemic of cholera occurred in New York City. The cause of cholera at that time was unknown, but in 1832, thousands of apparently healthy children and adults suddenly suffered severe diarrhea and vomiting, often dying within one day of being brought to the hospital. Because this disease hit hardest in low-income areas of the city, many blamed the epidemic on African Americans and immigrant Irish Catholics who lived there. John Pintard, a prominent citizen of New York, wrote at that time, "Those sickened must be cured or die off, and being chiefly of the very scum of the city, the quicker [their] dispatch, the sooner the malady will cease." Lacking adequate understanding of the cause of cholera, Pintard and

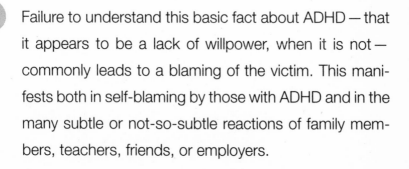

Failure to understand this basic fact about ADHD — that it appears to be a lack of willpower, when it is not — commonly leads to a blaming of the victim. This manifests both in self-blaming by those with ADHD and in the many subtle or not-so-subtle reactions of family members, teachers, friends, or employers.

many others of his time assumed that it was the fault of those affected. In 1854, a London physician discovered that cholera is caused not by some flaw in those affected but by a bacterium found in contaminated water.[39]

ADHD is not a life-threatening disease like cholera, but those who encounter this syndrome of chronic impairments in their child, spouse, students, employee, coworker, or friend often find it very difficult not to assume that if only this person who can focus so well on a few favored activities would exercise sufficient willpower, he or she could certainly perform much better on many other important tasks. Just as the cause of cholera was unknown in the early 1800s, so the roles of genetically based developmental delays in brain development, inefficient neural transmission at countless synapses, and impairments of functional connectivity from one brain region to another are not currently understood as causes of ADHD by most of the lay public or by many professionals. As a result, most with ADHD experience a persisting climate of skepticism about the legitimacy of the disorder and its treatment, coupled with a tendency for them to be blamed for it by others and by themselves.

2

eric

I'm in a great university where I want to do well, but I just can't get myself motivated to do the work. I did really well in high school; now my grades have tanked. I've been spending too much time hanging out with my girlfriend and smoking weed. I've tried some ADHD medicines, but they make me too jittery.
— 20-YEAR-OLD UNIVERSITY STUDENT

Eric wore a winning smile and spoke quickly as he explained the reasons for his failing out of his second year of university. "It's simple," he said. "I spent too much time with my new girlfriend, smoked too much weed, didn't complete my assignments, got depressed, and eventually I stopped going to my classes." To avoid being dismissed, Eric had taken a medical withdrawal from his university; he was now in my office with his parents seeking evaluation and treatment for himself. Clearly frustrated, he said, "I'm in a great university where I want to do well, but I just can't get myself motivated to do the work." We agreed to begin an intensive course of treatment, to be divided between skills development and psychotherapy. As his story gradually unfolded during treatment, it became clear that the underlying reasons for his failure were not so simple. His obvious problems of excessive use of marijuana and depressive symptoms were but the tip of an iceberg of struggles with insecurity,

43

frustration, anxiety, and shame that had been taking a toll on his body and self-esteem as well as on his schoolwork.

Eric was an extremely bright young man. His IQ score was near the top of the superior range, at the 97th percentile. He was charming and well liked by teachers and peers; he had been an outstanding player on the soccer and tennis teams of his very competitive high school. Diagnosed with ADHD in seventh grade, Eric had tried all available ADHD medications, but had experienced intolerable side effects that required his stopping each of them. His persisting ADHD symptoms were most apparent in chronic difficulties with completing homework. Eric's mother had been intensively involved in supervising his homework for many hours every day after school, until the end of tenth grade, when he overtly revolted and became so resistant that she and his father decided that they needed to delegate this stressful work to someone else. The nightly arguments and vituperation had become too exhausting.

To address these difficulties, from the outset of eleventh grade Eric's parents provided a tutor to help him five days each week to organize and focus on his homework. With this supportive scaffolding, he functioned quite well in a challenging high school curriculum. Eric's scores on standardized tests were in the top 5 percent, and, despite his unmedicated ADHD, his grades in high school courses were generally A's, with occasional B's. His outstanding high school record won him admission to an excellent university.

Shortly after he arrived for his first year of college, Eric met an older student, a senior named Jenny, whom he described as smart, hardworking, and very self-disciplined in doing her schoolwork. He attended most of his classes, but did little homework and spent every evening with Jenny, sleeping at her off-campus apartment every night. With her active encouragement and assistance, he attended his classes regularly and was able to keep up reasonably well with most of his assignments. Near the end of that year, however, Jenny ended their relationship, telling Eric that he was too irresponsible, not serious enough about his schoolwork, and not sufficiently independent. A few weeks later, he was hospitalized for two weeks with a severe episode of ulcerative colitis, probably exacerbated by stress, after which he was required to take prescription medication daily to prevent further gastrointestinal problems.

After spending the summer with his family, Eric returned to the university to start his second year. He joined a fraternity where he ostensibly found a community of male friends, but also many months of time-consuming pledge activities and not much support for academic work. His grades plummeted. He never felt very committed to the fraternity and spent little time interacting with his fraternity brothers.

Soon he met Lorna, a young woman who later turned out to have serious mood problems exacerbated by dependence on benzodiazepines (antianxiety medication) and marijuana. She moved into his room, where they spent most of their free time together, often smoking marijuana four to six times a day. They watched a lot of TV each day and avoided going out to interact with anyone else. Neither Eric nor Lorna did much homework. For a while, Eric woke up to go to his morning classes and was able to do reasonably well in a couple of courses that had dynamic teachers who really interested him. He got so far behind in his other courses that he felt ashamed and stopped going to class because he feared that the professors might ask him about his missing assignments.

This situation continued into the second semester, during which Eric fell so far behind in his work that he had to withdraw from several courses to avoid failing grades. Eric became increasingly depressed about his hopeless academic situation while feeling both comforted and trapped by his relationship with Lorna, who had become very needy and was quite upset when Eric was not in the room with her. Soon Lorna's addictions and emotional problems had escalated to the point where she had to take a medical withdrawal; she left the university over spring break of Eric's sophomore year. Without his constant companion, Eric became more depressed and escalated his marijuana smoking to even higher levels. He had to withdraw from two courses and soon recognized that he would be unable to finish the semester. This led to his being advised to take a medical withdrawal.

Within a few weeks, Eric experienced a serious episode of bleeding colon, which required another hospitalization. While in the hospital, he disclosed that for the previous several months he had failed to take the daily medications required to prevent such a recurrence. He had lost the prescriptions for his refills and felt too embarrassed to contact the physician to get them. Soon after he was discharged from that hospitalization, Eric came with his parents for a consultation with me.

○ fear of being alone

As Eric told his story, I was impressed struck by the dramatic contrast between his apparently outstanding performance in high school and his rapid decline in college. Obviously, his use of marijuana was excessive; this undoubtedly contributed to his lack of motivation to do his schoolwork, though it also helped him reduce his anxiety about leaving home and starting college. More striking was his quick attachment to Jenny and subsequently to Lorna. When Eric was with Jenny, he had been able to keep stable hours, used marijuana in a more limited way, and got most of his work done, as he had at home while in high school under the intensive daily guidance of his mother and, subsequently, his tutor. Apparently Eric needed a close, supportive relationship with daily contact to replace supports he had lost in leaving home and to sustain his efforts to get established in college. He lost that relationship with Jenny because his excessive dependence felt burdensome to her.

When Eric returned to college for his second fall term, he had quickly attached himself to Lorna, a young woman whose need for a close and exclusive attachment meshed with his own need for close, predictable, almost constant companionship. In subsequent conversations, Eric explained that he felt intensely bored, restless, and lonely when he didn't have another person with him for most of every day. Lorna became that person — an antidote to his painful and fearful loneliness.

When living at home, Eric had his parents, two younger siblings, and a few close friends with whom he had spent much time continuously since early childhood. There he also had daily contact with his tutor, a recent university graduate, for several hours each day. Eric spoke of how his tutor provided companionship and monitoring of his homework and studying, but also had played a huge role in helping him complete his work in high school. Often the tutor would help Eric so much with writing his essays and papers that he, rather than Eric, was the actual author. Nevertheless, Eric continued to do well on quizzes and tests, tasks for which the tutor could help him prepare, but could not do his work for him.

> Eric had to rely on moving around and keeping constantly active because he hadn't yet developed the capacity to recognize and cope with his overwhelming feelings of restlessness and excessive fears of rejection.

Despite Eric's very impressive intelligence, he was not able to remain reliably motivated to work. His strong anxiety about himself left him feeling the need for sustained daily support to stay on top of his academic work in high school. He reported that he chronically had great difficulty in sustaining focus to listen or read, was unable to take notes in class, and struggled to complete even short reading assignments. He had great difficulty in sitting down alone to do schoolwork for more than just a few minutes at a time. When at home, rather than studying alone, he often jumped into his car to go for long drives to relieve his boredom. He had to rely on moving around and keeping constantly active because he hadn't yet developed the capacity to recognize and cope with his overwhelming feelings of restlessness and excessive fears of rejection.

o changes in context

Whereas most students with ADHD can function reasonably well with the support of prescribed medication, Eric, unable to take available ADHD medications, needed intensive personal scaffolding in order to apply his impressive intellect to his academic assignments. In the context of high school, Eric had a strong scaffolding of support from his family and tutor. He also was intensively involved in athletics throughout the school year, often not getting home from school until seven in the evening, and he received frequent encouragement from coaches and peers, who recognized his impressive strength and skills in several sports and in interscholastic math competitions. He had an established group of friends, and, during his last two years of high school, he had intensive support each day from his tutor. In the context of this strongly supportive environment, Eric usually felt successful and was able to thrive in most domains except for writing his papers.

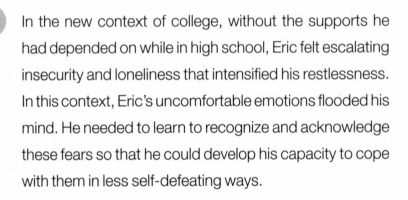

In the new context of college, without the supports he had depended on while in high school, Eric felt escalating insecurity and loneliness that intensified his restlessness. In this context, Eric's uncomfortable emotions flooded his mind. He needed to learn to recognize and acknowledge these fears so that he could develop his capacity to cope with them in less self-defeating ways.

The university was a totally different context. When Eric moved away from home to start college, he experienced a massive loss of support, both emotional and practical. He felt lonely and insecure in both academics and social relationships. Jenny gave some support for Eric's studies and provided some of the close companionship he longed for, but she was unable to tolerate his excessive dependency and ultimately dumped him. Lorna, quite bright but also very emotionally needy, was unable to offer any support for Eric's academic work. She did provide him with close companionship, but at the price of his curtailing most of his contact with other friends. In the new context of college, without the supports he had depended on while in high school, Eric felt escalating insecurity and loneliness that intensified his restlessness. In this context, Eric's uncomfortable emotions flooded his mind. He needed to learn to recognize and acknowledge these fears so that he could develop his capacity to cope with them in less self-defeating ways.

Some think of ADHD as a tumor that you carry, unchanging, from one situation to another. This view is an example of what social psychologists refer to as "the fundamental attribution error," a tendency to assume that a person's behavior is shaped primarily by factors within him or her—an assumption that fails to acknowledge how multiple situational (outside) influences combine to elicit and shape the individual's feelings and behavior. For example, when passengers are filing off an airplane arriving late at its destination, anyone who pushes past others to get off the plane is likely to be seen as rude and selfish; yet if the flight attendant announces that a few passengers need to get off quickly to make a tight connection for an overseas flight, those rushing to get off are seen in a more sympathetic light as reacting to a specific situation rather than as characteristically rude.

Context can make a big difference for anyone, but is especially important for people with ADHD. Context can enhance feelings of self-confidence and satisfaction; it can also intensify fear and self-consciousness. Especially during the transitions of early adulthood, most people with ADHD are strongly dependent on having a supportive social and emotional context in which to develop their slowly maturing capacity to manage themselves in daily life. Students with ADHD often report that they can work productively when with others who are working productively, but can't when they are alone. Some find that simply having another person in the room with them increases their ability to start tasks and sustain effort to complete them. Likewise, if they spend time with others who are disinterested in academic work or who party a lot, many decrease their work time and increase their partying time. It matters who you hang out with!

When Eric began treatment with me, we agreed to start with a change of his context. He moved away from home to live in an apartment near my office where he could make a fresh start utilizing intensive treatment and also take courses at a different college. At that point he also agreed to discontinue use of marijuana, at least for a while, and to curtail the multiple phone calls and text messages he had for months been exchanging daily with Lorna, his former girlfriend, since she had left the university to live at home.

o fears of being embarrassed or rejected

Initially Eric had little difficulty in completely stopping his previously heavy use of marijuana; however, he was very hesitant about curtailing his phone and text messaging with Lorna. He said that for the past few months he had felt burdened by her frequent calls and texts, yet he was afraid to break off their relationship completely "because I don't know if there will ever be another girl who will care about me."

At first, I thought Eric was joking. He was a handsome, witty, charming young man with a winning smile and excellent manners and conversation skills. It was hard to imagine that he would not be very appealing to most people he met. Yet Eric quickly made it clear that regardless of what others might actually believe, he worried chronically and intensely that other people, male or female, did not really like him, "I always think that if they say they like me or seem friendly, they are just acting that way because they feel sorry for me and don't want to hurt my feelings."

An example occurred one day when Eric was with me. He had just sent a text message responding to a girl who had sent a text inviting him to go with her to a party. When she didn't respond to his message within ten minutes, he became visibly tense and preoccupied, pacing and repeatedly saying, "I guess she doesn't really want me to go with her. She's probably found someone else already." Eric then gave me multiple examples of how he had struggled since early childhood with fears that others disliked him or thought that he was "totally uncool." "I've always been too scared to ask someone else to do something with me. I wait until someone asks me first, even when I really want to go out with them. And I seriously hate calling anyone up on the phone. I always figure that they're busy doing something more important than me. It makes me so nervous that I feel like I'm going to throw up."

Though he was obviously happy and relieved when he received a confirming text from that girl an hour later, Eric continued to obsess about whether she really wanted him to go with her. Afterward, he reported that their date had been a lot of fun and that she had said she'd like to get together again. Yet Eric explained to me that he was able to relax in such situations only after he had consumed a couple of beers beforehand, followed by several throughout the evening. For days after, he remained preoccupied with worries about whether the girl had been truthful when she said she wanted to see him again.

Over the course of many such incidents, it became clear that Eric had long been suffering from well-disguised but severe social anxiety. When he had attached himself to Jenny and then later to Lorna, he felt safe, because their daily times together left him with less worry about having to meet new people and with steady reassurance that someone did want to be with him, at least until she didn't. Constant companionship with a close friend was his way of protecting himself from his underlying social anxiety.

For Eric, such anxieties about being embarrassed or disliked were not limited to dating situations. He reported that an important reason for his stopping class attendance and eventually dropping some of his college courses was that when he did not hand in an assignment on time, he was afraid to return to the class. He felt certain that the professor would be annoyed with him and would possibly confront him with a humiliating inquiry about why he had not done his work on time. His efforts to avoid such situations quickly snowballed into repeated absences and eventually to withdrawal from the course.

A similar problem with his physician contributed to Eric's second bout of bleeding colon. He had lost the prescriptions he had been given for the daily medication intended to prevent recurrence of such an attack; he felt too embarrassed to contact the physician for new prescriptions. Instead, he went without the medication for months and had another attack. He remained excessively focused on his fear of appearing careless or foolish to his physician, meanwhile ignoring and minimizing the possible threat to his health. This social anxiety had been pervasive for many years, but Eric was very skilled at hiding it.

Significant social anxiety is a chronic difficulty experienced by more than one third of teens and adults with ADHD. They live almost constantly with exaggerated fears of being seen by others as incompetent, unappealing, or, as Eric mentioned, "totally uncool."

Significant social anxiety is a chronic difficulty experienced by more than one-third of teens and adults with ADHD.[1] They live almost constantly with exaggerated fears of being seen by others as incompetent, unappealing, or, as Eric mentioned, "totally uncool." Some of this is based on their fear that others will recognize their chronic problems with self-management or that they will say or do something that others will view as stupid or grossly inappropriate. Some behave impulsively often enough that such a fear is not unrealistic.

Many with ADHD have great difficulty in shifting their focus of attention from such fears. They lack that "top-down" ability to divert their attention away from those specific worries and to remind themselves of other reasonable explanations for others' behavior or attitudes toward them—for example, maybe the girl was not responding because she was away from her phone or busy with something else. Their attention tends to be biased to look for "clues" to support their expectations of ridicule or rejection. In ambiguous situations, they tend to be much more ready than most to assume the worst about how others may be feeling about them. Often these emotional problems are tied to impairments of executive functions that could put the matter into a broader, more realistic perspective by helping them recall other information, less self-focused, that might be relevant.

○ inability to relax to go to sleep

Although at the outset of our work together, Eric had been quite willing to discontinue smoking marijuana, it soon became clear that stopping solved some problems and created others. Every night for several weeks, Eric experienced prolonged delay in getting to sleep; often he was unable to get to sleep until four or five in the morning. This led him to sleep until shortly before noon and sometimes longer. Eric reported that he had great difficulty in getting to sleep ever since he had stopped smoking marijuana. He said,

> I'm glad I'm not smoking it because during the day, my head
> is much clearer now, but it's really tough for me to get to sleep
> without it. I lie down to go to sleep at a reasonable time, but I just

can't turn my head off. I just keep thinking. So I get up and watch TV or go online until about three or four in the morning, and then I sleep like a dead man. Over the past few years, the doctors have had me try a bunch of different sleeping pills, but none of them worked for more than a few days. Weed is the only sleeping pill that has ever worked for me since I was living at home and going to high school where I came home every day exhausted from our sports practice and games.

Difficulty in settling down to go to sleep is a very common problem among people with ADHD. Many report that they often stay up much later than they really want to or should. Typically they involve themselves in watching TV, reading, following Facebook, surfing the Web, or playing video games until they finally become totally exhausted, and then, at last, they are able to get to sleep without long hours of lying in bed staring at the ceiling unable to shut off their mind's incessant ruminations.[2]

At my suggestion, Eric started going to the university gym each day to run or swim and lift weights. This helped him get to sleep some nights, but even when he had exercised, Eric endured many nights of being unable to get to sleep until three or four. Following those nights of insomnia, Eric usually couldn't get himself up until noon the next day.

The first few months of our intensive work were during the summer, and the two courses Eric enrolled in at the university met in early afternoon. This meant that he was able to get to classes despite his insomnia, but we knew that he would need to develop a more conventional sleep schedule in order to manage the full load of classes he would be taking in the fall.

We tried all the usual "sleep hygiene" strategies of stabilizing bedtime and trying to establish a fixed nighttime routine, but none of these worked. We retried him on the usual sequence of over-the-counter sleep aids, such as benadryl and melatonin; then we tried prescription medications: clonidine, clonazepam, and zolpidem. None of these worked for more than a few days; several did not work at all. Small doses were totally ineffective, and larger doses left him too hung over the next day. After patiently trying these various options without success, and as the fall semester was drawing near, Eric argued that he had done well at completely refraining from marijuana for a couple of months, but now wanted to resume use of small quantities only at bedtime to help him get to sleep. I felt uncomfortable with this plan because I worried that it would lead to resumption of his excessive use, but, given the failure of other options, I thought that it might be worth a cautious try, so I agreed.

Some clinicians would strongly oppose such a compromise. They are committed to total abstinence as the only effective approach for anyone who has used marijuana or any other illicit drug excessively. Others hold to a "harm reduction" approach, which encourages the patient to reduce use of such a drug to a minimal level, but does not insist that he or she achieve and maintain total abstinence.[3]

Considering that Eric had been able to maintain abstinence for over two months and that our usual treatments for chronic insomnia had not worked, I felt that the harm reduction approach was a reasonable gamble. As it turned out, this approach worked well, and there were only very few occasions when Eric used marijuana excessively. By smoking a small amount of marijuana on those nights when he otherwise couldn't get to sleep, Eric was usually able to relax and fall sleep between midnight and one a.m.

o inability to get up and start the day

Getting to bed at a reasonable time was not Eric's only problem with sleep. From early childhood, Eric had suffered from chronic difficulty in awakening, regardless of how many hours of sleep he had. He found it almost impossible to awaken in response to an alarm clock, even when he had been able to get to sleep between midnight and one a.m. and didn't need to get up until seven hours later. Eric still slept through multiple alarms and, on most days, needed a person to awaken him if he had to get up any time before eleven. Such difficulties in awakening are chronic problems for many teens and adults with ADHD, regardless of how many hours of sleep they have had.

Only when he was able to get a student in the apartment next door to come in and personally awaken him was Eric able to get himself up before noon. Once asleep, he was a very sound sleeper and very slow to awaken. On several occasions, the neighbor student had awakened Eric, had a conversation with him as he was getting out of bed, and then left, only to find out later that Eric had flopped back on the bed and resumed sleeping, unable to remember the conversation when he awakened several hours later.

After many months of this assisted awakening, Eric gradually developed the ability to waken and get himself up with an alarm clock combined with leaving the blinds in his room open so that morning sunlight shone in. During winter months when he needed to get up while it was still dark, Eric was able to manage with a special alarm clock he bought online; it turns on an increasingly bright light one half hour before its alarm is set to ring. It took many months for Eric to adequately control his problems with getting to sleep and awakening. Often such practical tactics and some continuing support are needed to help those with ADHD address their problems with sleep and awakening effectively.

○ insensitivity to fear of causing a driving accident

Getting up in time to get to his morning classes was associated with another problem. Like many other young adults with ADHD, Eric tended to drive too fast.[4] He did this when he was hurrying to get to class after he had left in the morning with insufficient time, but he tended to ignore speed limits even when he was not in a hurry. This is another example of how people with ADHD often get stuck in their focus on one concern that holds immediate importance for them while not keeping in mind other concerns, such as, in this case, safety.

At times he drove his car home after drinking with friends, insisting that he was not impaired. His only motor vehicle accident occurred when he slid off an icy road into a ditch as he was driving too fast for conditions, but during one year he acquired four speeding tickets and one DUI violation. Until he drove his car into the ditch and his parents finally refused to pay his fines and court costs, forcing him to pay the expenses from his own savings, Eric did not recognize his risky driving as a problem. Only when he had the experience of having to pay the hefty fines out of his own pocket did the potential problems take on sufficient importance to break through his denial of risk. This frightening problem continued as a focus of our conversations for many months; there were no more speeding tickets or DUI violations, but it wasn't clear how much of this was due to Eric's changing his driving habits and how much was luck. His problems with his schoolwork were somewhat easier to track.

○ lack of motivation to work for longer-term goals

In the fall, when Eric started his full-time course load at the university, his problems with getting his homework done became apparent. He found it very difficult to set aside time to do schoolwork during those daytime hours when he had no classes. In the evening, he tended to work only when he had a gun to his head, tackling assignments only on the night before they were due. Like many others with ADHD, he had a lot of trouble with prioritizing his activities and planning realistically for the time required to do an adequate job. On several occasions, Eric stayed up most of the night working ahead on homework assignments listed on the syllabus for the next few weeks. He said that he would rather pull an all-nighter once in a while to get ahead than to have to face homework on a daily basis. Needless to say, this strategy often left him behind in his assigned reading, and he frequently turned in papers having put in much less care than was required to do a good job.

For tests announced in advance, Eric usually scored very high, despite his taking only sparse notes in class. He was quite good at recalling what the professor had said in class, even though, according to his own report, Eric was often using his computer online during class, surfing or playing games to combat his boredom when the instructor was not an especially lively and interesting lecturer. Long reading assignments were very difficult for Eric; rarely could he sustain focus on a textbook or novel for more than fifteen minutes at a time.

To address this, we retried Eric on stimulants and found that he could tolerate very small doses of a short-acting amphetamine like Dexedrine or Adderall without adverse effects. This was significantly helpful to Eric for overriding his academic apathy, getting himself started on academic tasks, and sustaining necessary effort. However, his very sensitive body chemistry made it difficult to manage his medication dose and timing. One day when he inadvertently took a larger dose (one that would still be considered small for most adults), Eric experienced rapid heartbeat and shortness of breath that caused him to take himself to the emergency room. He was released without delay once it was determined that his symptoms were a transient response to a dose of stimulant too high for him; his cardiovascular system was otherwise in good shape.

After his ER visit, Eric continued to use small doses of amphetamine to help him focus on reading or writing assignments, but he remained careful to avoid increasing the dose or taking several doses closely spaced. Eric's responses to stimulant medication indicated that he had a body chemistry that was very sensitive to stimulants, whether in the form of medications or caffeinated beverages. This regimen of limited use of stimulant medication was helpful for improving Eric's ability to focus on specific academic tasks, such as completing a reading assignment or writing a short paper once he got started, but it was not sufficient to alleviate a larger problem: unless provided considerable support, Eric lacked motivation to function day to day as a student.

Eric's comment, "I'm in a great university where I want to do well, but I just can't get myself motivated to do the work" highlights his dilemma. When thinking about his life in broad terms, Eric clearly recognized that he was fortunate to be enrolled in an excellent university. He spoke of how his parents were spending a lot of money to provide this opportunity for him and how he knew that graduating from this university would offer him status and better options for postgraduation employment than he would otherwise have, yet these longer-term benefits were not sufficient to motivate him to engage himself in the daily tasks required of a serious student.

"Right now," Eric said, "I just don't give a damn about getting to class or doing the long, boring reading assignment or trying to write a paper on a topic I really don't care about." He emphasized that he felt a disconnect between his longer-term goals and the immediate tasks required to make progress toward accomplishing those goals. "For me," he said, "there are no consequences right now for getting that stuff done. It's not like I have a job where I get a paycheck at the end of the week if I do well, and get fired and have no money so I can't put gas in my car tomorrow if I don't get my work done today."

Eric's challenge is a clear example of a problem faced by many young adults, especially those with ADHD who feel and act apathetic toward work.[5] It is often very difficult for them to feel motivation strong enough and consistent enough today for doing tasks that will pay off for them only much further down the road. If the task today is not intrinsically interesting to them, they find it very difficult to get started and to sustain sufficient effort to complete those tasks that are likely to offer them substantial payoff years later.

impatience with waiting

Extraordinary impatience and difficulty in sustaining effort over the longer term such as Eric experienced can be seen clearly in some individuals from early childhood. Research with preschool children has demonstrated that even very young children differ in their ability to resist the temptation to grab an immediately available reward rather than wait to get a larger reward a few minutes later. A research team headed by Susan Campbell evaluated over a thousand children whom they studied from birth through third grade. When these children were thirty-six months old and again at fifty-four months, they were presented with brief tasks that tested their ability to wait for rewards and to resist temptation. Here are a couple of the tests they conducted.

> Eric's challenge is a clear example of a problem faced by many young adults, especially those with ADHD who feel and act apathetic toward work. It is often very difficult for them to feel motivation strong enough and consistent enough today for doing tasks that will pay off for them only much further down the road.

At age thirty-six months during a visit to the laboratory, each child was allowed to play just briefly with a very attractive toy. The evaluator then placed that toy just out of the child's reach and told the child not to touch it while she did some paperwork in the corner of the room. Meanwhile, the child was given several other toys to play with. In two-and-a-half minutes, the examiner went back and let the child play again with the attractive toy. Reviewing videotapes, researchers measured how long the child was able to hold back from handling the "forbidden" toy while the examiner was busy across the room.

At fifty-four months, the child returned to the laboratory and was asked to play "the waiting game." The child was seated at a table where there were two dishes. One contained a small amount of candy that could be eaten right away, but only after the child rang a bell to call the examiner. The other dish held a larger amount of candy, which the child could have if he or she waited to have any candy until after the examiner returned to the room to end the game seven minutes later.

Several years later, while in third grade, these children were evaluated using parent and teacher ratings to identify which were having academic or behavioral problems that met formal diagnostic criteria for ADHD. Significantly higher rates of ADHD and academic problems were found in those children who at thirty-six months were not able to wait two-and-a-half minutes to play again with the attractive toy, and in those who at fifty-four months chose to eat the smaller plate of candy immediately rather than to wait seven minutes for the larger plate of candy. Many children who eventually develop ADHD suffer from excessive impatience from their earliest years.[6]

Similar results have been found in numerous studies of children with ADHD at various ages. As a group, children with ADHD tend to become frustrated more quickly than a matched group of the same age when they have to wait for something they want. Given a choice between a bigger prize available after a brief wait or a smaller prize available immediately, children with ADHD tend to take the smaller immediate prize rather than wait a bit to get the larger prize.

This preference for relatively smaller rewards received sooner rather than larger rewards to be given a bit later has been described as increased "delay aversion" in children and adolescents with ADHD. The claim is that the individuals with ADHD, compared to others of the same age, tend to experience rapidly increasing frustration and other negative emotions when they have to wait for something they want. To minimize this negative emotion, they are more likely to choose an immediate reward, even if it is smaller than what they could obtain if they were to wait a bit.[7]

Most research on delay aversion has been done with younger children, and some researchers suggest that older children with ADHD are not as prone to opt for the smaller and more immediate reward, at least not in the simple choice testing situations used in research thus far. However, despite methodological problems, there is considerable research evidence that children, adolescents, and adults with ADHD tend to respond to potential rewards with less sensitivity than individuals without ADHD.

It is possible that the increased impatience with delay found in children with ADHD is simply an aspect of a broader problem they have with anticipating reward. This would suggest that people with ADHD are not as sensitive to pleasure from anticipated rewards and thus are more likely to opt for a lesser reward they can enjoy immediately. This would be consistent with findings from a study that used PET imaging to show that neurotransmitter chemicals that activate reward-recognizing circuits in the brain tend to bind on significantly fewer receptor sites in people with ADHD than in a similar sample of people without ADHD.[8]

This and other imaging studies suggest why people with ADHD often tend to be less able than others to anticipate pleasure or register satisfaction for tasks where the payoff is delayed. An important effect of this may be that people with ADHD often have great difficulty in activating themselves to get started on tasks that are not especially interesting to them and in sustaining motivation for tasks where the rewards for doing the task are not imminently available.

It may be that individuals with ADHD are not "wired" to be as sensitive to potential rewards compared to immediately available rewards as most others of the same age. Recent brain imaging (fMRI) studies have shown that neural networks that alert the brain to anticipated rewards and to register pleasure or satisfaction tend to be significantly less sensitive in adults with ADHD than in controls.[9]

Clearly exemplifying these difficulties experienced by individuals with ADHD in working for anticipated rewards, Eric explained to me one day,

> For me there are no payoffs and no consequences if I miss classes or don't get my work done. Final grades, graduation, and getting a job seem like they are a hundred years away. It's hard for me to care about doing stuff I don't like when the payoffs and consequences are so far away. I need something immediate. Maybe I shouldn't even be in school. Maybe I should just get some kind of job where I would get a nice paycheck if I just show up on time and do my job.

○ changing the time frames for incentives

Eric's family is well off financially, and he had never held a job to work for his own spending money. His parents provided him a credit card, and they unquestioningly paid all his expenses, reasonable and not so reasonable, while he was in college. After Eric did poorly during his first semester of intensive treatment, when he had to withdraw from three of his five courses to avoid failing them because of undone assignments and excessive absences, I had a conference with Eric and his parents.

With my encouragement, Eric's parents decided to take up his challenge to set up more immediate payoffs and punishments for his doing well or poorly during each week of the following semester. They cancelled his credit card and arranged for him to earn the money he needed by working as a student. They stipulated that each week he would collect a reasonable sum of spending money for each day that he provided evidence of attending his classes and working productively on his assignments.

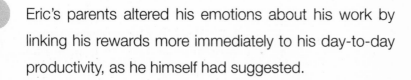

Eric's parents altered his emotions about his work by linking his rewards more immediately to his day-to-day productivity, as he himself had suggested.

If he did not go to class on any given day or did not show evidence of productive work—for example, appropriate underlining of reading assignments, research notes, or drafts for assigned papers—he would not be given any spending money for that day. His spending money for each week was determined by the quantity and quality of his academic efforts. This was not payment for high grades; it was payment for productive work. In this way, Eric's parents established a reinforcement schedule to provide him more immediate payoffs and undelayed penalties based on his day-to-day work as a student. With this system, Eric's parents addressed his problem with sustaining motivation in a way that he noticed and responded to. They altered his emotions about his work by linking his rewards more immediately to his day-to-day productivity, as he himself had suggested.

It took many weeks to work out an effective system to evaluate Eric's productivity and to provide him appropriate positive and negative consequences, but this approach seemed over time to give Eric what he needed to improve his motivation to do his assigned work, even when he clearly did not feel like doing it. These more immediate reinforcements, not so different from paying a young adult to do any other job, seemed more effective than any incentives that would have required him to wait months to receive the promised reward, such as payment for acceptable final grades.

Numerous times in the early weeks of the second semester, Eric earned no money because he failed to do the work to complete his daily assignments. He had no funds to buy gas or go out with friends. Soon these more immediate positive and negative consequences led him to work more productively so that he could more consistently earn the money he wanted. For him, doing his schoolwork eventually became more like earning money on a regular job, where failure to show up or to do one's work brings rapid penalties.

Given the difficulty many young adults with ADHD have in working for longer-term goals, some of them may need similar arrangements for more immediate and consistent reinforcement. Unfortunately, few families have the means to implement a plan similar to Eric's. For most of those students with ADHD who have severe problems sustaining adequate motivation to do postsecondary academic work, the only practical option may be to work full-time in a job, if they can get one, where they may develop the self-discipline to get up and go to work each day, putting up with those frustrations to earn a weekly paycheck. For some, such work experience may motivate them to return to college to work as a full-time or part-time student. For others, it may be the beginning of a work history that is never supported by education beyond high school. Some individuals, with or without ADHD, are quite successful in a career without a college or university degree; others are not.

o   o   o

This brief description of Eric and his experiences cannot encompass all the many facets of his strengths and his difficulties. Yet it does illustrate some of the complex ways in which his heightened sensitivities and some lack of sensitivity, his hopes and anxieties, his shame and his pride, his impatience and his determination interacted to shape his responses to an important life transition and to his early experience in intensive treatment.

Eric's experience with ADHD was unusual. Because his body was so sensitive to the medications currently available to alleviate symptoms of this disorder, medication had to play a very limited role in his treatment. Most people with ADHD are able to gain at least some benefit from medication treatment. For some, the benefits are huge; for others, the positive effects are moderate; and for still others, like Eric, the benefits are more limited and modest. Eric's experience is also unusual in that he had the opportunity and family resources to engage in a protracted period of intensive treatment for his ADHD, an opportunity in which he fully engaged himself, usually with candor, patience, and delightful good humor.

Eric returned to his first university after one year of treatment with me, and he graduated successfully two years later.

What Helped Eric?

- Change of context — a new living arrangement while continuing in a different full-time college
- Abstinence from marijuana, followed by a harm reduction approach to use marijuana only as a sleep aid
- Talk therapy focusing primarily on severe but unrecognized social anxiety
- Daily assistance with awakening until he could awaken independently
- Low dosing of stimulant medication to fit bodily hypersensitivity
- System of immediate rewards contingent on working effectively as a student

3

karen

My parents always taught me that I have an obligation to behave and achieve in ways that would not bring shame on my family. When I failed out of college, they helped me prepare to try again. I wanted very much to do it, but on that critical day when I was supposed to start the last two courses I needed to get readmitted, I was too afraid to walk in the classroom door.

—22-YEAR-OLD UNIVERSITY STUDENT

Karen's parents had been very pleased when she began her undergraduate studies at a prestigious university; they were shocked two years later when they learned that Karen was being required by the university to take a leave of absence because of poor academic achievement. Karen had not told them about her being placed on academic probation in the middle of her second year because of too many missed classes, too many papers turned in late or left undone, and an excessive number of low scores on examinations. Karen's grade-point average had dropped below the minimum required to continue there as a student, and she was told that she would need to complete a year of successful full-time studies at some other university in order to gain readmission. Karen had explained her failures as due to escalating depression for which she felt too ashamed to ask for help.

Despite their disappointment, Karen's parents had been supportive. They scolded her for not letting them know earlier of her academic difficulties and depression so that they could have provided assistance, but they recognized her feeling ashamed and quickly refocused to help her arrange the required year of studies at another university. At the time of their consultation with me, Karen had completed the year of studies at this alternative university and had earned good grades in most of her courses. However, she had failed two courses because she had been unable to complete the final exams within the allocated time. This meant that she needed to pick up two additional courses in summer school in order to gain reentry to the university where she had begun her undergraduate work.

The reason Karen and her parents sought consultation with me was that after enrolling in the summer school to take the two courses she needed, Karen was unable to get herself to go to the initial meeting or any subsequent session of either class. After several days of arriving on time and sitting on the steps of the classroom building, unable to enter, she gave up and continued for almost two months to live in her off-campus apartment, pretending in phone conversations with her parents that she was attending the classes, though she never even enrolled. Her parents discovered the problem only after about seven weeks when they found that the check they had given Karen to pay the summer school tuition had never been cashed by the university.

When the parents confronted Karen, she acknowledged with many tears and much shame that she had been unable to overcome acute panic attacks suffered each time she tried to enter the summer school classroom building. Each day for two weeks, she had walked to the classroom building on time, determined to go to the class. As she approached the door, her heart suddenly began to beat very rapidly; she was unable to catch her breath, and broke into a cold sweat. She felt that she was having a heart attack. These terrifying sensations lasted about ten or fifteen minutes each time and abated only when she gave up on her intention to enter the class that day and returned to her apartment. (Psychological factors that contribute to such experiences are discussed later in this chapter.)

In my office, Karen and her parents explained that she was now not allowed readmission to the university where she had begun; they did not know what to do. In our conversation, together with her parents and alone with me, Karen believably emphasized her readiness to face at last the problems that had now twice disrupted her studies. Tearfully she acknowledged, "I know I've needed help for a long time, but until now I haven't been able to say so. I know my parents wanted to get me help, but I felt too ashamed to accept it. I desperately wanted to fix it all myself."

After a comprehensive clinical evaluation, I found that Karen was an extremely bright young woman; her verbal IQ was at the 99th percentile. Yet she was suffering from three undiagnosed overlapping problems: attention deficit disorder, chronic anxiety with panic disorder, and chronic low-grade depression. She and her parents agreed that she would move to an apartment near my office and enroll in a local university to take a full-time course load while engaging in intensive treatment with me. Her hope was that she could complete this treatment in one semester with grades strong enough to allow her to reenter her first university. I cautioned that my office is not a setting for miracles, but agreed that we could consider Karen's options after we evaluated how she responded to appropriate medication and intensive talk therapy.

As we began our work together, Karen described her difficulties with her studies in more detail. She explained that she had found the transition from high school to college extremely difficult. She had done quite well in a very competitive high school that was highly structured and had mandatory tutoring. There her grades were high, and she enjoyed a lively social life with many friends. She was active in sports and had been captain of two varsity athletic teams in her school, stopping participation only after a back injury shortly before her high school graduation.

From her first weeks at college, Karen had felt intensely intimidated and overwhelmed by the less structured, much more demanding academic setting, where competition among students seemed cutthroat. She told how she had struggled from her earliest weeks. She said she was afraid to talk at all with faculty or to speak up and ask questions in class because all her classmates seemed so much smarter. She spoke of how helpless she felt in organizing and starting assigned papers without the support of tutors such as she had during high school. Most problematic, she said, was feeling overwhelmed and unable to keep up with heavy reading and writing assignments in multiple classes. She explained that it usually took her twice as long as her classmates to complete reading assignments because she often had to reread the assignment multiple times in order to understand and remember what she had read.

o   problems with reading comprehension and recall

Many students with ADHD report this problem of needing to reread assignments. For Karen, as for many others, this was not a matter of having difficulty recognizing and understanding the words she was reading; she was a very fluent reader. Her problem in reading was a chronic difficulty with sustaining focus and holding in mind what she had just read; it was as though her eyes simply slid over the words, passively recognizing them but not fully grasping and encoding the meanings in memory. This problem is especially vexing for people with ADHD when they are reading materials that are not especially interesting to them.

Another student once described to me his similar experience by saying, "When I'm reading something I'm not intensely interested in, it's as though my mind is licking the words and not chewing them." He understood the meaning of each word as he read it, but he was not able to keep the meanings in mind long enough to grasp and remember the content.

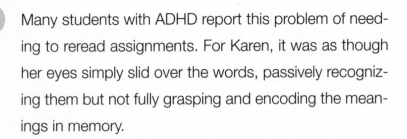

Many students with ADHD report this problem of needing to reread assignments. For Karen, it was as though her eyes simply slid over the words, passively recognizing them but not fully grasping and encoding the meanings in memory.

Scientists who study dyslexia have recently begun to emphasize the critical importance of attention in reading comprehension. They recognize that the ability to decode words on the page is not sufficient for adequate comprehension — fluency and focused attention are also essential. These capacities are closely linked to the individual's ability to hold focus, to sustain processing speed, and to use working memory, all of which tend to be among the executive functions impaired in ADHD.[1]

○ extended time accommodations for examinations

Our research group at Yale studied reading problems of students with ADHD by comparing the performance of 145 students thirteen to eighteen years old, all of whom had ADHD, on a standardized test of reading comprehension, with and without extended time. All took the test with the usual twenty-minute time limit; those unable to finish in that time were allowed an extended limit of twelve more minutes. Although the verbal comprehension abilities of these students were in the high-average range, 53 percent were unable to complete the test within twenty minutes, and only 42 percent were able to obtain a reading comprehension score that was within 15 points of their verbal ability score on an IQ test. When the students were allowed the additional twelve minutes, the percentage able to complete the test rose to 78 percent, all of those improving their test score to within 15 points of their verbal ability score.

When students unable to finish in the standard time were asked to explain their need for extra time, most said that they needed to reread many of the passages multiple times in order to answer the test questions. Because their IQ index scores for processing speed and working memory were significantly lower than is usual for students of their ability level, it is likely that their rereading was an effort to compensate for their difficulty with keeping information in mind and their relative slowness in processing visual information.[2]

Karen explained that her difficulty in completing timed tests was also complicated by worry about whether she would be able to finish in time. She said that often in the middle of such a test she would be saying repeatedly to herself, "Oh my God, I'm not going to be able to get finished in time, I won't even be able to get to try a bunch of the questions." These worries would take up a lot of space in her mind, limiting the amount of space for her to think about and remember what she was reading. To address her chronic difficulties with inattention and to improve her focus for reading comprehension, Karen and I agreed that she would start a trial of sustained-release methylphenidate to see if that might help alleviate her ADHD symptoms. She did this and soon reported significant improvement in her ability to focus and to sustain attention to her reading and other academic tasks. I also provided Karen with documentation of her disabilities and need for extended time on tests and examinations. She submitted this documentation to her university and was granted extended time for all tests and examinations.

○ social and performance anxiety linked with guilt

Many worries often gobbled up a lot of space in Karen's mind. One of her most persistent worries was that she might embarrass or bring shame upon her family. Her mother often reminded her of the importance her parents placed on acting responsibly and doing well so that members of their extended family would not be critical. Karen thought that this recurrent emphasis might be due to her mother's having grown up in a family with lower social status than Karen's father; her mother seemed to worry a lot about whether she and her children would be criticized by members of the father's family. Karen's strategy for dealing with this was usually to refrain from telling her parents about any difficulties she was having. This was a significant factor in Karen's not telling her parents about her problems at college until they became unavoidably obvious.

As we talked about Karen's long-standing and excessive worries about doing well and keeping her parents happy, I could see that Karen was suffering from chronic anxiety. This became especially clear after Karen reported a brief panic attack as she was working to make arrangements to reenter her first university for the spring term. I suggested that it might be useful for Karen to start a trial of fluoxetine (concurrent with her sustained-release methylphenidate) to reduce her chronic anxiety and to try to prevent further panic attacks. She agreed, and began this regimen. Within a few weeks, Karen reported that she felt considerably less anxious; she also experienced no adverse effects from either medication. A few weeks later, Karen told me that she had begun to feel more comfortable in approaching her professors and in speaking up in class, interactions she had rarely engaged in previously.

o family worries and family roles

Karen was not the only person in her family to worry excessively; her parents seemed to worry a lot also. After she left home to go to college, they felt a continuing need to maintain very close contact with her. They called her or expected her to call them at least once or twice each day. Some of their wish for frequent contact was clearly to provide support for Karen, who was living far from home. However, these frequent contacts also reassured and supported the parents as they struggled and coped with the daily challenges of their own lives. Parents are generally strengthened when they learn that their son or daughter is doing well. Karen developed considerable skill in reassuring her parents that she was doing well, even when she was having great difficulty in school.[3]

> In each family, children and adults tend to take on and maintain specific roles as they interact directly and indirectly with one another over time. Often these roles are acknowledged only in recurrent jokes and nicknames that family members exchange with one another.

In each family, children and adults tend to take on and maintain specific roles as they interact directly and indirectly with one another over time. Often these roles are acknowledged only in recurrent jokes and nicknames that family members exchange with one another. Someone may be seen as "the good one," "the nasty one," "the troublemaker," "the fearful one," "the complainer," "the strong one," "the weak one," "the rule enforcer," "the defiant one," "the messy and disorganized one," "the prude," "the fixer," "the stingy one," "the generous one," "the selfish one," "the fragile one," "the invulnerable one," and so on. Often a given family member carries multiple roles depending on the situation, sometimes happily, sometimes with resentment, and sometimes without awareness.

Family roles may evolve, being modified or exchanged over time in response to situational stresses or as family members get older or develop changing relationships with others within or outside the family. Yet often some of these roles are repeatedly reinforced and strongly internalized as family members continue to interact with one another according to unrecognized scripts consistent with their expected roles.

Karen had a younger brother who was quite hyperactive and difficult for his parents to manage during his childhood. Being older, with a mild temperament and cooperative attitude, Karen readily was seen as "the good child" about whom her parents did not need to worry, the one who could always be counted on to cooperate without a fuss, the one who did not present significant problems for her parents. From her early years, she was delegated in her family to be successful and problem free, a role that made it extremely difficult for her to acknowledge to herself and to her parents when she was having trouble. Until her early twenties, she fulfilled her delegated role without significant incident.[4]

o destructive avoidance and denial

Karen's avoidance of acknowledging imperfections intruded even into her therapeutic work with me. Although she was quite articulate in explaining her past difficulties to me, she was not able to be so forthcoming in explaining her current problems in school. As her first semester went on, Karen continued to talk about her wish to return to her first university after her current semester of work in the university near my office. She described her visits with the dean of her first university to discuss plans for reentry at the start of the spring semester and said she was quite confident that she would have strong grades to make this possible.

In our twice-weekly meetings, I regularly inquired of Karen about her current coursework and looked at some of the papers she was working on. Her papers were very well written, and she was generally able to talk quite articulately and interestingly about her current course reading and class discussions. Near the end of the semester, Karen reported that she was struggling with her economics course and was afraid that her final grade might be a C, but she expressed confidence that this would not be a problem for her being readmitted to her first university because all her other grades would be higher.

When grades were posted at the end of the semester, Karen reported that she was unable to access her grades because of a paperwork problem having to do with a form required by the university health service that she had never filed. Having seen this problem with a previous patient, I trusted her report. Soon after, Karen announced that she had decided to spend one more semester at the local university before returning to her first university. She said she felt that the additional semester of studying there while working with me would better prepare her for the more competitive university to which she planned to return. This revised plan sounded quite reasonable, so I took her report at face value. Over the next six weeks, we discussed the courses Karen had selected and begun for her spring term; she told me details about the readings she was doing and the term projects she planned to do.

> It was almost time for midterm exams when I discovered that Karen had been lying to me about her current functioning in the same way she had twice lied to her parents.

Six weeks into the spring semester, I received an email from Karen's parents saying that the check they had given her to pay for her second semester had not yet been cashed by the university. I confronted Karen, and, after a few efforts to deny the obvious, she acknowledged that she had never actually paid tuition for her spring classes, that she had failed her economics course, that she had gotten an incomplete in her history course due to never having handed in a required paper, and that she had stopped attending spring term classes after the second week. What she had told me about her courses beyond that point was a fabrication based on her having picked up and read the syllabus for each course. It was almost time for midterm exams when I discovered that Karen had been lying to me about her current functioning in the same way she had twice lied to her parents. I had fallen for it, and now it was much too late for her to enroll in those courses.

Once again there were many tears and much talk of shame, but Karen had placed herself in a very difficult position. She reported that she herself did not understand why she had let things slide in preparing for her econ exam and in completing the history paper. She said she did not know why she had not told me the real reason for her deciding at the last minute to stay at the local university for another semester, rather than returning to her first university for the spring term. She said that she herself was puzzled about why she had not completed enrollment for the spring term at the local university and about why she had not been able to tell me or her parents about her not getting herself started in her spring classes. This time there were no panic attacks — the fluoxetine seemed to be helping that — but there was, once again, failure to get started in classes she wanted and needed to take.

It certainly was difficult to understand why Karen had once again sabotaged her efforts to return to her first university. One possibility was that as the time for her planned return drew closer, she became increasingly frightened of the possibility of failing again if she returned to that very competitive environment. This might explain her failure to prepare adequately for her econ exam and to complete that paper in history, a course in which she had been doing quite well. However, that did not explain Karen's failure to enroll in the spring term classes at the local university.

Some observers might attempt to apply psychodynamic explanations to Karen's puzzling, self-damaging behavior. They might think of her as being immobilized by conflicting emotions. They might wonder whether her avoidance of starting her spring classes was a way of punishing herself for having once again disappointed her parents by not returning as planned to her first university. Was it a way of breaking out of her long-standing role as "the good and flawless daughter"? Was it a way of trying to escape from being too closely monitored by her parents and, perhaps, by me?

One or several of these motives might have been involved in Karen's actions, but she reported that there was no time when she consciously thought about such issues. She said that one day in the second week of spring classes, she had missed a train and returned from an out-of-town visit with friends too late to be able to get to two of her classes. She then felt so embarrassed that she avoided going to the next meeting of each of those two classes and then felt too embarrassed to report this to me. Karen may indeed have consciously thought about these events in this way, but her explanation did not account for the fact that she never took her parents' check to the university bursar to pay for spring tuition.

To some, this omission may suggest that Karen had strongly con-flicted feelings about completing her degree. They may assume that with-out consciously intending to do so, Karen acted in a way that brought both the long-dreaded embarrassment to her parents and punishment by loss of face upon herself.

o inadequate modulation of anxiety

Using speculations about emotional conflicts to explain Karen's persist-ing difficulty in dealing with her anxiety is not very helpful. Such expla-nations do not adequately take into account the intense power of anxiety or the pervasive effects of major failures in the brain's system for regulat-ing emotion. Often such efforts to provide psychodynamic explanations for puzzling behavior are used as a not-so-subtle way to blame the vic-tim of severe anxiety or other problems caused by inadequately regulated emotions.

To understand the puzzling, self-damaging behaviors of people in situations similar to Karen's, it is essential to recognize the critical role of the brain's alarm and gating mechanisms for regulating emotion. The human brain has a mechanism that allows it to modulate the intensity of experienced anxiety, frustration, discouragement, and so on. This enables a person to feel a little anxious for small stresses, moderately anxious for moderate stresses, and severely anxious for severe stressors. For some people, this system often behaves like a defective smoke detector.

> For some people, the brain's gating mechanism for regulating emotion does not effectively distinguish between seriously dangerous threats and much more minor problems.

Smoke detectors are designed to emit a loud, piercing sound when they detect smoke indicating that the building is on fire. Some defective smoke detectors sound that alarm in response to a thin wisp of smoke resulting from a piece of toast slightly overcooking in the toaster. For some people, the brain's gating mechanism for regulating emotion does not effectively distinguish between seriously dangerous threats and much more minor problems. These individuals are quickly thrown into panic mode by thoughts or perceptions that do not warrant such a reaction. Suddenly they experience the bodily sensations of rapid heartbeat, shortness of breath, and so on that normally would accompany only perceptions of a serious and imminent danger to life. This is what happened to Karen on the steps of the classroom building when she was unable to enter to start her summer school courses.

When Karen walked away from the building without entering it, she felt shame and frustration, but also powerful relief of the anxiety that had overwhelmed her when she was sitting on the steps trying to force herself to enter. For someone in this sort of situation, the relief brought by such avoidance is a powerful reinforcer; it collapses the mounting tension and greatly increases the likelihood that she will once again resort to avoidance when confronted with similar stressors. The avoiding individual may feel bad about having failed to confront her fears and walking away from the challenge, but she also tends to feel a massive sense of relief that she has, at least for that day, dodged the bullet that she feared was going to destroy her.

When the "top-down" mechanism for regulating anxiety works as it should, it allows cognitive space for a person to think about how to deal more rationally and realistically with stressors that otherwise may immobilize reasonable thought and planning. This is the mechanism that allows us to say to ourselves in a situation of frustration or worry, "Calm down, it's not that big a deal, I need to figure out some sensible way to deal with this mess."[5] When Karen attempted to enter the classroom and start the courses she needed to return to her original university, fulfilling her hopes and intentions, this top-down mechanism collapsed within her.

For most of us, most of the time, this gating mechanism for regulating emotion works adequately. When I was a very young boy, I removed from a cabinet most of a set of crystal goblets that were a treasured gift my parents had received as a wedding present. I arranged them in a row with different levels of water in each, then tapped them with a table knife to make music. In the process, I accidentally broke several of the goblets. It is not unusual in such situations for a parent to feel like lashing out in a strong verbal attack, laying a heavy burden of guilt on the child; some parents might also feel a strong impulse to hit and possibly hurt the child. Yet most parents can modulate their response, taking into account that the child probably did not intend to do such damage and did not realize the value of the object. They are able to keep in mind their wish to protect the son or daughter from any disproportionate verbal or physical attack that would cause long-term negative effects.

This top-down control system usually allows us to avoid excessively extreme impulsive reactions to stressors that may otherwise bring intense fear, anger, shame, and discouragement. This mechanism also clears the way for us to think in more realistic and practical terms about how to handle a problematic situation that requires some corrective action in order for us to avoid making it worse.

Yet for some people, especially many with ADHD, this top-down mechanism is often ineffective; it does not prevent an intense cascade of emotion that floods the person so completely that he is unable to think clearly about his response. Quickly he is overwhelmed by panic or anger or hopelessness that may be quite disproportionate to the actual situation. At that point, he is unable to keep in mind other facts and feelings that are also relevant and important; he may act impulsively and make choices that may seriously worsen his situation, later producing strong feelings of regret and remorse when the negative consequences of his actions and choices cannot be undone.

When Karen realized that she had failed her econ exam, she felt a sustained and intensely disproportionate flooding of anxiety and shame. As I have said elsewhere, I might compare this flooding to a virus's gobbling up all the space on a computer's hard drive, but that simile does not capture the full magnitude or intensity of Karen's reaction to this situation. Usually a computer crash can be fixed readily, and lost data can, one hopes, be restored by a backup system. That sort of flooding is usually transient and generally can be repaired.

○ desperate efforts to cope

When Karen recognized that she had failed her econ course, her emotional shock was much more like an overwhelming tsunami that suddenly and irretrievably washed away all her chances of getting back into the first university, all her hopes of restoring her good standing with her parents, and all possibilities of her getting her life back on track. This intense and pervasive emotion utterly overwhelmed the rational thought processes that otherwise might have allowed her to consider alternatives and engage in productive brainstorming with others who might have been able to help her.

Trapped in paralyzing shame and fear of exposure, Karen fell back on her well-practiced but ineffective strategies of avoidance and denial. She told herself that somehow she would soon figure out a way to fix this problem herself, before anyone else found out. She vowed that somehow she would be able to return to her first university as planned. Operating with this determination, she avoided paying the tuition for spring term at the local university. For her, making that payment and thus finalizing her enrollment would have constituted unavoidable recognition of what she was desperately trying to ignore and deny: that for a third time she had failed to complete satisfactorily the academic goal she had set out for herself and to her parents.

Karen's experience is an example of intense emotion disrupting rational thought and driving a person's behavior solely on the basis of wishes and fears rather than on a realistic assessment of the situation. In a very real sense, Karen was trying to keep this failure secret not only from her parents and her therapist but also from herself. Having read the syllabi for courses she had planned to take, she used imaginative lies to paint a convincing picture of herself doing the work for five courses while, in fact, she had not been attending any of them. By keeping this failure secret for more than six weeks, Karen rendered herself unable to complete the additional semester of coursework that, had it been successfully completed, could well have gotten her back into her first university in the following fall. She also seriously undermined her parents' growing trust.

Karen was an international student at her university. Because her home was outside the United States, she was required to maintain good academic standing to meet the requirements of her student visa. Her failure to enroll in a full-time load of courses at her university constituted a violation of the terms of her visa, so she was required to abruptly leave the United States and return to her home country. It was much too late in the semester for her to enroll in the courses she needed. She returned to her family in her home country. Before her departure, I spoke at length with her and her parents about the importance of Karen's revising her plans, not continuing further at that point in full-time academic studies, and working in business for a time while taking only part-time academic courses.

For several weeks, I heard nothing from Karen, but one month after she arrived home, I received a phone call from her and her parents. Happily they reported that she had been able to find a full-time job. It did not pay much, but it gave her an opportunity to work in a field that strongly interested her. She was able to reconnect with some of her old friends at home and had many opportunities to work collaboratively with others, while also receiving much closer daily supervision. Already her job supervisor had given her a promotion with added responsibilities. She also had enrolled in a community college and had begun a night school course to resume work toward her college degree, this time at a slower pace. This more structured situation seemed a good fit for Karen at this point in her life. I hoped that from this base she would be able to gradually develop her capacity to work more independently and to more adequately manage her strong anxiety so that she would be able more fully to realize her impressive potential.

What Helped Karen?

- Change of context — a new living arrangement while making a third attempt to continue full-time college
- Talk therapy focusing on pressures of family expectations and shame
- Medications to alleviate ADHD impairments, depression, and excessive anxiety (only partially successful)
- Psychoeducational testing to support receiving the accommodation of extended time for taking tests
- Counseling after third failure in full-time college studies to revise goals and plans, undertaking a more manageable part-time school experience
- Undertaking full-time employment in business where more structure and more immediate rewards and consequences are provided
- Structure of returning to live at home temporarily with family while restabilizing after third academic failure

4

martin

I'm in Mensa, but I earned no credits in my first two years at college—I was too baked to get myself to class. Now I'm doing well in a few courses where the professors are really interesting, but I can't get started on writing papers and often skip class. . . . With my miserable academic record, what's the use in my trying to graduate?
—23-YEAR-OLD UNIVERSITY STUDENT

Martin was a handsome but somewhat reserved young man when he came with his parents for an initial consultation with me. At that time, he was in the middle of his second year of college. His father emphasized that since his earliest years, Martin had been seen by his parents and teachers as extremely bright, but unable to sustain attention to tasks, quite absentminded, not very hard working, and not very good at getting along with his peers. He recalled a time in second grade when the teacher had spoken of Martin as "the little professor" who could answer many questions, but acted aloof from his classmates.

Over the years, Martin's parents had sought consultations with several different doctors to determine how they could help their son develop his extraordinary intelligence. One psychiatrist saw him as simply stubborn; another suggested that he might be "a bit autistic." His parents questioned whether Martin might have an attention disorder, but the doctors said that someone so very bright could not have such a problem. No doctor had any suggestions that seemed helpful.

○ risks of high IQ with ADHD

In describing reasons for seeking consultation with me, Martin's father emphasized the discrepancy between Martin's high IQ and his achievement throughout his schooling. This is a burden carried by many of those who have both high IQ and ADHD. At least until their ADHD is diagnosed and treated, they tend to suffer repeated reminders of how they are not performing up to the level expected by those who know that they are extraordinarily intelligent. They tend to feel disappointed in themselves, and they sense the disappointment of their parents and teachers.

Often this discrepancy leads parents and teachers to try to encourage the underperforming student's efforts by reminding him of how smart he is. Research suggests that this approach is generally not as helpful as one that encourages the student when he works hard, emphasizing that he can improve his performance by continuing to work hard. Studies have shown that students who see their intelligence as a given, fixed quantity demonstrate different brain-wave patterns and less motivation in response to discouraging feedback than do those who see their intelligence as a capacity that can be improved with learning and hard work. These studies found that students who grow up thinking that each person is born with an unchanging level of intelligence are likely to give up in frustration more quickly after encountering negative feedback, assuming that their intelligence is just not sufficient to the task. In contrast, students who have learned to think of intelligence as a capacity that can be improved with continued effort are more likely to keep working after experiences of frustration or negative feedback, trying to improve their future performance.[1]

It is not unusual for people with high IQ to be seen as unlikely to have an attention deficit disorder. Our research group at Yale and others have published research showing that people with high IQ, even some quite accomplished and able to focus well for a few specific activities, can suffer from significant attention problems. ADHD impairments are not limited to any particular level of intelligence; they can affect anyone from those with the highest IQ to those at the lowest end of the range.[2]

Many doctors and educators have not yet reached this understanding. They assume that a high level of intelligence confers protection against attention problems, and they do not recognize that a student can be very bright and focus very well for a few specific activities, including standardized tests, and still have significant difficulty in deploying his impressive intelligence for most activities of daily life, including some that the student himself considers quite important. Often these difficulties are taken as problems resulting from boredom or lack of willpower, when they are actually problems with chemical dynamics of the brain.[3]

o avoidance of social contacts

Martin's grades in elementary school were good, though well below what his parents expected. Throughout those years, he had very little contact with peers outside the classroom, and he was not active in any clubs or sports. At home, Martin was not very affectionate with family members and spent most of his free time reading, watching television, and using the computer.

Martin's parents had been concerned for many years not only about their son's failure to perform academically up to their expectations but also about his lack of interest in engaging with others of the same age in friendships, sports, clubs, or other peer-group activities. They lived very near a park where other children often went to play, yet Martin consistently avoided going out to join in informal play or to participate in sports. Martin refused to get involved in such activities and often complained about other students at school teasing him.

Martin's parents thought that their son's avoidance and difficulties with peers might be a result of other students' being jealous of their son's precocious cognitive abilities, but they also worried that perhaps something was missing in his ability to interact with others his age. The suggestion of one doctor who evaluated Martin that the boy might be "a bit autistic" worried them.

In his initial interviews with me, Martin did not appear at all autistic. He seemed a bit rigid and overly formal in his speech patterns, but he did maintain eye contact and was engaged; he also seemed quite droll and was able to engage in witty, ironic humor. Yet there was still some of the "little professor" style that had been commented on by his second-grade teacher, and some hints of insensitivity to the feelings and concerns of others.

Martin was socially isolated, living in a single apartment and interacting very little with other students, even those who rented apartments in the same building. He candidly acknowledged that he was smoking marijuana heavily and, with much shame, confessed that he rarely left his apartment to go to class or interact with other students.

When Martin was twelve years old, his parents sent him to boarding school, hoping that the more structured, round-the-clock situation would be helpful both for his academic development and for improving his ability to get along with peers. Initially Martin was very shy and uncomfortable; he was a bit small for his age, and classmates often teased and bullied him. After some months, he gradually interacted more with his dorm mates, but he suffered some emotional scars and never made any close friends. In their reports, teachers commented on his being quite bright but extremely inattentive and very inconsistent in academic work, often late with homework and other assignments. Nevertheless, in that highly structured setting, he completed his high school studies with high marks and then was admitted to a competitive university.

o initial assessment

When he came with his parents for an initial consultation with me, Martin and his parents were frustrated with his poor performance in college.

His grades were low, primarily because he rarely attended class and often didn't prepare or complete assignments. This university had no dormitories; students were required to find apartments in the city and make their own arrangements for meals. Martin was socially isolated, living in a single apartment and interacting very little with other students, even those who rented apartments in the same building. He candidly acknowledged that he was smoking marijuana heavily and, with much shame, confessed that he rarely left his apartment to go to class or interact with other students.

After a comprehensive evaluation, I found that Martin was, in fact, an extremely bright young man; his IQ scores were in the top 3 percent of the population. He was appealing and showed a good sense of humor and a wide-ranging understanding of current events. He referred to himself as a "news junkie" who regularly followed the news in print, on the radio and TV, and online. He noted that if his studies continued as they had been going, he would never earn his degree. Yet he also claimed that he did not feel lonely, and emphasized that he was a very independent fellow who did not like to rely on anyone for help and who felt determined to fix his problems himself.

At the conclusion of that initial consultation, I urged Martin to taper down and discontinue his use of marijuana. His chronic use of marijuana had been helping diminish his feelings of loneliness as well as his feelings of shame and hopelessness about his academic failures, but it was also diminishing Martin's ability to mobilize himself to deal constructively with his problems with school and social relationships.

This evaluation also confirmed Martin's suspicion and that of his parents that he was suffering from a significantly impairing attention deficit disorder of the nonhyperactive type. I suggested that he begin a trial of medication treatment for his ADHD as soon as he was able to significantly reduce his excessive use of marijuana. I explained that medications for ADHD could not be effective for someone heavily using marijuana. Because his university was very far from my office, I urged him to seek and engage in treatment with a local doctor who could help him address his marijuana dependence, his ADHD, and his discomfort in social interaction with peers.

Martin said he was quite interested in trying medication treatment for his ADHD and stated his determination to stop his use of marijuana altogether. He was not so optimistic about how he could improve his avoidance of social interaction with others or his lack of motivation for getting out of his apartment to attend classes and work on his academic assignments. Despite the serious difficulties he was facing, Martin emphatically stated his wish to return to his university and try to make a go of it on his own. His strong determination to fix everything without depending on anyone else, even in this time of failure, was quite striking.

Martin said he would keep in touch with me by email, but I heard nothing further from him until the end of that academic year, when he wrote, "I've crashed!" and explained that he had not been able to get the treatment I had suggested, had not been able to reduce his use of marijuana, and had earned no credits for that year of university studies. He asked if he could return for further consultation with me. We agreed that he would move to New Haven to attend summer school at a local university while working intensively with me to gain a clearer understanding of his problems and to develop a longer-term plan.

o   new start in a new context

When he arrived, Martin did not want to elaborate much on his feelings, but one day, soon after starting work with me, he mentioned that his favorite song was Nina Simone's "Ain't Got No, I Got Life," which includes these lyrics: "Ain't got no friends, ain't got no schooling / Ain't got no love, ain't got no name . . . Why am I alive anyway?" and then concludes with "I got my brains . . . I got life . . . and nobody's gonna take it away." This song seemed to give expression to his difficult-to-describe feelings of failure and loss as well as his determination to hang on and try to make things better.

In the summer school courses, Martin was very successful. He stopped using marijuana, attended every class, and kept appointments with me daily. Living in a dormitory with other summer school students, he made a few friends with whom he ate and frequently went out. One night he phoned me to report that he had left the club where he had been having beers with some friends; the friends had begun dancing, and Martin did not know how to dance. Fearing that he might be forced to try to dance, he fled the situation, but with my encouragement, he returned, telling them he couldn't dance that night because his leg hurt. The next day, fully on his own initiative, he signed up for a dancing class at the university gym. He clearly wanted very much to push himself to learn how to interact more comfortably with his peers. Later he commented, "I was such a dork when I first came here. It took me a long time to get over that."

In this new living situation, having stopped his use of marijuana, meeting daily with me, and using medication helpful for his ADHD, Martin showed strong motivation to improve his life situation in a way that he was not previously able to do.

Before the two-month summer session ended, Martin, his parents, and I agreed that he would move to New Haven, enroll full-time in a local university, and work intensively with me to continue treatment for his ADHD, try to understand and resolve his social and emotional difficulties, and complete his university degree.

To address his ADHD symptoms, Martin had started on a regimen of extended-release methylphenidate. Because this had been only minimally helpful, we then moved to a extended-release amphetamine. This was somewhat helpful, but only when the dose was increased to more than the usually recommended maximum. Martin's body was not very sensitive to these medications, and he burned through them quickly over the day. Eventually he needed to be on a maximum dose of immediate-release amphetamine to start the day, followed by a maximum dose of extended-release amphetamine, which was followed by another maximum dose of immediate-release amphetamine in late afternoon to provide coverage for homework and any evening activities. Dosing of stimulant medication cannot be adequately determined simply by the patient's age or weight; it depends on how sensitive the individual's body is to that particular medication.

o struggles with excessive privacy and fears of dependency

When he began full-time study at the local university, Martin's longer-term problems gradually became more apparent. For me, the process of forming an effective working alliance with Martin for psychotherapy was frustratingly slow and difficult. After some bursts of candor in his initial sessions, Martin tended to be extremely private, reluctant to share even trivial information about his daily life and very reluctant to share his emotional reactions. One day, with a smile, he described himself in these terms: "I'm a very private person, private even about being private. I hide a lot, but I don't want people to think I'm hiding anything."

Only occasionally was Martin willing or able to drop his well-developed façade of self-confidence, often bordering on arrogance, to share a glimpse of his underlying struggles, particularly with anxiety and shame. He once confided, "I don't often show it, but underneath I'm really kind of fragile." He was not willing to elaborate, and he then quickly closed down that candor; the next morning, he reported that he had vomited several times during the night "for no discernible reason."

When Martin described himself as fragile, he did not have in mind his physical strength. He is a tall, well-built, strong young man. In that brief comment, he seemed to be referring to fragility of his inner strength, the confidence and hope that are essential for a person to keep trying in the face of discouragement and failure. Multiple studies have shown that for most people, their sense of competence and self-confidence tends to be rather fragile, readily shaken or shattered by experiences of failure or by discouraging feedback from teachers, parents, or peers. This vulnerability seems to be heightened in students identified as exceptionally bright and in people burdened by stereotypes (such as those related to an ADHD diagnosis) that cause them and others to expect them to be unable to function with much success.[4] Rarely was Martin able to acknowledge this sense of fragility, even to himself. In many ways, his avoidance of this was adaptive.

Over several years of treatment with me, Martin's very cautious reluctance to share personal information persisted — interspersed, when he was able, with brief episodes of self-disclosure and collaboration. These moments of connection fueled an unspoken but slowly growing sense of a strengthening relationship between us. It gradually became clear that Martin had never before had a continuing relationship that involved much sharing of personal feelings or even of details of daily life. For him, this intensive and sustained relationship with me presented an unprecedented challenge and a not always welcome opportunity to grow beyond the detached isolation that had been his primary mode of operation since early childhood, even within his family.

○ burdens of perfectionism and poor planning

Martin was now carrying a full load of five courses, rather than the two courses he had taken in summer session. Reluctantly he reported that he was falling behind in preparing for three of his classes because he was spending too much time preparing for the other two. I asked to see his notebooks for each class. Martin's written work for two of the courses was extremely thorough and immaculate; he had taken careful notes at each lecture and then had typed all the pages, carefully ensuring that each was perfectly formatted. He had taken elaborate notes on assigned chapters of the textbook, formatted them perfectly, and illustrated each page with relevant diagrams he had searched for on the Internet. His notes for those two courses were so careful and elaborate that they could have been marketed as textbooks; his notes for the other three courses were very fragmentary and superficial.

When I questioned him about this imbalance, Martin shrugged, saying, "If I can't do it carefully to get the formatting just right, I can't do it at all. It's got to be 'just so.'" He explained that when taking notes during a lecture class, if he made a spelling error or accidentally wrote outside the margins, he felt the need to tear up that sheet of paper and start all over again, trying to reconstruct his notes for the lecture. He described several additional ways in which he felt compelled to act with similar exactness. He chuckled as he recalled that at Christmas he made it his job each year to arrange everyone's presents under the family tree in concentric circles, grouped according to recipient with exactly measured distances between each of the gifts. He also described his compulsion to go on weekly cleaning binges in which he tediously cleaned and straightened up his apartment. He smiled as he announced, "I guess I have a bit of OCD."[5]

Twice weekly we reviewed his academic work. In these conversations, Martin often recognized that he was not keeping adequate track of his assignments and was not effectively allocating his time. His stimulant medication for ADHD was apparently improving his ability to focus during class and to read or prepare assignments, but the medicine had not adequately helped him prioritize his tasks. Often he concentrated too much on work that interested him and not enough on other assignments that were important and about to be due. Repeatedly he announced resolutions that he would hereafter carefully keep a calendar and to-do list for his academic assignments, but he found it very difficult to do this on his own. When I attempted to help him structure this task, Martin became annoyed and reminded me that he needed to learn to take care of these things for himself.

o social insensitivities and unrecognized emotions

Fully as problematic as his academic struggles were Martin's difficulties in dealing with other people. He did not live in the university dormitories; he rented an apartment near my office. Over his first year, he rarely went out with other students after class or in the evening. He mostly kept to himself. Other students in his new university and several of the faculty he encountered experienced him as bright but aloof and a bit arrogant. He tended to be impatient with making small talk and engaging in other interactions that can help people feel more comfortable with one another. He would finish others' sentences and frequently said "I know" before they had finished speaking. He was often extremely sarcastic with others, making jokes that were witty but often stinging and offensive.

Martin seemed unaware of or uncaring about how his words or actions would be likely to affect others. He would promise to call people and didn't follow through or would agree to participate in a class work-group session and then not show up. Sometimes this was just forgetfulness, typical of those with ADHD. Yet often it came across as disregard for the feelings of others involved.

One particularly unfortunate instance involved Martin's getting acquainted with a professor whose work especially interested him. After talking with the professor several times, he expressed his interest in working as his research assistant. He was given the position, took the training, and began running subjects for the research project.

Martin had little to say about this work when I inquired, but several weeks later he broke the news to me that, without giving notice, he had stopped showing up for the work and had been avoiding contact with the professor for several weeks. We spent some time talking about how his dropping out of the position without notice would be likely to affect that professor and others to whom it might be mentioned. We also discussed alternative strategies for trying to repair the relationship with that professor, but Martin felt too embarrassed to talk with him ever again.

Martin's avoidance of contact was also characteristic of his dealings with his family. Rarely did he speak about them or reach out to make contact with them. On the rare occasions when his parents would call him, he often was quite brief in his comments or would allow their call to go into voicemail as though he were not at home. Only occasionally would his underlying concern for them be visible. When he learned that his younger sister was struggling in school, he took pains to stay in close touch with her with frequent phone calls. When he received word that his elderly grandmother had fallen and become more demented, he clearly was upset and reluctant to talk at that moment, though in subsequent days he spoke of several enjoyable times he had spent with her.

Many such examples strengthened my impression that although Martin often seemed out of touch with his emotions and usually had trouble expressing them, he was not lacking in the capacity to make and sustain connections with other people. In his meetings with me, Martin sometimes was quite engaged in productive conversation, though he often showed up late, missed appointments with no notice, or came to sessions unwilling to talk much, clearly indicating his wish to end the session and depart. It seemed that Martin could tolerate only limited doses of social and emotional engagement with me or others, often avoiding contact. In discussions, he would usually take flight from talk of anything emotional. He preferred to keep conversation at a factoid or abstract, impersonal level, wrapping his more personal life in a cloak of secretiveness and excessive privacy. He explained this as a style that was typical of the interactions of his family.

Several months into our first year of work together, I asked Martin to read and discuss with me a popular book on emotional intelligence. After reading a section describing the importance of using empathy to guide one's behavior, Martin commented, "This is a whole dimension of life that I have never learned much about and am not very good at." He was clearly interested in mastering this domain, yet he did not find it easy to engage with any consistency in the kind of introspection and self-disclosure needed.

Off and on over many months, we discussed possible reasons for Martin's excessive privacy about facts of his daily life and about his emotions. Martin mentioned that his father had few friends and rarely showed affection or any other emotion other than frustration and annoyance, even toward his wife and children. He said he felt certain that his father loved and cared deeply about his family, but Martin claimed that much of his father's concern for him took the form of criticism and constant reminders of Martin's need to improve in his schoolwork and cooperate more in household routines. Martin responded to this with a pattern of fierce arguments with his father about politics or news while holding back from giving his father any information about school or details of his daily life. This carefully practiced strategy helped Martin avoid giving his father information that he feared might later be used to criticize or humiliate him.

Martin's strong tendency to withhold from me and most others any information about his daily life, especially any facts or emotions that might possibly be seen as weaknesses, illustrates the power of early family relationships to influence a person's behavior in later life with other people. John Bowlby, a pioneer researcher on emotional attachments between people, has described how each person, through his or her experiences during childhood and adolescence, develops certain expectations about how he or she is going to be seen and dealt with by others. These expectations often persist without much change over the years. This may cause the person to deal with new friends, teachers, dating partners, spouses, and others while operating with those old assumptions, which may not adequately fit the current situation.[6] This can create self-fulfilling prophecies that seriously interfere with the new relationship. It is using the map of an old neighborhood to try to navigate a new and different territory.

This problem of staying stuck in old patterns and roles of interaction persisting from childhood or adolescence is worsened considerably for individuals like Martin, who have had little experience interacting with peers as they grow up. One important function of our childhood friendships with peers is to compare notes with one another about ourselves and our families. Visiting frequently at a friend's home; watching the friend interact with his or her parents and siblings; observing how they argue, how they show affection, how the friend is spoken to, what he or she is not allowed and what he or she can get away with; and seeing the friend's reactions to tales and observations of our own family — these experiences can offer an eye-opening perspective on how patterns in our family are not the only ways that people interact. Such experience offers us an ongoing, broader perspective from which to reevaluate ourselves and our parents, possibly correcting distortions and realizing alternative ways to think and act within the context of close relationships.[7]

Martin had not had the benefit of close relationships with peers as he grew up. This left him stuck in relatively unchanged expectations and patterns of behavior that he had developed in his family during childhood and adolescence. In dealing with me and others, Martin tended to remain locked into the same guardedness and distance he had developed in interacting with his father, trying to avoid any possible humiliation.

Importance of early peer relationships was demonstrated by researchers in New Zealand who followed a cohort of more than a thousand children over a nine-year period. Their study showed that children who have problematic peer relationships at age nine tend to have significantly less success in school and employment than those who get along reasonably well with their peers during childhood. Those who were rejected by their peers at age nine tended to do more poorly in school, were more aggressive with others, and had less adequate skills for social relationships than those more successful in peer relationships at age nine. The 10 percent of children who were least successful in peer relationships at age nine were nearly five times more likely to become unemployed upon leaving school.[8]

These problematic self-perpetuating patterns in interpersonal relationships can be modified, but the process of changing such engrained patterns usually requires intensive, long-term interaction in a therapeutic relationship, professional or otherwise. It is not easy for a person stuck in such patterns to learn to see how a current relationship is not as similar to problematic earlier relationships as it may appear to him.

○ immobilizing emotions and avoidant behavior

A more extreme version of Martin's avoidance of engagement was a series of episodes in which he went into "hibernation," closeting himself in his apartment, shutting off his phone, spending all of one or several days sleeping most of the time, missing his classes, and doing no work. On several such occasions, I had to go to his apartment to get in touch with him. His mood during these intermittent episodes was extremely depressed, lethargic, and irritable.

Initially Martin insisted that his hibernating behavior came without any noticeable reason, that he was not experiencing any upsetting feelings. His emotions tended to hit him indirectly with repeated episodes of jaw clenching, nausea, vomiting, and extreme fatigue. Eventually it became clear that at such times he was covertly anxious, overwhelmingly demoralized, and often quite ashamed in a stressful situation he had created for himself—for example, when trying to prepare for a major exam in a course for which he had not done nearly enough of the assigned reading, or getting close to the deadline for a paper he had not yet begun to prepare, suddenly realizing that he had sabotaged the possibility of getting a decent grade.

Gradually Martin began to recognize that he had a long-standing pattern of being immobilized by depression and withdrawal at times when he was faced with anticipated stress, consequences of his self-sabotage, or other events that brought strong, unrecognized emotions. Yet generally he referred to such understandings with a smile as "just your psychological theories." He could not easily tolerate acknowledging vulnerability to fear or shame or failure.

○ renewed marijuana use and increased social interaction

In the summer after his first year of study at the new university, Martin got acquainted with some friends with whom he began to feel comfortable. They were stoners, students who smoked marijuana daily; some smoked several times each day. Soon after he began hanging out with them, he was back into smoking marijuana on a regular basis. On the surface, this behavior was simply a resumption of the excessive marijuana use in which he had been disastrously immersed for two years at his previous university.

Although this return to smoking weed posed a significant threat to Martin's academic productivity, it was different from his earlier pattern in one significant way: this time he was smoking and socializing with others. He started hanging out with peers. Relaxed by the marijuana, he began to enjoy talking and joking with these friends, hearing about their experiences of past and present, and sharing with them a few of his own. He also began, for the first time, to do some dating with girls in the group. He was beginning to engage in social interactions with peers at a more grown-up, age-appropriate level, and he felt proud of it. When he and a girl agreed to announce that they were "seeing each other," he mentioned to me, "This is really doing a lot for my self-esteem."

Despite these social benefits, resumption of using marijuana did take a significant toll on Martin's schoolwork. Most problematic was its relieving his anxiety too much: he did not worry enough about some things he needed to worry about. He did not adequately feel the importance of getting to class consistently and completing his assignments regularly. When I confronted him about these problems as resulting from his frequent episodes of excessive smoking, Martin initially argued that his use of marijuana did not hurt his work, but as we reviewed the frequency of his failure to prepare adequately for tests and his often apathetic attitude toward preparation of assigned reading and papers, he soon agreed that he needed to sharply curtail his use of marijuana if he was going to be successful in fulfilling his goal of earning his degree. However, he found that changing his pattern of marijuana use didn't come quickly or easily.

There is considerable research to suggest that smoking marijuana tends to reduce anxiety; yet, especially for chronic users who smoke a couple of times weekly or more, marijuana tends to produce an "amotivational syndrome," an apathetic "Oh well, whatever" attitude that undermines effort and diminishes emotional awareness of the likely consequences of failing to fulfill commitments. It blocks emotions that are important for sustaining motivation and effort. This effect has been shown not only in self-report data provided by chronic smokers but also in laboratory studies with both adolescents and adults. Moreover, even after a month or more of no marijuana use, chronic users tend to demonstrate subtle but persisting impairments in attention, processing speed, working memory, and other executive functions.[9]

Use of higher levels of THC, the active ingredient in marijuana, tends to cause greater cognitive impairment.

It should be noted, however, that studies of the effects of marijuana smoking on cognitive functions do not show that all levels of use of marijuana are equally impairing. Use of higher levels of THC, the active ingredient in marijuana, tends to cause greater cognitive impairment; in other words, impairment is dose related. One study comparing the effects of moderate and higher levels of marijuana smoking in people who regularly used marijuana demonstrated that those who smoked smaller amounts were significantly less impaired than those who used a higher dose. Smoking cigarettes with higher levels of THC was associated with more risk-taking in decision making and more impairment in cognitive-motor tasks that are important for coordinated movement (for example, in driving).[10]

For an individual like Martin who suffers from chronic EF impairments associated with ADHD, chronic marijuana use tends to significantly worsen symptoms of ADHD and substantially diminishes the effectiveness of medications intended to alleviate ADHD.

Martin came to realize that his resuming frequent marijuana use, even if not daily, was worsening his ADHD problems and undermining his academic performance, yet he found it very difficult to reduce his smoking. Marijuana significantly improved his ability to relax and reduced feelings that caused him stress—his shyness in new social situations, his uncertainty about what to say and what to do when hanging out with peers in unstructured social situations, his tendency to get stuck in second-guessing himself about what he had said or done, excessive urgency about getting things done perfectly, and his long-standing feelings of embarrassment or shame. Any time he stopped smoking marijuana for more than a day or two, these uncomfortable feelings intensified. Martin then began to act more irritable and moody, triggering a feeling of increased urgency to smoke again.

There was another way in which Martin's smoking weed seemed to function for him. Especially during his first couple of years in treatment with me, Martin would binge in using marijuana at the worst possible times, just prior to the deadline for completing a term paper or the night before an exam for which he had not adequately studied. Initially, when confronted about such incidents, Martin would deny that there was any significance to the timing. Eventually it became clear to both of us that his bingeing served as a self-handicapping measure that allowed him to say to himself and to others, "Oh, I could've done much better on that big exam [or could've written a much better paper] if I hadn't gotten really high for a couple of days before." This was an attempt to protect a bit of self-esteem when Martin felt challenged in ways that he feared could cause him an undeniable defeat.[11]

As he gradually comprehended the strong negative impact that his episodes of heavy marijuana smoking were having on his school functioning, Martin tried repeatedly to keep track of exactly when he smoked and to limit himself to smaller quantities. He cooperated with periodic urine testing and attended self-help groups for addicts. At times Martin was able to get his smoking under better control, yet he continued to have episodes of excessive use, some of which were damaging to his academic work. His repeated difficulty in doing this seemed to result not so much from his enjoyment of marijuana as from his lack of more effective ways to deal with his unclaimed anxiety and other uncomfortable emotions.

Over several years, Martin's grades at college continued to be quite uneven. In those courses where he found either the subject matter or the professor especially interesting, he did very well, earning A's or B's. In some other courses, Martin was able to do well despite lack of interest because he was bright enough to score high on examinations, even if he didn't prepare carefully. Yet in some other courses, he failed to hand in critical assignments or exceeded the limit for missing class sessions and had to take a failing grade or withdraw from the class and lose credit. Despite his often extreme inconsistencies, Martin never let his overall grade average drop below a C; much below his potential, but enough to maintain good standing at the university.

At the outset of his junior year, Martin moved into a rented house with seven of his male and female friends. Over that year, he had opportunity to see firsthand the diverse ways in which each of them dealt with and sometimes failed to deal with the demands of schoolwork as well as the frustrations and pleasures of sharing daily life. He observed who worked hard and consistently on their studies and who blew everything off, who was sharing in the responsibilities of keeping up the house and who was leaving the work and financial burdens to others, who lifted up the moods of housemates and who dragged them down.

This communal life helped Martin catch up a bit in learning about the diverse ways in which his peers coped with the various stresses they encountered in hooking up and breaking up with boyfriends or girlfriends, dealing with professors, managing their money, and interacting with their families. He also found ways to cope with their kind and some-times unkind ways of giving feedback to him. These were all valuable lessons, especially for Martin, whose childhood and adolescence had provided him little opportunity to get an intimate look at how others his age dealt with the responsibilities and stresses of daily life.

In the midst of all this, Martin gradually emerged as a leader and support for his friends. When there were problems with their difficult landlord, Martin organized a response and conducted the necessary negotiations. When one of the housemates became severely psychotic after overdosing on drugs, Martin helped talk him down and connected him with his family so he could receive the necessary treatment. When another housemate became seriously depressed after her boyfriend dumped her, Martin spent many hours over several weeks helping her get herself together.

Despite these various benefits of living with his friends, Martin also struggled with some significant problems while living in that house. More than a few of those friends were heavy drug users, often smoking marijuana or doing other drugs in the house. Martin did not get caught up in using heavy drugs, but he had continuing difficulties in controlling his use of marijuana. Sometimes he managed it so that he could still do his work; at other times he let responsibilities slide in ways that significantly hurt his grades. He still maintained his overall C average, but he did not pass two courses that were graduation requirements for his major.

recognizing missed opportunities and adopting a new attitude

When he came to the outset of what was to be his final year of under-graduate studies, Martin was forced to accept that his C average was not sufficient for him to graduate. Because he had not satisfactorily com-pleted those two courses that were specifically required for his major, he would have to do an additional year to complete his degree. Martin was demoralized. This was the point at which he expressed the lament quoted at the outset of this chapter: "It's going to take me seven years to get my B.A. With my miserable academic record, what's the use in my even trying to graduate?" He wondered whether his parents would be willing to pay for the additional year of coursework required, considering that he had not adequately fulfilled his responsibilities. Painfully he acknowledged, "For so many years, they've given me so many great opportunities—boarding school, the old university, coming here and going to this university—and I've pissed so much opportunity away! I haven't really made good use of what I've been given." He wavered at the edge of guilt-ridden depression and considered giving up on his goal of completing his degree, but after a few weeks of such wavering, he vowed that he was determined to do what needed to be done.

Martin's final year of undergraduate studies was an important one for him in several ways. He moved out of the house where he had been living so he could avoid living with friends who smoked excessively; instead he moved into an apartment he shared with one other friend whom he felt sure would not incite him to smoke too much. He went almost daily to the gym to work out so he could improve his physical condition and relieve stress. Martin also developed and sustained a satisfying relationship with a young woman who had recently graduated from college and was working full-time in a responsible job. He recognized her as someone who took her work responsibilities seriously and wanted to continue her education further, but who also knew how to enjoy life.

Feeling a new appreciation for the value of completing his degree, Martin took his responsibilities for each course much more seriously; he was careful about his class attendance and about meeting deadlines for assignments. He did not totally abandon his problematic habits of waiting until the last minute to write papers or to prepare for exams, but he worked about as effectively as many other students his age, and he earned much higher grades that were more consistent with his actual abilities.

o   o   o

Causes for these multiple improvements in Martin's functioning are not easy to determine. After almost seven years of undergraduate studies, including five years of treatment, he seemed almost suddenly to be growing up, making overdue gains in maturity. Martin attributed much of his progress to having a continuing relationship with the first girlfriend he really respected and wanted to stay close to and to emulate in his attitude toward work. That relationship provided him with a consistent opportunity to develop both emotional and physical intimacy, from which he gained not only considerable satisfaction and nurturance but also significantly enhanced self-esteem and improving ability to interact with a partner at an adult level. As he spent time with his girlfriend and her family, he also had an opportunity to observe differences in family styles and learn some more adaptive ways in which family members can think about and interact with one another.

Undoubtedly other factors also contributed to Martin's growth. There were a few professors who provided a very useful mix of pressure, support, recognition, and inspiration. The patience and willingness of Martin's parents to keep funding his extended studies and treatment also played an essential role, not only economically but also as tangible evidence of their trust in his often-obscured potential. I would like to think that the five years of work Martin and I did together also contributed.

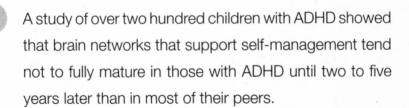

A study of over two hundred children with ADHD showed that brain networks that support self-management tend not to fully mature in those with ADHD until two to five years later than in most of their peers.

Another factor may have been brain development. A study comparing repeated brain images of more than two hundred children with ADHD between five and twenty years old with a matched group of children without ADHD showed evidence that brain networks that support self-management tend not to fully mature in those with ADHD until two to five years later than in most of their peers. These differences in brain maturation appeared, not in all areas of brain, but in those specific portions of the brain that are important for control of cognitive processes and for planning.[12] It may be that Martin's prolonged delay in getting better control of himself to deploy his strong intellectual abilities was partly due to his brain structures' needing more time to mature than is typical of others his age. Interestingly, Martin's father described himself as having had a similar transformation from being a "weak and lazy" student to becoming a strong and hardworking student at about the same age.

Upon graduation, Martin still needed to strengthen his work ethic and efficiency, improve his awareness of his own emotions, and interact more sensitively with others. Yet over the span of five years, despite many frustrations and failures, he grew impressively in each of these domains. After graduation, he gained admission to a master's degree program in which he consistently worked hard and earned good grades. He successfully completed his master's degree within the standard two years for the program.

What Helped Martin?

- Change of context to sustain intensive psychotherapy while attending college full-time
- Initial abstinence from marijuana use followed by harm reduction approach to reduce addiction
- Intensive talk therapy to address shame over failures, defensive sarcasm, denial of addiction, avoidance of social interaction, poor planning, and excessive perfectionism
- Gradual development of friendships and group living with male and female peers
- Medication adjustments calibrated to address extreme insensitivity to stimulants
- Monitoring and support to sustain effort in school despite shameful episodes of failure

5

sarah

I've been married twenty-five years, have three great kids, and had a decent career as a journalist, but I just got fired because I couldn't prioritize and keep up with my work. Since menopause I've had trouble keeping track of things and getting work done. I've always had some trouble with these things, but it's recently been getting worse.
—50-YEAR-OLD HOMEMAKER AND MOTHER

Sarah had never been fired before. After completing college, she took a job as a staff writer for a weekly newspaper and moonlighted as a writer for a local radio station. She then moved up to work as a reporter for a prominent daily newspaper, where her output of news and feature stories won her recognition as a talented and productive journalist. This continued for almost ten years until her husband was transferred to an executive position in another state. Shortly after they moved, Sarah became pregnant with the first of their two children and chose to remain at home to be a full-time mother, a task she truly enjoyed.

Over the next twenty years, Sara nurtured her children and was active as a leader in church and community activities. After their younger child graduated from high school, Sarah decided to return to working full-time so that she could help cover the cost of the two college tuitions. Soon she was hired as a writer for a weekly newspaper.

Sarah was enthusiastic about resuming work as a journalist, but, returning after a hiatus of twenty years, she found the work much more difficult than her previous job on the daily paper.

Frequent phone calls disrupted her concentration repeatedly throughout the day, and she had a lot of trouble prioritizing tasks and using her time efficiently. Often her assignments were not ready in time for deadlines; this brought harsh criticism from her editor. Feeling frustrated and humiliated, Sarah began to experience migraine headaches. At the start of her third month on the job, she quit, saying that despite the emotional support of her family, she simply couldn't bear the stress she felt on this job.

Sarah was afraid she would run into similar problems in any position as a journalist, so she decided to enroll in the local community college, where she began courses to qualify herself as a paralegal. Her writing skills and long hours of work yielded high grades that developed into a GPA of 4.0. Soon after passing the licensing exam, Sarah was hired to work as a paralegal in the practice of an attorney in a neighboring town. Although she had done well in her community college courses, Sarah felt swamped and increasingly anxious as she struggled to keep up with the multiple demands of her new job. She was making many errors, each one escalating her anxiety and her fear of making further mistakes. The attorney for whom she was working complained bitterly of Sarah's lack of time management skills and her failure to complete tasks within the allotted time. After three months, he fired Sarah, telling her that she was too forgetful, too disorganized, and too slow to work in a busy office as a paralegal. Two weeks later, she came to my office for an initial consultation.

At the outset of our consultation, Sarah reported that she had scarcely slept the night before because she was intensely worried about the possible outcomes of our session. "I'm hoping you will find that I have ADHD, because if that's not it, then I probably have early-onset Alzheimer's. And that would be terrifying!"

As she told the story of her efforts to return to the workforce, Sarah emphasized the embarrassment and shame she felt in not being able to do work that she had considered much less challenging than tasks she had done quite successfully twenty years earlier. "It takes me so long to get started on tasks, and I get distracted and sidetracked at every step. I feel I'm constantly fighting brush fires, fighting to get one controlled and then discovering that two or three others are now flaring up. I can't keep priorities in mind, and often I totally forget what the boss has asked me to do if I don't write it down right away. I'm not that old; I'm just fifty, and my memory is a sieve!"

As Sarah described her current situation, it certainly did not sound as though she was in a state of general decline. She reported good health and appeared quite lively and energetic; she spoke of her planting and maintaining a huge vegetable and flower garden every year. She told me about her running several miles two or three times a week, reading voraciously, and enjoying getting together often with a group of good friends. She noted that her enthusiasm for these activities had been dropping considerably over the past couple of years, but she was still pushing herself to keep up most of what she had always done, even though she had been feeling increasingly depressed.

○ ADHD-like symptoms not emergent until midlife

To learn whether Sarah had struggled with symptoms of ADHD earlier in her life, I asked about her experiences in school. She reported that she had done well in high school, carrying a B average and successfully completing several advanced placement courses. Following high school, she entered a competitive liberal arts college, planning to prepare for medical school. After struggling with several math and science courses, she decided to follow instead her strong interest in reading and writing. She gained recognition for her contributions to the campus newspaper and literary magazine. This paved the way for her working in journalism after she completed her degree. Throughout her schooling, none of Sarah's teachers had ever suggested that she demonstrated difficulties with focus or with organization and completion of her assigned work.

When I evaluated her with questions about her current functioning, I found that Sarah clearly was suffering from severe impairments of those executive functions (EFs) usually impaired in ADHD:

- She complained of much difficulty in getting herself started on tasks until they were becoming an emergency.
- She found it virtually impossible to focus for long on any task that was not really interesting to her.
- She felt unable to prioritize tasks, often spending excessive time on unimportant tasks while avoiding more urgent responsibilities.
- She often got stuck on one task, unable to set it aside and move on to something else that required her attention.
- Often she had difficulty sustaining her effort for tasks that could not be completed quickly.
- She reported that her memory for some things from long ago was surprisingly strong, yet her ability to keep things in mind moment to moment was frustratingly poor.
- She also reported that over the past couple of years, she had often found herself unable to recall names of people she knew well or a word she needed to express a particular thought.

After taking this history, I asked Sarah to respond to the forty items of my rating scale for ADHD symptoms in adults.[1] On that measure, a person can score between 0 and 120; any score of 50 or above suggests that the respondent has a significant likelihood of having ADHD. Sarah's score on that rating scale was 93. She was reporting high levels of chronic difficulty with a wide variety of EF impairments that are typical of adults with ADHD.

I also administered to Sarah a standardized test of verbal working memory. For this test, I read to Sarah two short stories, each with just twenty-five word units (small groups of words that convey a specific fact or action). Immediately after reading each story, I asked Sarah to repeat the story back to me, as close to verbatim as possible. After a delay of twenty minutes, without reading the stories again, I asked her to repeat again whatever she could remember of the two stories. Using the published scoring criteria for that scale, I was able to compare Sarah's immediate and delayed recall of the stories with norms for individuals of her current age.

Sarah's immediate recall placed her at the 37th percentile (meaning that she scored worse than 63 percent of others her age), but for the delayed recall twenty minutes later, she was able to recall considerably less of the stories and scored worse than 84 percent of others her age. On this verbal memory test, most people score near their verbal comprehension index score on the Wechsler Adult Intelligence Scale IQ test: Sarah's score on that IQ measure was in the very superior range, stronger than 98 percent of her peers, but, like many others with ADHD, she had a lot of trouble with remembering these two brief stories just moments after hearing them.[2]

> Sarah didn't seem to have had any noticeable signs of ADHD when she was younger. She manifested most of the symptoms of ADHD in her recent history, around the same time that her menopause began.

Although Sarah didn't seem to have had any noticeable signs of ADHD when she was a child, adolescent, or younger adult, she manifested most of the symptoms of ADHD in her recent history and in her current performance on the measure of verbal working memory. She dated these symptoms as arising at around the same time that her menopause began with diminishing frequency of menstrual periods.

○ onset of symptoms of ADHD

According to the version of the manual used for psychiatric diagnosis at that time, the diagnosis of ADHD required that at least some of the symptoms of the disorder be noticeable before age seven. This was a carryover from the earlier conception of ADHD as a developmental disorder of early childhood. The most recent version of that manual modified this requirement to say that it should be sufficient for some of ADHD symptoms to be noticeable by about age twelve years.[3] This is somewhat better, but it still presupposes that by puberty or earlier, at least some of the symptoms should be apparent in any person diagnosed with ADHD.

Some people with ADHD don't manifest significant impairments until they experience the stresses of adulthood, when they encounter increased challenges to their EF abilities.

There is a fundamental flaw in this assumption that ADHD symptoms are always apparent in childhood or early adolescence. The infrastructure of the brain that supports the EFs impaired in ADHD does not fully mature until the late teens or early twenties. Although some people with ADHD manifest symptoms in early childhood, many others function without any apparent symptoms until they are faced with the increasing demands for self-management that emerge gradually during adolescence and early adulthood. Some children are honor students in elementary school while they are in a single classroom most of the day with one teacher who can perform most EFs for them. Yet those same students may be significantly impaired in self-management and fully meet diagnostic criteria for ADHD when they are in secondary school with multiple classes, each with a different teacher, an environment where students need to take much more responsibility for managing themselves. Still others with ADHD don't manifest significant impairments until they experience the stresses of adulthood, when they encounter increased challenges to their EF abilities.

This delay in recognition of impairments of ADHD-related EFs could be compared to electrocardiogram (EKG) assessments. A person lying still on a table might show a perfectly clean EKG. Yet the same test administered while that person is running on a treadmill may reveal occluded arteries that were not noticeable until the individual's cardiac function was challenged by increasing exertion. Significant problems in the cardiovascular system or in cognitive function may not be noticeable until the individual is challenged by increasing demands on that functional system.

A research study identified a group of adults who fully met all the diagnostic criteria for ADHD, including having some symptoms apparent before age seven.[4] The researchers compared those adults with another group of adults who met all diagnostic criteria for ADHD except for the "some symptoms apparent before age seven" criterion. There were no significant differences between the two groups in their level of functional impairment, patterns of co-occurring psychiatric disorders, or number of blood relatives who also had full ADHD. A subsequent study showed no significant differences between those two groups in their profiles of personality characteristics.[5] These studies make clear that a person may suffer significant impairments of ADHD that do not become apparent until long past the age of seven.

o a co-occurring disorder

Like most others with ADHD, Sarah also had another psychiatric problem. For two years previous to her consultation with me, she had been dysthymic. Dysthymia is a medical term for low-grade chronic depression; it does not involve the severe disruptions of daily function-ing, sleep, and appetite found in major depressive disorders, and it does not include suicidal thinking. Usually people who are dysthymic can still get themselves to work and complete most of their daily tasks, yet they tend to suffer almost every day from depressed mood, low energy, and debased self-esteem, and find little enjoyment in activities that previously were pleasurable for them. Usually they can pull out of their dysthymic mood when doing something really interesting to them, but otherwise they tend to feel "down in the dumps."[6] It's not unusual for people with untreated ADHD to suffer from dysthymia; it is often an aspect of their reaction to living with the frustrations and stresses of untreated or inadequately treated ADHD.

Sarah's dysthymia had begun shortly after she resigned from the newspaper job she attempted when she had gone back to work, about the

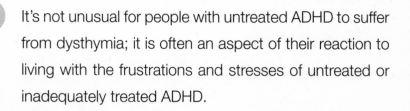

It's not unusual for people with untreated ADHD to suffer from dysthymia; it is often an aspect of their reaction to living with the frustrations and stresses of untreated or inadequately treated ADHD.

time she had given up on trying to return to working as a journalist and decided instead to learn to become a paralegal. Dysthymia seemed an understandable reaction to the disappointment and profound discouragement Sarah experienced when she found that she was no longer able to function in the role of a journalist, an occupation in which she had been so successful twenty years before.

Emotional stress can certainly contribute to development of dysthymia or other psychiatric disorders, but often stress is multilayered. One stressor can be intensified by another stressor in the background.[7] Sarah's stress over failure in her attempt to return to work as a journalist occurred in the context of another major stress at that time: her younger child had just made the transition off to college. Although most parents feel some liberation and relief as they begin to experience the "empty nest," most also feel some loss.

For twenty years, Sarah had been directly engaged with her son and daughter almost every day. She awakened them each morning; prepared their meals; monitored their comings and goings for school and social activities; provided guidance; enforced expectations; listened to their footsteps, their voices, and their music; and shared directly in many of the ups and downs of their daily life. Now she was gradually grieving the loss of those pieces of her life. Her failure to recapture the satisfactions of working effectively as a journalist had greater impact because it came at a time when she was already feeling another major loss.

Although these combined stressors contributed to Sarah's dysthymia, they did not account for all of the cognitive impairments she was experiencing at the same time. Dysthymia often includes problems with concentration, but it does not generally bring the larger syndrome of problems with memory, organization, prioritizing, and so on.

o   menopause and midlife onset of ADHD-like symptoms

When I inquired about Sarah's schooling, work, and other life experiences, neither she nor her husband could recall any significant difficulties with ADHD symptoms during any earlier time in her life.

Like anyone else, she had experienced occasional problems with inattention, planning, and memory, but these had not been chronic or severe until just a few years before her consultation with me at age fifty. In other words, Sarah's problems with EF impairments associated with ADHD appeared to have a midlife onset.

Sarah was not the first middle-aged woman who had appeared in my office complaining of midlife onset of attention and memory problems. Many competent, successful, well-educated women — physicians, attorneys, scientists, professors, and business executives — had come with similar complaints of cognitive difficulties emerging for the first time during their mid- to late forties or early fifties. Virtually every one of these women presented with the same concern expressed by Sarah at the outset of her consultation with me: "Do I have ADHD, or am I suffering from early onset of dementia?" Most were not only frustrated but also terrified that they were permanently losing critical mental functions.

What all these women had in common was that they were either in the midst of their menopause or had been through menopause and were no longer having any menstrual periods. Some younger women who had undergone surgically induced menopause had brought similar complaints.

role of estrogen in cognitive impairments of menopause

In 2000, I published my initial observations about this phenomenon of perimenopausal and menopausal women with midlife onset of a constellation of cognitive impairments similar to what is commonly found in ADHD.[8] In that brief report, I noted that a possible mechanism for this midlife onset of chronic cognitive difficulties in women might be the menopausal decline of estrogen, a hormone that is a facilitator for the release of dopamine in the female brain. Dopamine is a neurotransmitter chemical manufactured in the brain. It plays a critical role in facilitating communication in neural networks that service executive functions of the brain. Basic research in neuroscience suggests that in the female brain, estrogen facilitates and modulates the release of dopamine, especially in brain areas associated with EF, in a variety of complicated ways.[9] If this is so, significant reductions or inconsistency in estrogen levels such as occurs in a woman's body during perimenopause and beyond may contribute substantially to worsening ADHD symptoms in women with ADHD and may even produce midlife onset of ADHD-like symptoms in some women who have not previously manifested ADHD symptoms in any significant way.

Estrogen's impact on cognitive functioning had already been demonstrated in earlier controlled studies of verbal memory in women. Researchers in one study read two stories, each just a couple of paragraphs, to women before their estrogen level was reduced by surgery or chemical suppression; their recall of comparable stories was then tested after their estrogen level had been suppressed. Results showed that the women had much more limited recall of details in those stories after their estrogen level was reduced than they had in the testing prior to estrogen suppression. It was also shown that administration of additional estrogen after suppression tended to improve story recall significantly.[10]

Another study used fMRI to show that administration of estrogen to postmenopausal women increased activation in specific brain regions during verbal and nonverbal working memory tasks.[11] Subsequent to my brief report in 2000, a number of studies have elaborated on cognitive impairments suffered by many women during perimenopause and on the impact of estrogen on these impairments. Much of the research literature is contradictory, but indications are that there may be a critical period for effectiveness of estrogen augmentation. Estrogen replacement therapy may be helpful in alleviating cognitive impairments of perimenopausal women, but such treatment is reported to be less effective for some women, and perhaps even harmful for older postmenopausal women.[12] Given these ambiguous findings and the fact that some women and their doctors are apprehensive about estrogen augmentation, it would be helpful to identify alternative treatments to alleviate cognitive impairments in peri- and postmenopausal women.

Medications used for treatment of ADHD may be an option to be considered.

Over the past ten years, the impact of estrogen on cognitive functioning has also been studied in women who have undergone chemotherapy for breast cancer or lymphoma. Many, though not all, women who undergo treatment with estrogen-suppressing drugs report and demonstrate that such chemotherapy produces "chemofog," substantial impairments in their cognitive functioning, particularly their working memory, executive functioning, and processing speed.[13] There is evidence that genetic factors may render some women more likely to experience such impairments.[14] A preliminary study has shown that dexmethylphenidate, a stimulant medication used to treat ADHD, may be useful in alleviating some of these cognitive impairments in women undergoing chemotherapy.[15]

o o o

Sarah had not undergone cancer surgery or any chemotherapy, but she did note that she had become aware of increasing difficulty with attention, working memory, and organization of daily tasks at about the same time that her periods were becoming more erratic and then eventually stopped. Yet she did not assume that cessation of her menses had anything to do with her becoming increasingly forgetful and disorganized. She started experiencing hot flashes at that time and was awakening more frequently during the night; these problems were clearly linked in her mind to her declining estrogen, but she did not think of her increasing cognitive difficulties as due to those hormonal changes.

As I mentioned earlier, Sarah was terrified that her cognitive problems were due to early onset of Alzheimer's dementia, a disorder with which her mother had suffered for nine years before her death. Sarah began to cry as she spoke about her mother's long decline. "I just would not be able to go through that process of my mind slowly dying long before my body actually dies. It would be too hard on me and way too hard on my family." She had felt some relief when a friend suggested she might have just an attention deficit disorder, but in her private thoughts, she felt that she was headed for a cognitive decline similar to what she had seen in her mother.

○ treatment for midlife-onset cognitive impairments

Some of my colleagues and I conducted a pilot study at Yale on women like Sarah who reported midlife onset of problems.[16] We recruited a small group of women who had complaints of midlife onset of difficulties with attention, concentration, and memory without any history of having had ADHD in childhood or adolescence. At the outset, we administered some neuropsychological tests often used to assess such problems; we also elicited their responses to my rating scale for EF impairments associated with ADHD. Each woman then underwent a six-week trial of treatment with atomoxetine, a medication often used to treat ADHD, and another six weeks of taking a placebo with a washout period between. Neither the patients nor the staff running the study knew when the woman was taking the active drug and when she was on placebo. We readministered the neuropsychological tests and the rating scale at the conclusion of each phase of the study.

When we compared the responses of the women when they were taking atomoxetine against their responses to the placebo, we saw improvement in the rating scale scores. Participants reported that they noticed significant improvement in working memory and in attention. There were no significant changes in their scores on the neuropsychological tests. This pilot study was small and had some methodological limitations, so the results must be seen as suggestive but not definitive. A larger study of the same type, but utilizing a stimulant medication, is now under way.

As just noted, although the women in this pilot study reported improvements in cognitive functioning on the rating scale, there was no significant change shown on the neuropsychological tests used in the study. This is not surprising, because in other studies of women reporting cognitive problems in menopause, these tests, often referred to as "tests of executive function," have not been very consistent in capturing impairments or improvements. These "EF tests" typically involve simple cognitive tasks, such as sorting different types of cards, reading words printed in different colors, drawing complex designs, and the like, in a private room with a psychologist within less than an hour. Critics have argued that such tests are not valid measures of the complexities of how a person's attention, working memory, planning, and so on function over time in dealing with the complexities of daily life.[17] In contrast, there is substantial evidence that older children, adolescents, and adults with ADHD-associated EF impairments can usually report their functional difficulties with EF accurately on ADHD rating scales; some of those scales have also been shown to be sensitive to changes in EF resulting from treatment with ADHD medications. Further research is needed to test this finding in peri- and postmenopausal women.

Sarah was not involved in our pilot study of treatment for women with midlife onset cognitive complaints, but we did offer her a trial of treatment with a stimulant medication approved for treatment of ADHD. With support from her primary care physician, Sarah began a trial of dexmethylphenidate given at a low dose in an extended-release formulation. As noted earlier in this book, the effective dose of stimulant for any patient depends not on age, weight, or symptom severity but on how sensitive that individual's body is to that particular medication. Thus, when starting any patient on stimulants, it is important to begin with a very low dose and then gradually increase as needed to slightly higher doses in a stair-step fashion.

> Sarah also noticed that the stimulant had an unexpected benefit: it helped reduce her hypersensitivity to worry and criticism.

After a couple of weeks, Sarah reported that 10 mg of this extended-release formulation was helpful in improving her ability to sustain focus and effort for work tasks, though she did not feel that it helped her processing speed significantly. She tried a slightly higher dose of 15 mg, but that caused her to feel a bit racy and caused a slight elevation of her blood pressure, so she resumed the 10 mg dose. A few months later, she went back up to the 15 mg dose and found it more effective without the racy feeling and without the elevation of her blood pressure. Early on, Sarah felt frustrated because the morning dose of the stimulant wore off in late afternoon, leaving her feeling a bit irritable and tired for a couple of hours. This was readily improved by adding a 5 mg dose of the immediate-release version of the same medication to be taken at about four in the afternoon, before the unpleasant "rebound" from the morning dose occurred. Sarah also noticed that the stimulant had an unexpected benefit: it helped reduce her hypersensitivity to worry and criticism. She and members of her family found that she seemed more calm most of the time when she was on this medication.

Often long-acting formulations of stimulants wear off around midafternoon; for most patients, a small dose of short-acting stimulant can extend duration of coverage for evening activities while also alleviating the rebound problem. Careful fine-tuning of dose and timing is needed to optimize a patient's response to stimulant medications.[18]

After Sarah was stabilized on the stimulant, she reported that her cognitive functions had improved considerably each day during the period when the medication was active. Medications for ADHD cure nothing; if effective, they simply alleviate ADHD symptoms during the period of time they are active. This is similar to the way eyeglasses can improve vision while they are worn, but do not cure the persistent impairments of vision in any lasting way.

Sarah noted that each day while the stimulant medication was active, she was better able to get started on tasks and to resist excessive distractions. She said she could recall more easily what she had heard and what she wanted to say and do. She found it easier to sustain effort for a task and to bring tasks to completion within a reasonable time. She said she did not feel that she was as effective as she had been twenty years earlier, but she felt that she was generally functioning as effectively as she had been before she entered the perimenopausal transition.

About a month after Sarah was stabilized on stimulant medication, she reported that the anxiety and depressive feelings that had plagued her for a couple of years prior to her coming to see me were still persisting as she was mobilizing herself to seek yet another job. On my suggestion, her primary care physician prescribed for Sarah a trial of fluoxetine, a medication that often works well to alleviate both depressive symptoms and anxiety. She found this helpful for about six months and then gradually tapered off its use. At that point, she had obtained a new position at another newspaper and was functioning quite well on the extended-release stimulant medication in the morning and a small dose of immediate-release stimulant in the afternoon. Once the stress of seeking and getting started in a new job was behind her, the stimulant treatment apparently provided enough control of her emotional difficulties that she no longer needed the fluoxetine.

o   o   o

Unlike others whose stories are included in this book, Sarah did not technically meet the currently established diagnostic criteria for ADHD because she did not have a history of ADHD impairments during childhood, adolescence, or early adulthood. Nevertheless, her cognitive self-management impairments that emerged around her menopause were virtually identical to those of adults who fully meet diagnostic criteria for ADHD.

Sarah's story, like our small pilot study, suggests that medications used for ADHD may be helpful to some of those women who experience midlife onset of ADHD-like EF impairments. Due to safety concerns, many women are reluctant to take estrogen replacement on an ongoing basis after menopause, and estrogen replacement therapy is not always effective in treating EF impairments for these women. Because it seems that many women suffer these EF impairments during and after perimenopause, a need for further research on the usefulness of ADHD medications for treating these impairments is clear.

What Helped Sarah?

- Talk therapy to recognize and provide support for her grief over empty nest and feelings of embarrassment and fear related to her diminished ability to perform tasks that were previously easy
- Rating scale and clinical interview evaluation of current cognitive strengths and weaknesses to rule out early-onset dementia while identifying midlife onset of ADHD-related EF impairments and intact cognitive strengths
- Education and reassurance about the way menopause and estrogen were related to her midlife onset of symptoms of EF impairments
- Prescription and fine-tuning of stimulant to help alleviate ADHD-type impairments
- Concurrent prescription of SSRI medication to alleviate depressive and anxiety symptoms

6

mike

My dad always said that I'm smart but just lazy; maybe he's right. I got put on academic probation, and now I have to drop out. I'm always spacing out and can't get myself started on anything until the last minute. I tried my friend's ADHD medicine and it helped a lot, but my dad doesn't want me getting evaluated for ADHD because he says the meds are like steroids.

—21-YEAR-OLD UNIVERSITY STUDENT

Mike was a lanky young man with thick black hair and a wide smile. In our first consultation session, I asked Mike and his parents to tell me about how they decided to come to see me. Mike was explaining how he had just dropped out of the state university because of low grades when his father interrupted to speak to me:

I don't want to be rude, but I have to tell you up-front that I'm not much of a believer in this ADHD stuff. This boy is really smart and he has great potential, but he hasn't got any big psychological problem, and he certainly doesn't need any medicine. He simply hasn't learned yet how to do stuff he doesn't feel like doing.

Mike responded with downcast eyes:

That last part is true. When the professor is really interesting and it's a subject I like, I can get good grades just like I did in high school—that's when I get an A! But if I'm stuck in a class that's boring, I just can't keep pushing myself to keep going to class and doing the reading and getting the papers done. That's when I get the D's and F's. I've wasted so much of your money.

Mike's mother joined in to say,

That's why we told you we just can't afford to keep paying the tuition. This has been going on for four semesters now, and you've earned credits in only half of your courses. We don't have money to waste on these courses that aren't going to get you any credits. We know you're really smart. We think you just weren't ready to go to college. You need to work for a while so you can grow up a little more first. I think it's just immaturity.

Mike responded,

You always keep telling me that I'm so smart. If I'm so smart, why can't I get the work done and pass these courses? I don't feel very smart at all. I think I should just give up on college and get a full-time job.

Clearly these parents were frustrated with Mike's having lost so many credits by not doing what they assumed he could do if only he tried harder. Equally clear was Mike's shame, his hopelessness, and his increasing inability to believe that he was as smart as his parents and teachers had been telling him.

My first task in talking with Mike and his family was to acknowledge their shared frustration and increasing disappointment. Only then could we get started in trying to figure out why this young man who had graduated from high school with honors had been struggling with such frustrating inconsistency and disappointing failure in his first two years of college. I told his skeptical parents that we needed to get more information before any of us could know whether Mike's problems with college were due to immaturity or ADHD or some combination of factors.

After taking a careful history of Mike's strengths and difficulties, I administered normed rating scales, asking him and his parents to rate how much difficulty he had been having with the many different functions associated with ADHD as we now understand it. I emphasized that it made no sense for us to discuss treatment, with or without medication, until we had a clearer understanding of his specific problems. I also suggested that Mike take a full IQ test to give him and his parents a realistic basis for thinking about how strong his cognitive abilities actually were. Mike and his parents agreed to go forward with this plan.

A week later, Mike returned to take the IQ test. As we were starting, he joked that the test scared him because he was afraid that it was going to prove that he was way below the smarts level that his parents and teachers thought they saw in him, that maybe it would show him to be "retarded." In fact, his performance was quite impressive in both the verbal and visual-spatial domains. His parents joined us after the testing so that they could all hear the results together. I explained the scoring system for the test and then asked Mike to guess where he had scored. Reluctantly he guessed that he might have come out slightly above the middle of the average range. He was shocked and his parents were quite surprised when I showed them that he had actually scored in the very superior range, stronger than 99.9 percent of students in his age group. Immediately they asked, "How can Mike be so much smarter than most kids his age and yet not be able to succeed in a lot of college courses that all the rest of them managed to pass?"

To respond to that question, I showed them Mike's scores on the normed ADHD rating scale we had worked with in the initial session; scores given by Mike and by his parents both placed him in the "high probability of ADHD" range. I also showed them that their answers to the items from the psychiatric manual's diagnostic criteria for ADHD fully met the cutoff for diagnosis. We also looked at Mike's score on the normed verbal memory test in which I read two brief stories to him, each containing twenty-five word units, and then, after reading each one, asked him to repeat that story to me as close to verbatim as possible. (This was the same test I administered to Sarah, whose story you read in Chapter Five.) On that measure, Mike had scored in the 9th percentile, worse than 91 percent of people his age in the general population. My explanation of these measures and of the latest understanding of ADHD helped Mike and his parents see that although he was clearly extremely smart, he also suffered from significant impairments of EF that constitute ADHD. After hearing this, Mike's father acknowledged that his earlier skepticism was based on a totally different understanding of ADHD than what I had just explained.

> Studies of children and adults with ADHD have demonstrated that people with high IQ not only can have ADHD but also are likely to struggle in school much longer than many others before their ADHD impairments are recognized, diagnosed, and treated.

Parents and teachers often find it difficult to believe that students who are very bright can be suffering from ADHD, especially if they're not troublemakers. Often people assume that anyone very intelligent can use that intelligence to avoid difficulties with organizing and prioritizing, using working memory, following through to finish tasks, and performing other EFs that are critical to success. Research has shown, however, that EFs are a separate domain within the broader group of cognitive functions. Correlations between measures of EFs and IQ scores are not statistically significant. A large study of children with ADHD and a control group demonstrated that group differences in EF were not explained by group differences in IQ, and vice versa. That same study showed that EF and IQ are relatively independent of each other in individual children.[1] Other studies of children and adults with ADHD have demonstrated that people with high IQ not only can have ADHD but also are likely to struggle in school much longer than many others before their ADHD impairments are recognized, diagnosed, and treated.[2]

After I explained to Mike and his parents our new understanding of ADHD and how it's related to chemical problems in the brain, I asked Mike how he felt about the possibility of undergoing a trial of medication to see if it could help to alleviate his ADHD symptoms. I explained potential side effects and possible benefits; I also explained that we couldn't be sure that medication would be helpful, but that odds of its being at least somewhat helpful were about eight out of ten.

Mike quickly said that he would like to try it, but his father countered that he wasn't very comfortable with the idea of Mike's taking such medication and wanted some time to think about it before they made any decision. Mike told his parents that he had once taken a tablet of Adderall, a medication for ADHD, that he had gotten from a friend. He said that it helped him a lot with his schoolwork that day. His dad insisted that he still wanted to think about the whole issue before he would allow Mike to get any prescription.

Mike's experiment with ADHD medication not prescribed for him is an illustration of a pattern of use that is widespread on many college campuses and in many high schools. Often students "borrow" or buy ADHD medications from friends with ADHD who have had it prescribed to them. In some cases, as with Mike, there is just a single trial; in others, the unprescribed use is often repeated. Media reporting on this often assumes that students are taking unprescribed ADHD medications to party with them, to try to get high. However, a number of studies of stimulant use and misuse among students in colleges and universities have reported that a large majority of those students who take stimulant medications not prescribed for them seem to be taking them not for recreational purposes but to support and improve their academic functioning as they study for a test or stay up for an all-nighter to complete a term paper.[3]

Mike came back alone for his next session with me. He reported that his father was still very skeptical about the medication option. He had compared it to a baseball player taking steroids, but he said he wouldn't stand in the way if Mike wanted to give it a try. His mother had also reluctantly agreed.

Mike and I talked about how we couldn't be sure that medication would be helpful to him, that it tends to be significantly helpful to about 80 percent of people with ADHD who take it, so long as their medication is adequately fine-tuned for their specific body chemistry. I explained that the effective dose of stimulant medication for a person has nothing to do with how old he is, how much he weighs, or how severe his symptoms are; effective dose is instead determined by how sensitive that person's body is to that specific medication. We also went over possible indicators of having too much or too little.

After our discussion about medication, Mike decided to try it. However, before I actually wrote the referral note to ask his physician to prescribe it for him, Mike brought it all to a stop.

> On second thought, I'm not sure I really need the medication if I'm not going to be going to school. First, I have to decide what to do about school—should I go to our local community college where the tuition is really cheap and try to get some decent grades so I can eventually go back to the university, or should I just forget about going to college and get some kind of job and make a career out of that? I know I scored high on that IQ test, but that's no guarantee that I'll be able to make it through college. Maybe my parents are right. I just don't know if I really belong in college.

In this question about whether or not to proceed with his plan to try medication treatment for his ADHD, Mike was raising a much bigger question: he was wondering whether there was any real basis for hope that he could be successful in college.

conflicting hopes and fears

I asked Mike to tell me how he was thinking about the decision he was trying to make. He said he was going back and forth between two different pictures of how things could turn out. In one picture, he imagined himself as someone who would return to college while taking the ADHD medicine, be able to do the work consistently, and emerge as a successful graduate who had experienced a difficult, frustrating start, but who eventually was able to put on a cap and gown and walk up to collect his diploma. In this picture, he envisioned belatedly fulfilling his parents' and his long-held dreams as a very bright young man who was simply a late bloomer.

> Psychologists have demonstrated that most of us carry within us a variety of possible selves, a wardrobe of fantasies about what we might become, pictures both of who and what we hope to be and of who and what we are afraid we might become.

Yet Mike said that he hesitated even to start trying the medication and going back to school, even at the lower-priced local community college, because he also had in his mind a picture of himself as a loser who keeps on losing, a gambler who keeps feeding money into the slot machine until he has spent his last dollar, one who just doesn't know when to cut his losses, call it quits, and move on to something else.

Mike said that he kept thinking he might end up as what his parents had repeatedly warned him he was becoming: a lazy loser with great potential who just never got it together. Mike told me about an uncle on his father's side who tried college several times, but never finished his degree. This very bright uncle ended up working as a janitor in an elementary school rather than as the successful professional his teachers and family had expected him to become. This uncle was Mike's alternative possible self.

o possible selves

Psychologists have demonstrated that most of us carry within us a variety of possible selves, a wardrobe of fantasies about what we might become, pictures both of who and what we hope to be and of who and what we are afraid we might become. We may base these possible selves on elaborated images of specific people we've actually known in the past or present, heard about from others, or seen in the media.

They might include images of an attractive, physically fit athletic self; a self-confident, popular social self; a wealthy self who doesn't have to worry about keeping up with any bills; an assertive self who can forcefully confront those who are frustrating; or a married self with an enviable partner. Simultaneously, we may carry images of possible selves that represent more negative outcomes: as an unattractive, onetime athlete who has gotten hopelessly out of shape; a shy, friendless, and isolated self; an impoverished self who is unable to keep up with even the most basic expenses; a bullied self who is unable to speak up to stop those who are disrespectful or rude; a lonely self who is left without any partner or who makes do with an undesirable partner.

A team of psychologists who pioneered use of the possible-selves concept wrote that

> an individual's repertoire of possible selves can be viewed as the cognitive manifestation of enduring goals, aspirations, motives, fears and threats. Possible selves provide the self-relevant form, meaning, organization and direction to these dynamics. As such, they provide the essential link between the self-concept and motivation.[4]

Mike and I spent several sessions talking about these conflicting pictures he had of himself. I emphasized the importance of the phrase "at this time" to look at his situation, trying to help him keep in mind that although his academic track record since high school had been weak and very inconsistent thus far, that did not need to be taken as the final verdict on his future. We talked about how well he had scored on the IQ test and about the differences as well as the similarities between himself and his unsuccessful uncle.

o persistent social anxieties

I also questioned Mike about whether he could see any other factors that might have complicated his difficulties in making a successful adjustment to the university. His first response was to sheepishly admit that there had been many times when he had gone on binges of smoking marijuana with a couple of his stoner friends. He had managed to keep this secret from his parents because he knew they had strong feelings against any drug use. He had also withheld information from me in my initial evaluation, even when I asked him in private session about drinking and drug use. He explained that he had never been a consistent smoker of weed, but that there had been two or three episodes each semester when he had gotten into it, and when he had started, it was daily use for about a week, often at critical times in the semester when exams were being given and papers were due.

In a nonjudgmental way, I asked Mike about how he decided when he would use weed and when he wouldn't. His answer was direct: "I smoke when something is freaking me out." He told of how he had always tried to put on a very laid-back front for other people, including his parents, while he actually had always worried a lot about what other people, peers, teachers, and other adults thought of him.

When I asked for examples, Mike recalled his early high school years when he was repeatedly teased by others for being short and physically immature. He had not fully hit puberty until his junior year, several years after almost all other boys in his peer group. Although he had grown rapidly after his seventeenth birthday and was eventually more than six feet tall, he said he still had bad dreams about walking down school hallways as a midget and getting shoved against lockers or having his books and notebooks knocked out of his hands onto the floor while everyone was changing classes. He spoke of how he hated going to the locker room for gym class, where he was required to undress in front of classmates, all of whom were more fully developed sexually than he was for most of his first three years of high school.

Recalling his discomfort in the locker room led Mike to tell of a more pervasive shyness. He said,

> It wasn't just about being the runt of the litter in junior high and high school. I was always really shy, even in elementary school. I never knew what to say when I had to talk to anybody that I didn't already know pretty well. I was too small to play any sports. I just didn't know how to act cool. I never volunteered to answer questions in class, even when I could have given better answers than what most of the others were saying. I would answer only when the

teacher called on me. I felt awkward and always figured that everybody could see that I was a dorky wimp. I didn't want to say too
much because then they would figure I was a brown-noser.

o illusion of transparency

Mike's assumption that others could readily notice weaknesses he perceived in himself is an example of what psychologists call the "illusion
of transparency" or the "spotlight effect."[5] Several studies have shown
that many people, especially those who suffer from Social Anxiety Disorder, assume that others can discern far more about their uncomfortable
internal state than actually is the case.

> A national epidemiological study of people with ADHD
> found that social anxiety is the most common of all psy-
> chiatric disorders co-occurring with ADHD; almost 30
> percent of adults with ADHD report also having social
> anxiety.

Prevalence of social anxiety — excessive worry about how one is perceived by others — is markedly elevated in individuals with ADHD. A
national epidemiological study of people with ADHD found that social
anxiety is the most common of all psychiatric disorders co-occurring
with ADHD; almost 30 percent of adults with ADHD report also having
social anxiety. This is considerably higher than the rate for this disorder
in the general population, where a previous epidemiological study found
the incidence to be about 13 percent.[6] This may be because those with
ADHD often live with considerable fear that their inattention problems
will be noticed by others and cause them embarrassment.

Mike reported that his strong fears of being embarrassed were one
of the reasons he often stopped attending some of his college courses. If
he overslept for a morning class or didn't have a paper ready to hand in
when it was due, or if he felt unprepared for a quiz or test, he would often
skip that class session and then feel afraid to attend the next meeting.

He worried that in class he might be confronted by the professor for his failure to do what was expected. In this way, a single missed class often led to another and another until sometimes it felt to Mike as though it would be less shameful to withdraw from the course completely than to go back to the class and risk a humiliating confrontation.

○ anxiety, marijuana, and medications

After we had spent several sessions exploring Mike's anxiety problems and his episodic use of marijuana to reduce that anxiety, he announced that he wanted to stop using marijuana altogether. I cautioned him that it might be better to taper down his use gradually so that he could adjust to the change with less stress. Two weeks later, Mike returned and reported that, despite my advice, he had stopped smoking marijuana cold turkey and had stayed away from it completely, even though he had been experiencing a lot of insomnia and agitation every day since.

He was proud of his accomplishment and felt quite determined to continue his abstinence. He had started a strenuous program of exercise, which seemed to be gradually reducing his difficulty in getting to sleep. He did, however, ask if I could arrange for him to try some medicine to cut down his excessive worrying "about everything under the sun." I contacted his physician, who readily agreed to prescribe for Mike a trial of fluoxetine to reduce his excessive anxiety. I also explained to Mike that it would probably take at least a few weeks for him to feel the full benefits of this medication.

A few weeks later, Mike reported that he was already feeling some reduction in his worry. He also told me that the domain in which his anxiety was most intense was dating. Although he was able to carry on casual conversations with girls he met in his classes or when hanging out with friends, he had very little dating experience. He saw himself as one who could be a friend to girls, but not a good boyfriend. In high school, he had been "going with" a girl for about six months during his junior year, but she eventually dumped him to date someone else. Mike's hunch was that she was more experienced sexually and wanted to have a boyfriend who was more ready for sexual involvement than was Mike at that time.

In his next session, Mike slumped into the couch, stared at the carpet, and hesitatingly said, "Sometimes I think I might be gay. I really hope I'm not, and I don't really think I am, but sometimes I wonder about that." I asked what he thought would be so bad about being gay. He said, "Probably nothing except that my parents would freak out for a while. I know a couple of guys who are gay, and they seem OK." I asked what made him think he might be gay, whether he'd had some sexual experiences with other guys or found himself thinking about doing that when he masturbated. I mentioned that such experiences were common among many guys, some of whom eventually found that they were gay and others who turned out not to be. Without any hesitation, he said, "Nope, even when I was little; I never had any sexual experiences with any other guys, and when I jerk off, the movies I run in my head are always about me or some other guy having sex with some hot girl."

"So what makes you think you might be gay?" I asked. Mike answered directly:

> Because I just don't have the balls to ask some girl out and then have sex with her. I get my eye on some girl who's really hot and friendly, and I just don't make the moves to get to know her or to let her get to know me. I guess I'm afraid I wouldn't know that to do if she said yes.

As we talked further about this, it became clear that Mike's fear that he might be gay was not based on homosexual interests he was unable to claim. It was a way of thinking about himself as a defective male, as though any guy who is not proficient in developing and maintaining sexual relationships with girls is not just shy, but homosexual. I explained that although it is certainly true that some males who are gay are fearful of sexual relationships with females, that is not what makes them gay. I tried to help him understand that homosexuality is about what turns the person on, not about what he or she feels afraid to do. I assured him that sexual shyness can be found in people of any sexual orientation and that many gradually get over it if they can persist in developing friendships with potential partners before trying to rush too quickly into explicitly sexual relationships.

A few weeks later, Mike returned and reported that the fluoxetine he was taking seemed to be kicking in. "Stuff that used to bother me way too much doesn't bother me that much anymore." With a broad smile, he told of how he had gotten a part-time job at a local gas station where he was not only pumping gas but also helping do minor repairs in their garage. More important to him was that he had worked up his courage to start a casual conversation with Barbara, an attractive girl who came by that station frequently to buy her gas. Gradually their conversations had become increasingly longer. That had led to their meeting up for lunch together and a plan to catch a movie on the following Saturday night. "And I did it all without getting that feeling that my heart was pounding too fast and thumping like it was going to jump out of my chest."

Mike said he wasn't sure what was making those moves easier for him. "Maybe it's that medication, or maybe it's all the exercising I'm doing every day, or maybe it's this therapy and just figuring out that a lot of other people get nervous like I do. She told me that she feels that way sometimes too and that she knows a lot of other kids our age who are the same way."

Two weeks later, Mike asked me to give him the letter to ask his physician to start him on some ADHD medication to take concurrently with the fluoxetine. He said he had decided to enroll in several courses at the local community college for the fall term that was about to begin. He told me, "I'm really feeling a lot better these last few weeks. I don't feel so self-conscious. It's easier for me to talk with people; I don't have to fake it so much."

Regardless of what factor or combination of factors was causing Mike's improved mood and increasing self-confidence, he was clearly experiencing some desperately needed success, which was helping him get a bit unstuck from the morass of discouragement he had been stuck in a couple of months earlier. He was beginning to feel that his more positive images of his possible self might be attainable.

○ reconsidering vocational goals

A week later, Mike returned with his papers to enroll in the community college. He explained that he was having a hard time deciding which courses to take. His math grades in high school had been very good. Since starting college, he had been planning to become an accountant and had declared accounting as his major. Yet in looking over his transcript to prepare for enrollment in the community college, Mike noticed that most of the courses he had done well in thus far were in history and English; most of his low grades and withdrawals were in courses in math, economics, and accounting. When he told his parents that he was thinking of switching to become a history major, Mike's father had told him he should continue with his accounting major because it could get him a good job after graduation; he also said that he thought it important for Mike to finish what he started and not be jumping from one thing to another.

Mike told me that he had been interested in history all his life, often reading about it and watching the history channel on TV. He described how he had gotten especially interested in the complex causes of our wars in Vietnam and Iraq. I asked him what he might do for a career if he finished college with a major in history. Mike answered quickly with a broad smile, "I'd like to be a high school history teacher. I think I could make history come alive for those kids." He then announced that he was going to sign up for a couple of history courses in the coming semester and not be held back by his father's preferences.

At the end of that semester, Mike had earned A's in both of his history courses and B's in the two others. He had spent a lot of time outside of class talking with one of the history professors whom he really admired. At the end of that term, Mike changed his major to history. During the following semester, he missed only one class, handed in all his assignments, and earned a solid B+ average.

Mike was proud of his grades, but he was also very proud of his ongoing relationship with Barbara. After a weekend trip with her and her parents, Mike exclaimed over how both her parents really liked him and that it seemed clear that he and Barbara were becoming a couple with a future. Mike reported that they were seeing each other almost daily, were becoming very close friends, and were enjoying an exciting and very satisfying sexual relationship.

With all the time Mike was now spending with Barbara, keeping up with a full-time load of courses, and working part-time at the garage, he was feeling quite busy and generally happy. One day he said that he felt it might be time for him to cut back and taper off his therapy sessions with me. Then he said,

> Before we stop meeting regularly, there's one more thing I need to sort out with you: I've never really understood why I didn't go away to college right after graduating from high school. I was on the honor roll and getting better grades than a lot of my friends who ended up going away to college in that first September after we graduated. But I didn't even apply. I just commuted to the local branch of the state university and kept living at home.

○ covert binding in family loyalties

I asked Mike what he remembered about that time. He recalled that his parents kept telling him that he was too immature to go away to school. They told him that they would only pay for him to start out as a commuting student. "So I just accepted that and took some courses there while I was working almost every day as a dishwasher at a pizza place," Mike said with a shrug and a sigh. "And that's when I started hanging out with a few friends who were heavy stoners. They weren't going away to college either. Most of them didn't have the smarts, and they just didn't care."

I asked what else Mike could recall from those days. "Oh, yeah," he said, "that was the time my mom was really depressed. She had to go into the psych ward at the hospital for a few weeks and then she came home on a lot of medication. It was a pretty bad depression. She had to quit her job, and mostly she just sat around staring at the walls and crying, or else she was asleep." This was the first time Mike had talked about his mother's major depression; neither he nor his parents had mentioned it in the initial evaluation session when I asked about stresses in the family over the past few years. I asked Mike how his father had reacted to his mother's depression. He told me that his father just got really quiet and pretty much kept to himself. Most nights he would just drink a six-pack and then fall asleep watching TV. It was like he didn't know what to do and say to her or to me. So I tried to help out with talking with her and getting her meals and being sure she was taking her medications.

The mystery of why Mike had not gone away to college right after graduating from high school no longer seemed a mystery. The explanation that Mike and his parents had been working with was that Mike was "too immature" to go away to college when his friends left in the September after high school graduation. The story of the mother's severe depression and his father's helplessness after she returned from the hospital suggests another explanation. Mike assumed the role of caretaker and support for his severely depressed mother and felt an obligation to stay home and care for her, even though it meant deferring his long-held plan to go directly on to college. This was not recognized explicitly by Mike or by his parents, even after the fact; they continued to explain his staying home as a sign of his immaturity when, in fact, it was a sign of his strength and loyalty to his family.

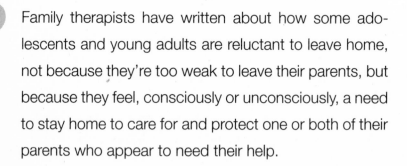

Family therapists have written about how some adolescents and young adults are reluctant to leave home, not because they're too weak to leave their parents, but because they feel, consciously or unconsciously, a need to stay home to care for and protect one or both of their parents who appear to need their help.

Most psychologists rarely speak of loyalty as a factor in the struggles of some adolescents and young adults to launch themselves into adult life. Yet unrecognized loyalty can be a powerful force to delay some individuals in the process of growing up. A few family therapists have written about how some adolescents and young adults are reluctant to leave home, not because they're too weak to leave their parents, but because they feel, consciously or unconsciously, a need to stay home to care for and protect one or both of their parents who appear to need their help.[7]

Even when the young person fully recognizes and struggles consciously with these conflicts between, on the one hand, a wish to stay at home to provide care for an emotionally or medically ill parent or a needy or wayward sibling and, on the other hand, a wish to leave the family and move on to pursue education and develop a more independent lifestyle, reconciling them can be quite difficult. These conflicts are much more problematic when the problem is buried in silence, not acknowledged honestly by family members.

In those situations, as in Mike's family, the one who stays may be labeled as weak, immature, or too needy of continuing parental support, while the needs of the parent or sibling remain "undiscussable" and unrecognized. For this reason, the loyalty conflict may remain invisible and extremely difficult to change. The individual thus bound may continue to see himself or herself as weak and unable to cope or to relate effectively with peers or other adults, locked in protracted dependence on the one who is unrecognizably dependent on him or her.

Mike and I spent several sessions discussing the difficult dilemma he had been facing when his mother was so depressed and his father was so unable to help her. We talked about how he had begun to buy into the view that he was too immature to move on to college. We also talked about how he had begun to act out the part of an immature and irresponsible student, fulfilling his parents' attribution.

o   o   o

In the ensuing months, we tapered down the frequency of our meetings, while his relationship with Barbara continued to strengthen and his grades continued to improve. Two years later, Mike wrote me to announce that he had just graduated with honors from the university, had successfully completed his student teaching, was continuing in his relationship with Barbara, and would be starting a new job in September as a high school history teacher.

What Helped Mike?

- Talk therapy to address social anxiety, marijuana use to reduce anxiety, reassessment of vocational goals, insecurities about sexuality, and covert binding in family loyalties
- Family therapy sessions to help Mike and his parents recognize that difficulties in college were due primarily to ADHD impairments and not to laziness or immaturity
- Rating scale and clinical evaluation of current cognitive strengths and weaknesses, with explanation to Mike and his parents about ADHD in very bright individuals
- Therapeutic clarification of conflicting views of "possible selves" and hopes for the future
- Prescription of SSRI medication to reduce excessive anxious ruminations and social anxiety
- Exploration of conflicting feelings about medication to alleviate ADHD impairments followed by prescription and fine-tuning of appropriate stimulant medications

7

lisa

Other kids don't seem to get my jokes and aren't interested in who I am. I try to make friends, but no one ever calls me back when I call them. I try to talk with my parents about it, but my dad doesn't understand kids, and my mom's always yelling at me. ADHD meds help me get schoolwork done, but they don't help with social stuff.
— 15-YEAR-OLD HIGH SCHOOL STUDENT

Lisa was fifteen years old when she came with her parents for a first visit to my office. She was quite small for her age; I would have guessed her to be several years younger. In her hands she was carrying two small dolls, replicas of Homer and Marge, the two parents in the animated TV show *The Simpsons*. She gave a broad smile when she saw that I recognized the characters, and then tossed her head as though to say, "So what?" Her father quickly told her to put the toys away. She ignored him. Her mother then looked at her sternly and said, "I'm telling you, put those things away NOW!" Lisa sighed, rolled her eyes, then set the dolls down beside her.

When I asked Lisa why her parents had brought her to see me, she said, "They made me go to some child psychiatrist all last year because they thought I have Oppositional Defiant Disorder and ADHD. It was a waste of time, same as the psychology clinic they took me to before that." I asked, "So what are you hoping we might be able to do here?" Lisa's response was immediate: "Get my parents to stop fighting all the time, get my grades higher, and fix it so all the kids don't treat me like a leper."

○ triangular family conflict

Quickly Lisa's mother responded, "We wouldn't be fighting so much if you were doing what you're supposed to." Her father added, "You need to learn how to treat your mother and me with respect." In a few short minutes, Lisa and her parents had demonstrated how the three of them tended to get locked into battles, triangular warfare, that distracted from problems in their marriage and the other two problems Lisa had mentioned, her underachievement in school and her chronic trouble getting along with her peers.

This discussion continued with the mother complaining that her husband was unable to be firm with Lisa, that he couldn't get her to do her homework, and that he tended to give her whatever she demanded, however unreasonable. She mentioned that at times Lisa pushed or hit her father to get him to take her out to McDonald's for burgers after school. Lisa's father acknowledged that he found it easier to give in to his daughter than to put up with her protracted demandingness. Lisa added, "Yeah, and then my mother gets mad and yells at my father for being a wimp."

On the surface, it appeared that Lisa was simply a disrespectful early adolescent, an only child, whose parents were struggling to cope with her chronic defiance and her refusal to put sufficient effort into her schoolwork. Underneath that, all three family members were clearly suffering. Each of the parents seemed quite bright, but quite distant from and very frustrated with one another as well as with Lisa. My initial impression of Lisa was that she was very bright, but also rather depressed in an irritable way, painfully aware of her inability to form satisfying relationships with peers and worried about her current inability to perform academically as she was now starting her first year of high school.

o   stimulant "rebound" and late-afternoon irritability

One year earlier, Lisa had been started on medication for her ADHD by her previous therapist. She was taking a long-acting stimulant that had helped considerably to improve her focus and effort for her academic work during the school day. However, like many students taking these longer-acting stimulant medications, Lisa found that the positive effects of the medication tended to wear off at the end of the school day, after which she experienced a "rebound" of fatigue and excessive irritability that severely affected her behavior and focus each day when she got home after school; this irritability continued into the evening. Unfortunately, the physician prescribing that medication had not recognized or provided any treatment for this rebound problem.[1]

Although medications for ADHD are not marketed to improve mood, many patients find that stimulant medications improve their "top-down" control of emotions so that they are not so readily flooded by feelings of frustration or irritability. For some patients, however, stimulant medications wear off too abruptly, suddenly leaving them more vulnerable to excessive moodiness. Often this can be alleviated by an additional small dose of the short-acting formulation of the same medication taken shortly before the time that the longer-acting dose is wearing off, so the patient experiences a smoother drop-off from the medication and is less vulnerable to "crashing" emotionally.

My first intervention was to ask Lisa's physician to provide a "booster dose" of the short-acting version of the same stimulant medication, to be taken immediately after school so that Lisa would have more adequate medication coverage in the late afternoon and early evening when she needed to do her homework and interact with her parents. Fortunately, the booster dose helped considerably to reduce Lisa's irritability after school; it also helped her in completing her homework more efficiently with less conflict between herself and her parents.

o unraveling family polarization and conflict

As we talked about the chronic conflicts between Lisa and her parents, it quickly became clear that the parents were polarized regarding how to deal with Lisa. As in many other families with exceptionally oppositional children, one parent had consistently taken on the role of "the enforcer" while the other was locked into the role of "the marshmallow."[2] Lisa's mother was quick to confront Lisa when she was speaking at all disrespectfully, was not meeting expectations, or was slow to comply with directions. She shouted a lot, took away privileges, and issued other punishments, often receiving disrespectful and hateful responses from her daughter in return. Lisa's father rarely confronted Lisa and almost never punished her, regardless of how demanding or disrespectful she was being. Even on occasions when Lisa had been shouting at him and pushing him, he eventually relented and gave her what she had been demanding. Following such incidents, he then reported Lisa's misbehavior to her mother and expected the mother to confront Lisa about it. Meanwhile, Lisa herself joined her mother in criticizing her father for being too weak and ineffectual.

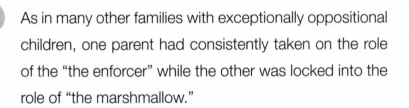

As in many other families with exceptionally oppositional children, one parent had consistently taken on the role of the "the enforcer" while the other was locked into the role of "the marshmallow."

Both parents clearly loved their daughter and wanted to help her function better, but for several years, both had been caught up in chronic conflict with one another regarding how best to deal with Lisa. The father felt that his wife was frequently too intense in confronting Lisa; her mother was chronically enraged with the father for his failure to discipline his daughter while leaving all the disciplinary tasks to his wife. There were also many indications that these parents had been unhappy with each other since long before Lisa's birth. Lisa was caught up in her parents' ongoing marital conflicts.

As Lisa reported in our initial meeting, when she acted up toward her father, it provoked her mother to show intense anger toward both the father and herself; this often left father and daughter aligned as dual victims of the mother's chronic anger. It appeared that Lisa was enmeshed in the chronic marital conflicts of her parents, sometimes provoking them to act against one another and, at other times, drawing their anger toward herself.

To address these family issues, we began a mix of conjoint family meetings with Lisa and both parents, occasional meetings with just the parents, and more frequent individual meetings for Lisa with me. The family sessions focused on ways the parents could change their patterns of interaction with Lisa by working to keep a more united front in dealing with her inappropriate and disrespectful behavior. We also discussed strategies Lisa could use to extricate herself from the conflicts between her parents by not intruding herself into their disagreements. My goal in this was to help the parents recognize the need for them to establish themselves as a parenting team trying to help their daughter learn how to function more effectively with them and with those outside their family, especially her peers.

o   stresses of social ineptness

In our individual sessions, Lisa often complained that classmates, both girls and boys, tended to dislike and ignore her, not responding to her efforts to develop friendships and join in their activities. One of the first examples of her peer problems that she presented was from a trip her class had recently taken to an amusement park. In the bus on the way to the park, Lisa made an obscene gesture behind the back of one of the group leaders who was very popular with the students. Others on the bus told the leader, who then confronted Lisa; she initially denied and then soon acknowledged having made the gesture.

She told me that when her assigned group got off the bus that day, they quickly ran away and "ditched me so I had to walk around all day at the park by myself. It was the worst day of my life." When I asked Lisa about why she had made the gesture on the bus, she said, "I was just challenging authority. That's what teenagers do." Until she had been dumped by her group, Lisa had not realized that her classmates were not likely to consider her gesture funny or appropriate, especially because it was aimed at an adult most of them really liked.

In sessions over subsequent months, we discussed additional examples of situations where Lisa had felt hurt and surprised at the reactions of peers to her efforts at humor. At times, her humor was quirky, but quite funny; at other times, it was clearly inappropriate and misguided. We needed to discuss many examples to help Lisa develop a clearer sense of what sort of jokes are likely to be funny to others and which are likely to bring more negative reactions. These judgments can be difficult to teach some individuals. It would be easier to teach some eight-year-olds how to factor a quadratic equation than to teach people with problems like Lisa's how to know when a joke is likely to be considered funny and when not. Many complex calculations are involved, even though for most people, those judgments are made intuitively.

Several studies have found that children with ADHD tend to have more frequent and more difficult problems in getting along with their peers than do most children without ADHD. Even in summer camp situations where they are interacting with a new group of peers and can make a fresh beginning with no bad reputation to start with, those with ADHD tend to act in ways that cause peers to quickly reject them. They often push too much to get attention for themselves and often don't share the concern of their peers for fairness. Such rejection can start very early.

One study found that many kids with ADHD were disliked and rejected by peers from the first day of camp, several days earlier than others, and that this rejection tended to persist until the last day of camp. Often they annoy peers not only by being too demanding but also by not following the usual informal rules of peer interaction. Children who suffer such rejection from peers often tend to remain more enmeshed in their families and to miss out on many of the interactions with peers that would enable them to learn skills of cooperation, negotiation, and conflict resolution that are critical for essential social functioning throughout life. Some researchers have emphasized that such social problems are manifestations of executive function impairments characteristic of ADHD.[3]

o problems of asperger's syndrome in people with ADHD

As I heard more from Lisa about her problems with peers, it became apparent that her difficulties in social interaction were more severe than most other children her age with ADHD. Lisa seemed to have considerable trouble anticipating how others, particularly her peers, might respond to her efforts at humor, though she sometimes could see the problem after the fact. She commented, "There's something about me that repels people . . . I'm just weird. Like in my writing for English class I often put in details that gross people out, even when I thought they were funny. Lots of time its stuff like on *The Simpsons*." She seemed genuinely puzzled at why others her age wouldn't find her efforts at humor as amusing as she did.

As she gave more examples, it became clear that in her isolation from friendships with peers, Lisa had immersed herself in watching the exaggerated satirical style of humor characteristic of *The Simpsons*. She then imitated this style in her interactions with her parents and her peers, unable to see that often this would appear juvenile and ridiculous to other kids her age. Her parents reacted to Lisa's Simpsonesque humor with annoyance, but they had not been able to help her see how it was likely to annoy or look pathetic to other high school students.

Lisa's peer communication problems were more severe than those of most other adolescents with ADHD; in some ways she seemed to interact with peers more as would a child with Asperger's syndrome, one who desperately wants more social interaction with peers but does not understand how to make it happen.

Some 20 to 50 percent of children with ADHD also meet diagnostic criteria for an autism spectrum disorder. These children tend to have much more significant

> deficits in their abilities to size up social situations, notice how others are reacting to them, put themselves in the shoes of others, and flexibly shift their roles and behaviors in interaction with others in their age group.

Although many people with ADHD tend to have difficulties in peer relationships, for some, such difficulties are due to more severe problems in social communication that are typical of individuals on the autism spectrum (for example, Asperger's syndrome). Recent reviews of research comparing children with ADHD and children with autism spectrum disorders found that 20 to 50 percent of children with ADHD also meet diagnostic criteria for an autism spectrum disorder.[4] These children tend to have much more significant deficits in their abilities to size up social situations, notice how others are reacting to them, put themselves in the shoes of others, and flexibly shift their roles and behaviors in interaction with others in their age group.

Although some are quite bright, these children who are more severely impaired in terms of social skills fail to learn the informal rules of social interaction that most other children, including many with ADHD, pick up simply by observing the interactions of others, especially among their peers and slightly older children. Even when they are told about inappropriate social behavior, some children with these more severe problems just don't "get it" and are not able to readily deploy alternative ways of acting. It is only with much effort and many, often painful experiences that some of them can learn to use their intellect to pick up and apply in their actions the social skills that are intuitive for most of their age mates. Lisa did not fully meet diagnostic criteria for an autism spectrum disorder, but she did have some of these more severe social problems in her childhood and early adolescence.

o impact of delayed pubescent development

Lisa's social difficulties were also complicated by her small stature and immature physical development. She looked like a girl several years younger than her age. She recognized this and felt ashamed of it, though she and her parents never spoke of these issues. The combination of her physical immaturity and her social immaturity put Lisa at substantially increased risk for scapegoating by her peers at an age when most boys and girls are acutely conscious of their pubescent status or lack of it. Some who had heard about Lisa's fascination with *The Simpsons* started calling her Maggie, the baby of that cartoon family; others simply referred to her with contempt as "runt" or "weirdo." Especially during junior high and high school, some adolescents are merciless in their ridicule of classmates who look and act like younger kids.

Recognizing the severity of Lisa's difficulties regarding physical immaturity, her pediatrician arranged for Lisa to consult with a specialist, who found that Lisa's bone age was more than three years behind her chronological age. That physician prescribed growth hormone treatments, which helped Lisa gradually catch up in her bodily growth and pubescent development. Within a year, she grew more than four inches and had begun to look more like the smaller of her female classmates.

Despite her physical growth and some efforts to curtail her more immature attempts at humor with classmates, Lisa continued to feel like a beleaguered outcast in her high school. Her widespread reputation as "the weird one" and her tendency to react to teasing with excessive and sarcastic intensity caused the scapegoating to persist. Despite all her difficulties, Lisa's mind was set on her eventually getting into a good college. Both of her parents were college graduates; her father had graduated from a very competitive university, and her mother was working part-time on a graduate degree. Lisa was hoping to follow a similar path of educational achievement, though her grades in her first two years of high school were not very high, mostly in the C range. At this point, I proposed that we do a battery of IQ and standardized academic achievement testing to get more objective information about Lisa's cognitive strengths and difficulties.

Lisa did quite well on the verbal comprehension and perceptual reasoning portions of the IQ test, scoring in the superior range for both. Like many other very bright students with ADHD, her scores were much weaker, though still in the average range, for the portions of the IQ test that assess working memory and processing speed, two aspects of EF often impaired in persons with ADHD. Lisa's achievement tests for reading and writing were in the average range; her math achievement was at the lower end of the average range. These achievement test scores were lower than would usually be predicted by such high verbal comprehension and perceptual reasoning scores on the IQ test, but this was not surprising, given the struggles Lisa had been experiencing with teachers, parents, and peers during earlier grades before she was medicated for ADHD.

o recognizing strengths and increasing hope

When I gave Lisa and her parents the results of her IQ and achievement testing, she responded with much pride for having scored quite high in the verbal comprehension and perceptual reasoning portions of the test. She said with a broad smile, "So maybe there's some hope for me eventually." I emphasized that those superior scores were indicators of her strong potential; I also showed her that despite her currently taking medication for ADHD, there was still evidence of her difficulties with working memory and processing speed in the testing, as well as some significant weaknesses in some academic areas. For her, these objective data about her cognitive abilities were important pieces of information. She began to talk of herself as an intelligent person, someone who could eventually do a lot better. This image of herself helped Lisa sustain hope for her future during the many months and several years when her current achievement was considerably below what she hoped for.

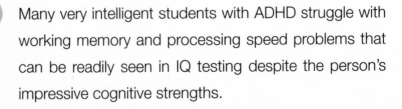

Many very intelligent students with ADHD struggle with working memory and processing speed problems that can be readily seen in IQ testing despite the person's impressive cognitive strengths.

Our ADHD research group at Yale has published studies of children, adolescents, and adults with ADHD and high IQ which indicate that many very intelligent students with ADHD struggle with working memory and processing speed problems that can be readily seen in IQ testing despite the person's impressive cognitive strengths.[5] This information can be helpful for these students, enabling them to see both their strengths and their difficulties. When I gave Lisa the results of her testing, I also cautioned her against bragging to classmates about her high test scores and reminded her that just being smart does not usually bring much success; consistent, significant effort and output are also required. Sometimes very bright students with ADHD, especially those with significant impairment in social interactions with peers, try to win respect from peers by bragging about their high IQ scores, a behavior that usually generates the opposite of the effect wished for.

o a fresh start in a new school

Concerned about Lisa's continuing underachievement and her increasing demoralization with school, her father suggested that Lisa might benefit from becoming a boarding school student. He had attended boarding school himself and had found it helpful for improving his social abilities as well as his academic work. Initially Lisa was fearful about living away from her parents, but she also was able to see boarding school as potentially a fresh start socially and as an opportunity both to strengthen her academic abilities and grade average and to extract herself from her continuing conflict-ridden enmeshment with her parents.

After visiting several schools, Lisa applied to one within a few hours of her home. She was admitted, though the school insisted that she would need to begin by repeating tenth grade. Although she was reluctant about repeating the grade, she agreed, and enrolled to begin at the start of the coming academic year.

Lisa came for a session with me after completing her first two weeks at the new school. She was enthusiastic about the place, the curriculum, the students, and the teachers. She enjoyed having a roommate and participating in the required athletic activities. She reported that most of the kids there were friendly and welcoming to her. She told me,

It's really good to have a bunch of kids around all the time to talk and do stuff with, a lot better than just staying around home all the time with nobody else to talk to, except for two parents who don't like each other very much.

Lisa also reported that she was not the only kid in the school with parents who didn't get along. In just the first few weeks, she had already had conversations with several other students who had told her about chronic battles between their parents, many of whom were divorced.

Over the next year and a half, Lisa brought progress reports indicating that she was getting considerably better at preparing for class, studying for exams, and engaging actively in class discussions. She still struggled with organization of her writing and getting homework assignments in on time, but written comments from her teachers included statements like "Lisa has been a joy to teach in American History. She has a wonderful sense of humor and a very pleasant manner"; "In Chemistry, she maintained a 92% test and quiz average, making her one of the top performers in this class."

Several teachers commented on Lisa's effort and enthusiasm — for example, "She was a wonderful student this term in video. She was enthusiastic and goal-oriented, making the best movie she could, taking the time to complete each project to the best of her ability." The coach for her cross-country team wrote,

Lisa was well-prepared for the season, having run a lot during the summer . . . She met or exceeded every expectation, establishing herself as the best runner in our conference. In addition to her success as a runner, she was often encouraging to other runners on her team and her day-to-day effort set an excellent example.

Overall, Lisa's grades were high enough that she made the school honor roll.

o shame, anger, and self-cutting

After she returned from Christmas break for the spring term of her junior year, Lisa's success at boarding school suddenly collapsed. Shortly before Christmas break, Lisa heard that several boys at the school had been making disparaging comments and spreading untrue rumors about her. Because she liked two of these boys and thought they liked her, she felt deeply hurt and angry. She posted on the screen saver of her computer the names of those boys and labeled them with an obscenity.

Not surprisingly, this was seen by another girl, who told the boys just after students returned from Christmas recess. The boys then confronted Lisa and continued to spread even more untrue rumors about her among the small student body of the school. Several of her friends turned against her, and Lisa quickly began to feel that she was once again being rejected and shunned by her peers, as she had been in the school she previously attended. In her hurt, embarrassment, and anger, she began making cuts on her legs, not sufficiently deep to cause serious bleeding or to require stitches, but enough to leave clearly recognizable marks on her legs.

Two days after doing this self-cutting, Lisa telephoned and asked me to hospitalize her because she was feeling a continuing compulsion to cut herself. I arranged for her parents to go immediately to the school and bring her to my office for an emergency visit. After talking with Lisa, it seemed clear to me that she needed to be in the hospital for just a few days to help her stop her unprecedented cutting and to help her stabilize so that she could return to school safely to deal with the social and academic problems that this situation would inevitably bring.

It is not easy to assess and treat cutting behavior. Some parents, teachers, and clinicians feel very frightened about cutting because they assume that it is a prelude to suicidal behavior; usually it is not. A population-based survey study of adolescents ages twelve to eighteen years found that almost 17 percent of the nonclinical sample reported at least one episode of nonsuicidal self-harm. The most frequently reported were self-injury such as cutting, scratching, and self-hitting, or ingesting a medication in excess of the prescribed or generally recognized dosage. The average age of the first incident was fifteen years. Several other studies of adolescents or young adults who were not identified as clinical patients found similar prevalence rates.[6] Data from a significant study showed that nonsuicidal self-injury is not always accompanied by severe psychiatric symptoms and, in most cases, is not followed by suicidal behavior. However, some who have self-injured are in considerable psychiatric distress and are at significant risk of serious self-injury or suicide. Assessing the level of any individual's severity and risk is not easy and requires careful clinical judgment.[7]

When Lisa was discharged from the hospital, she spent a few days at home prior to returning to the boarding school. We met several times to discuss strategies for dealing with reactions of classmates, teachers, and staff to her having been hospitalized and to the cutting and peer conflicts that had preceded it. Arrangements were made for Lisa to meet more frequently with a counselor near the school, but Lisa found it difficult to work with him.

Back at school, Lisa was having trouble focusing on her work and was late in handing in many of her assignments. Her grades were dropping considerably at the time when teachers were reminding students that their junior year grades were particularly important in making a good impression on college admissions officers. Over the next couple of months, some of Lisa's friendships were restored, but some of her classmates were more distant and disinterested in interacting much with her.

o overcoming rejection from school administrators

In late spring, Lisa and her parents received a letter notifying them that the school was not inviting her to return for her senior year. Lisa's grades had dropped somewhat, but they were not the reason for her not being invited to return. The headmaster explained that the administration was uncomfortable with Lisa's having had that episode of cutting herself, that she had not reached out to others on campus for help, and that the counselor whom the school had designated to meet with Lisa following her hospitalization had concluded that Lisa either was bipolar or had Asperger's syndrome.

Lisa's response to the school's decision was to ask me to write a letter on her behalf, and to draft a letter of her own, to the headmaster asking for reconsideration of their decision. She wrote a very thoughtful and articulate letter describing how much she felt she had benefited from her time at the school and reciting the many ways in which she had been successful prior to the cutting incident. She vowed that there would be no more cutting and that she would be putting far more effort into her schoolwork if allowed to return for her senior year. I wrote a letter supporting Lisa's request and challenging the counselor's diagnoses which, I felt, were based on insufficient understanding of this complicated girl.

After a series of negotiations between Lisa and her parents with the school administration, an agreement was reached for Lisa to return for the coming academic year as a day student. She was allowed to take classes and participate in the team sports and occasional evening activities, but she was not to stay overnight in the dormitories. Being a day student would have involved much too lengthy a commute for Lisa to make from her home. However, a close relative lived within easier commuting distance and was willing to have Lisa stay at her home each evening when she had classes the next day. On weekends, Lisa was to return home to live with her parents. There were also some conditions about her meeting with me frequently and self-monitoring her behavior with classmates so as to keep it "appropriate to the expectations of the school."

Lisa and her parents accepted these terms, and Lisa turned to the task of trying to find a college or university where she could be admitted to continue her education after graduation from high school. Although the college adviser at the boarding school suggested that Lisa apply not to a four-year university but to a two-year college in a special program for students with disabilities, Lisa was determined to enroll in a mainstream program at a four-year university, and I encouraged her to do so.

determination to show her strengths

Lisa was strongly determined to show the school that their fears about her were unfounded and that she was now able to work even harder and more effectively in both academics and sports than she did before her hospitalization. She worked out energetically during the summer so that she could return to run on the cross-county team, of which she had once again been elected captain. She also was determined to nurture her friendships with several of the students with whom she had begun to develop more mature reciprocal relationships.

Lisa graduated with high honors from the boarding school that year. The dean commented that she had never seen such a dramatic improvement in a student between junior and senior year. On the strength of recommendations from several of her teachers plus her own interviews, Lisa was accepted into a very respectable university, where she continued to do quite well academically and developed satisfying relationships with a number of other students. Because the university was at a considerable distance from my office, Lisa and I were not able to meet frequently, but she did return to see me at the end of her first semester, reporting that she was really enjoying college. She had earned all A's in her first-semester courses, and she spoke of several friends with whom she enjoyed spending free time. Proudly she reported,

> I've completely shed the image of that weird girl who is unpopular. I've learned that sometimes I just have to conform. Now I listen more and talk less. People see me as cool, laid back, and funny. I've got real friends and I'm having fun, but still doing well on my work.

Four years later, I received a letter of appreciation from Lisa's very proud parents announcing that Lisa had graduated summa cum laude from the university at the top of her class, already had a job as a teacher, and seemed to be doing quite well. Shortly after, Lisa herself stopped by to show me her diploma.

What Helped Lisa?

- Family therapy to identify triangular conflicts and polarizing of parents and to show need to change patterns of family interactions to reduce mutual provocation
- Education of family and prescribing physician about how rebound from stimulant medication for ADHD had been causing daily episodes of late-afternoon irritability and how

adding a "booster dose" of this medication could alleviate this problem

- Individual talk therapy to understand impairments in social interaction with peers, to increase awareness of social cues, and to coach behaviors to improve peer relationships
- IQ testing and recognition of cognitive strengths not evident in earlier school settings
- Growth hormone treatments for excessive delay in physical development
- Boarding school placement to increase socialization, provide a fresh start, and separate from parent conflicts
- Crisis intervention for self-cutting; support for dealing with overreaction of school administration and for making a successful academic, athletic, and social comeback

8

steve

My wife divorced me three months ago, and then a month later I got
fired from my job — both because of my ADHD! Meds help some, but
not enough. I get stuck doing some things and don't get around to
doing what's really important. I procrastinate, and everything takes
me way too long. I'm good at programming computers, but not at
programming myself.

—32-YEAR-OLD COMPUTER PROGRAMMER

Steve, a thirty-two-year-old software engineer, spoke with
sadness — but also with very noticeable frustration and annoyance — of
the recent loss of his marriage and his job. He spoke as though he had
been robbed of both by his ADHD and was annoyed because the medication prescribed by his previous doctor had not "fixed" his ADHD and
prevented those painful losses. Despite his ADHD, Steve had earned a
bachelor's degree in engineering and a master's in computer science.
ADHD medication had been helpful for his schooling, but it had not
been effective in helping him change the behaviors that had caused his
wife to divorce him and his boss to fire him from his job.

o impact of ADHD impairments on employment

Many recognize that ADHD often causes difficulties in academic
achievement and in parent-child relationships, but there has been

little research and not much discussion about the impact of ADHD on work performance. Findings from the few studies on ADHD and employment indicate that as a group, adults with ADHD are more likely to be unemployed, to have been fired from employment, to have excessive absences from work, to have poor job performance, to have difficulties interacting with co-workers, to have impulsively changed jobs, and to have chronic employment problems.[1] This is not to say that everybody with ADHD suffers from poor work performance; many are quite consistent and productive workers, and some are truly outstanding employees. Available data simply indicate that the executive function impairments of ADHD significantly increase the risk that affected adults will have significant problems with employment.

At the time we initially met, Steve was much more concerned about his having been fired from his job than he was about his wife's divorcing him. He explained that his supervisors had been consistently pleased with the quality of his programming work, often giving him particularly challenging assignments. However, these supervisors had become increasingly frustrated with Steve's chronic failure to meet basic expectations, such as arriving at work on time and turning in expense account reports on a weekly basis.

o difficulties in recognizing others' feelings

Steve had been warned about these chronic problems repeatedly, but had not made the required changes. He and his coworkers were expected to begin work at 9:00 each morning; Steve rarely arrived before 10:30. He explained that often he was out of bed by six, but then got sidetracked listening to the music of a particular CD repeatedly for more than an hour and then taking time to read and respond to multiple emails when he should have been on his way to work. He felt that he had solved that problem by working a couple of extra hours later at the office most days, but this was not the way his supervisor looked at the situation.

Reports for expense accounts were to be submitted weekly so that the company could maintain adequate records and prompt reimbursement of staff members like Steve, whose work frequently involved travels to other cities for assignments that often lasted several weeks. Steve said that he usually submitted his expense reports about one to two months after the deadline had passed and that his supervisor had confronted him on this several times. He seemed not to understand his supervisor's escalating annoyance over these matters. He did, however, recognize that his delays in filing his expense accounts were hurting him. He told me that the company had recently refused to reimburse him for $15,000 of business expenses because his submission was from the previous fiscal year and he had ignored their repeated warnings about the deadline.

In explaining his firing to me, Steve reported his feeling that he had no power to force himself to comply with these directives from his supervisor, even when they cost him a lot of money. Apparently he assumed that his feeling powerless about these problems would constitute an acceptable excuse to others, as it did to him. He did not seem to grasp that to anyone else, such persistent failure to comply with basic rules, especially after being warned repeatedly by his supervisor, would seem clearly to be inexcusably oppositional and defiant. Steve was fired from his job because, despite his technical competence, his recently appointed supervisor, unlike his previous boss, was unwilling to tolerate such chronically insubordinate behavior.

Steve blamed his problems at work on his tendency, as a person with ADHD, to easily become distracted. When I asked about this, he repeatedly spoke of "getting stuck" on particular activities, unable to switch focus when needed. He told me that he understood that he needed to get out the door of his apartment by eight in order to arrive on time at work, yet he was unable to stop himself from becoming involved in these various activities that prevented him from getting to work at time.

My initial evaluation of Steve indicated that he clearly was suffering from ADHD and was gaining some significant benefits from taking the stimulant medication that his previous doctor had prescribed. He said it helped him maintain his focus and improved his working memory when he was at work, but he also told me that it did nothing to help him to get started in the morning when he was trying to get off to his job. When I asked him what time he was taking the prescribed medication, he explained that he usually did not take it until he was walking out the door to go to work. I suggested to him and to his physician that Steve might benefit from taking his ADHD medication immediately upon awakening to see if that might help him avoid the excessive distractibility as he was getting himself up and ready to leave for work each morning. Steve saw his prescribing physician the next day and began this change in routine three days later.

○ complications from compulsivity

Steve's serious difficulty in "switching gears" to make transitions from one activity to another, almost regardless of what it cost him in his dealings with his employer, appeared on the surface to be a stubborn resistance to meeting basic requirements of work. It soon became clear, however, that as I had suspected, Steve was dealing with more than an issue of excessive distractibility or a chronic difficulty in planning his time. He was also caught up in a powerful compulsion to continue with activities in which he was engaged—a significantly impairing Obsessive-Compulsive Disorder (OCD), an exaggerated version of the "hyperfocus" ability reported by some with ADHD.

One of the problematic characteristics of OCD is cognitive inflexibility—that is, difficulty in being able to change the set of one's mind when circumstances require. This is somewhat like having a television whose channel selector often sticks and will not allow you to switch to another channel, even though you want to. In imaging studies, children with OCD have demonstrated this problem when they

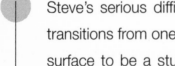

Steve's serious difficulty in "switching gears" to make transitions from one activity to another appeared on the surface to be a stubborn resistance to meeting basic requirements of work. But Steve was also caught up in a powerful compulsion to continue with activities in which he was engaged—a significantly impairing Obsessive-Compulsive Disorder.

are given tasks that require switching from one mental set to another; these studies have shown that this impairment is related to insufficient activation in the frontal regions of brain.[2]

Steve's problem of getting stuck was complicated further by a severe impairment in his ability to accurately size up the emotions of other people — in this instance, the frustration and anger building up in his supervisor. Underlying both of these issues seemed to be a quiet but powerful resistance to being pressured to meet others' expectations. When I mentioned these observations to Steve, he recalled that his father had a similar pattern of often not doing what he was supposed to do, at home or at work, even though he had been employed all his life as a police officer whose work involved enforcing rules on other people.

o   o   o

When I asked Steve why his wife had initiated their divorce, he told me that she had lost interest in him and found another partner.

> She always said that I'm super smart and hard-working, but that I didn't ever pay enough attention to her and that I was always getting too caught up in other things. After a while I just got sick of listening to her complaints, so I wasn't that unhappy when she found herself someone else who apparently could give her what she wants.

Initially it was difficult for me to determine whether Steve was feeling more sadness over the loss of his wife than he was showing, or whether he himself was so unhappy in the marriage that he was relieved to have her bring it to an end. I asked him about this, and he told me that his wife had been "constantly" complaining about his ignoring bills that needed to be paid, until she gave up and began taking care of all their bills herself from their joint earnings while continuing to complain about his not doing it.

Steve acknowledged that he had often procrastinated excessively in paying bills and taking care of other practical tasks. One year ago, he had been assessed heavy penalties by the IRS for his failure to file their joint income tax for three successive years, and he had recently been stopped by the police while driving because his car registration was more than a year out-of-date. He also noted that he frequently went without his ADHD medication for weeks at a time because he had not gotten around to arranging with his physician to obtain another prescription. In mentioning these examples, Steve clearly recognized that these behaviors were unreasonable and hurtful to him, but he said he felt helpless to change his ways, despite his repeated vows to himself to stay on top of such obligations.

After hearing about the severity of Steve's chronically excessive procrastination and his seeming inability to force himself to shift from one activity to another, I recommended that Steve begin medication treatment for his OCD problems in addition to his ongoing medication for ADHD. With his agreement, I suggested to his physician that Steve be given a trial of fluvoxamine, a selective serotonin reuptake inhibitor (SSRI) that had been approved for treatment of OCD.

Although, as we had expected, there was no immediate relief of his OCD impairments, after a couple of months and elevated dosing, Steve reported that he was gradually becoming better able to stop activities that were keeping him from getting to other tasks or activities that were more important. He also reported with some pride that he was now making daily to-do lists and actually completing most of the listed tasks.

o   loss of medication effectiveness

Unfortunately, these benefits from the SSRI did not persist very long for Steve. About six months after starting the fluvoxamine, Steve reported that the medication seemed to be losing effectiveness and was, in fact, causing him to feel rather lethargic and less motivated to do his work. Moreover, he was experiencing a resurgence of his OCD symptoms, getting stuck on repetitive activities that kept him from accomplishing what he needed to do. His physician agreed with my recommendation to taper down the SSRI gradually over a few weeks and then to start a trial of clomipramine, a different type of medication that is sometimes effective in treating OCD when SSRIs are ineffective. After he was on that medication for about a month, Steve reported that he was feeling less lethargic and sleeping better at night, and was significantly better at controlling his compulsions to repeat again and again activities that diverted him from what he needed to do. Meanwhile, Steve continued to respond well to the stimulant medication he was taking concurrently for his ADHD.

○ lack of empathy in a marriage

When he spoke further about the problems in his marriage, Steve reported that his wife frequently objected not only to his failure to take care of practical matters but also to his not spending enough time with her because he often went out to go rollerblading or to play volleyball with friends, activities in which she had no interest. He also recalled that his wife had often been frustrated by his spending too much time on his computer, often until the middle of the night. He mentioned that he often "got stuck" when using his computer, whether to surf the Web, view pornography, or play computer games.

As he spoke about these various complaints his wife had made about him, there was considerable irritation and resentment in Steve's manner, with little evidence of his feeling any empathy for her frustrations with him. He was focused almost exclusively on his trouble in dealing with his wife's frustration: "When somebody's criticizing you every time they say something to you, eventually you reach a point where you just want it to get stopped." He seemed glad to have the unhappiness of his marriage ended, though he did also express some sense of loss as he mentioned that he felt lonely in his apartment since she had left, and somewhat wistfully commented, "I guess it's too bad that we never figured out how we could communicate better with one another."

I asked if there had ever been a time when he and his wife had been able to communicate more effectively than they had over the past year. Steve told me that they had never had very good communication, even from the beginning of their relationship. He said that they had known each other since early childhood because their parents were friends with one another. When they finished their schooling, they both felt that it was time for them to marry, and both sets of parents had strongly encouraged them to go forward with marriage rather than to delay. As he told the story, it sounded as though he had never had strong interest in getting married at all, other than to avoid disappointing his parents. He thought that his wife may have had a similar lack of enthusiasm for the marriage, but had been hoping, for a while, that the relationship would eventually improve.

o   frustrations of ADHD impairments in marriage

There has been little research on the impact of ADHD on dating and marital relationships of adults with ADHD, except for some studies on the parenting skills of those who have children with ADHD.

One study that compared adults with and without ADHD found that those with ADHD were significantly less likely to report stability in love relationships and had higher rates of divorce.[3] Another study of adults in their thirties with ADHD found that less than 40 percent of them lived or had lived with a partner, considerably less than the 75 percent that was normative in that community at that time.[4]

Authors of that study had conducted clinical interviews with each participant. They suggested that many of those adults with ADHD appeared to be somewhat delayed in their emotional and social maturity, and many of the single participants reported that in their early to mid-thirties they were just getting ready to have a serious boyfriend or girlfriend. These researchers seem to have assumed that developing a sustained, intimate relationship with a partner is the normative pattern for all people. That assumption seems questionable in that many individuals with or without ADHD seem to lead adequate and satisfying lives without any ongoing intimate partnership.

One study that compared adults with and without ADHD found that those with ADHD were significantly less likely to report stability in love relationships and had higher rates of divorce.

In one of the few research studies published on the marital problems of adults with ADHD, spouses most often complained that the partner with ADHD[5]

- Had trouble organizing and maintaining the home, procrastinated, did not initiate or complete chores, was forgetful of tasks that must be done
- Got into frequent arguments, disagreements, and misunderstandings; was not available or supportive as a partner
- Was disorganized, seemingly lazy, incompetent, inflexible
- Didn't contribute enough financially and had poor financial management
- Was quick-tempered, unpredictable, moody, impatient, easily frustrated

These problems are certainly not unique to relationships involving a person with ADHD, but they were all present and problematic in Steve's relationship with his wife. For this particular couple, however, there seemed also to be two more fundamental problems. First, at the point in his life when he and I were meeting, Steve did not seem to be very interested in developing an intimate relationship with another person, particularly not with the woman who became his wife. Moreover, at that point in his life, he seemed to lack some of the basic building blocks of personality that are necessary to developing a mutually satisfying close relationship with a partner. Steve explained that his sexual orientation was clearly heterosexual and that he was fully aroused in watching heterosexual pornography, but he did not feel much interest in his wife, sexually or in any other way. He also felt that she did not have much interest in him. He reported that during his adolescence and college years, he had been involved in some short-term relationships with various women, but did not feel much interest in developing any longer-term dating relationships with any of them.

Second, in his relationships with both his boss and his wife, Steve seemed seriously impaired by a fundamental lack of empathy, a persistent inability to recognize how other people were likely to be feeling and why they acted as they did. He also consistently failed to show adequate willingness or ability to take into account the feelings and needs of the other person as he was dealing with him or her.

○ overlap of ADHD and autism spectrum impairments

Recent research has demonstrated that a sizeable percentage of people with ADHD also suffer from significant chronic problems in inter-personal relationships that are quite similar to those associated with Asperger's syndrome and other autism spectrum disorders. They tend to lack age-appropriate empathy and show persistent difficulties in social communication and social interaction. One recent review article asks whether autism spectrum disorder and ADHD are "different manifestations of one overarching disorder."[6] There are also genetic studies that demonstrate a significant relationship between autistic traits and ADHD, which seems to be accounted for largely by genetic factors.[7]

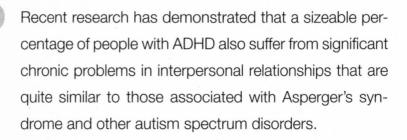

Recent research has demonstrated that a sizeable percentage of people with ADHD also suffer from significant chronic problems in interpersonal relationships that are quite similar to those associated with Asperger's syndrome and other autism spectrum disorders.

In talking with Steve, I did not feel that he was detached or disinterested in interacting with me. He had sought out the consultation for himself, and he sustained good eye contact and some warmth throughout our conversations. However, I was struck by his apparent inability to understand why his wife and his supervisors had been repeatedly annoyed and frustrated with him. I also noticed Steve's seeming lack of connection in his relationships with his wife and with his boss. His social impairments seemed most severe and most noticeable in those longer-term relationships where sustained and reciprocal interaction would be expected.

Steve reported that he enjoyed going out with a group of friends to participate together in activities. He showed some enthusiasm when he spoke about rollerblading with several of his friends and playing on a competitive volleyball team. He did not say much, however, about any personal conversations with friends. His interactions with them seemed limited to sharing participation in group activities, but not much in the way of moving past that into closer friendships. Steve seemed to be a very solitary person in his marriage, at his work, and when engaged in activities with friends. His activities with them seemed more like the parallel play of very young children who play beside each other but not interactively, until they learn the skills and pleasures of mutual play in games with shared activities and interactive imagining.

○ limited capacity for sustained intimacy

Tim Page, a very successful journalist and music critic, wrote a remarkable book called *Parallel Play*, in which he described his experiences growing up with undiagnosed Asperger's syndrome. His recollections of his difficulties with marriage seem similar in some respects to those experienced by Steve:

> When I was twenty-nine years old, I realized it was probably time to get married; the decision, I'm sorry to say, was just as cold-blooded and pragmatic as that. I married my best friend, a brilliant and intuitive woman . . . but my capacity for intimacy was then very limited and the marriage lingered but couldn't last . . . She wanted a life commitment and was determined to win me over . . . And then, suddenly and without warning, she had to leave and she was too regretful or too solitary or maybe too compassionate to tell me why.[8]

From his account, Page seems to have been taken by surprise when his wife left him; he was totally unprepared and bewildered by her sudden departure. It was not until later, in middle age, that Page found that his particular combination of strengths and limitations were aspects of Asperger's syndrome. One day, while reading a book about this syndrome written by medical specialists, he felt

> as though I had stumbled upon my secret biography. Here it all was—the computer-like retention, the physical awkwardness, the difficulties with peers and lovers, the need for routine and repetition, the narrow, specialized interests . . . I was forty-five years old when I learned that I wasn't alone.[9]

Page describes Asperger's as including

> early precocity, a great ability to maintain masses of information, a lack of ability to mix with groups in age-appropriate ways, ignorance or indifference to social norms, high intelligence, and difficulty with transitions, married to . . . ability to concentrate on the minutia of the task at hand.[10]

Note that lack of empathy does not appear on this list.

Steve had many of these characteristics of Asperger's in addition to his ADHD and OCD, but he was not severely autistic; in most social interactions, he probably appeared just somewhat shy or reserved. However, the interaction of the problematic effects of Steve's ADHD, the additional impairments of his OCD-related inability to shift focus, and his Asperger's-related difficulties in recognizing the emotions and perspectives of others led to Steve's sudden loss of his job and his marriage.

o carrying on despite losses

About six months after losing his job and separating from his wife, Steve was successful in locating a new job doing computer programming work similar to what he had been doing before. However, taking this job required that he relocate to live in a distant state, too far from my office to continue treatment with me. Over the next six months, he returned for a few follow-up sessions, during which he reported that he was continuing to take the stimulant medication to alleviate his ADHD symptoms and the clomipramine to help him avoid getting too caught up in his obsessive-compulsive behaviors. In his last follow-up visit with me, six months after he had moved away, Steve reported that he was working more efficiently in his new job, trying to pay more attention to what his supervisors wanted, and getting his expense reports in on time. He also mentioned that he had decided that another marriage was not something he wanted. He told me that getting together with a few friends to play volleyball was about all the socializing that he felt he needed, at least for the present. My response was to acknowledge that there are many different ways to live a life and that I did not see it as my responsibility to try to push him into any intimate relationships, unless he himself had that as his goal.

What Helped Steve?

- Talk therapy to confront defensive anger and excuse-making while identifying strengths for building more adaptive attitudes and behaviors in work and social relationships
- Modifying the timing of ADHD medications for improved coverage early in the day
- Identifying OCD problems of compulsive behaviors, cognitive inflexibility, and difficulties in switching from one activity to another that were present along with ADHD impairments
- Adding SSRI medication for OCD concurrent with ADHD medication, and switching to an alternative medication after SSRI lost effectiveness
- Education about the impact of autism spectrum impairments in empathy on problems that disrupted employment and marriage
- Support of efforts to get a new job and keep it while also supporting patient's decision to avoid seeking another marriage, recognizing his limited ability and lack of interest in such intimacy

9

sue

Until I got into middle school, I always got really good grades and never got into trouble. Now everybody thinks I'm hopeless just because I dress Goth and don't do much homework. My parents and teachers all look down on me just because of the friends I hang out with. They don't really know me or my friends!

—14-YEAR-OLD HIGH SCHOOL STUDENT

Sue was wearing black lipstick and was dressed in black jeans, a black shirt, and a black leather jacket when she and her mother came for her first consultation with me. Her appearance announced that she wanted to be seen as a "Goth." When I asked her why they had come, she quickly responded, "Even when I want to focus, I can't. My mind just wanders. And I'm pretty disorganized and always late. And I've always had a bad memory."

Sue wasn't wasting any time in setting our agenda. She seemed clearly to be seeking help for problems that sounded like ADHD.

Sue explained that she was currently in the middle of her ninth-grade year and that her grades had been declining since the start of seventh grade.

All the way through elementary school I was an honor student. Always got A's and good comments from my teachers on report cards. Back then I was sort of a teacher's pet. But when I

169

got into middle school, that all changed. I wasn't sucking up to the teachers anymore, and school got a lot harder, and I just didn't care about my work as much. I met some new friends who were more interesting, more real, than any I'd had before.

It is not unusual for children with ADHD, especially those who are not hyperactive and are very bright, to do quite well in elementary school, where they spend a significant portion of each school day in one classroom with a single teacher who can provide considerable structure and stability for each student in that stable group. The teacher gets to know each student and can support her in her academic work and in resolving difficulties in social relationships.

o problems emerging in middle school

In the transition into middle school or junior high school, most early adolescents are confronted not only with escalating academic demands in class and in homework requirements but also with a much more complex daily environment, with multiple teachers, increased need to organize materials and keep track of multiple assignments, hourly changes from one group and classroom to another, and expectations of more independent functioning with less intensive supervision from teachers and parents.

 Research has shown that the transition into middle school tends to be especially disruptive for children with ADHD.

Research has shown that the transition into middle school tends to be especially disruptive for children with ADHD. Although many show some gradual decline in their ADHD symptoms during middle to later childhood, the transition to middle school tends to disrupt that decline significantly and to cause increased impairment of functioning.[1]

While the transition into middle school is progressing, most children are either undergoing dramatic physical changes due to pubescent development or fretting about why they have not yet acquired the bodily signs of physical and sexual maturity. Concurrent with those changes of puberty, middle school students tend to seek increased autonomy from their parents while struggling to cope with the rapidly changing social dynamics of their peer group. For many, early adolescence is also a time of experimenting with new ways of thinking, talking, and acting both within their family and in the wider community. Highlighting this variability, the authors of an intensive study of teenagers that used an experience-sampling method to monitor subjective changes at different times of day during various activities noted,

> Teenagers are maddeningly self-centered, yet capable of impressive feats of altruism. Their attention wanders like a butterfly, yet they can spend hours concentrating on seemingly pointless involvements. They are often lazy and rude, yet, when you least expect it, they can be loving and helpful. This unpredictability . . . is what adolescence is all about. The years from twelve to nineteen are special because they offer a developing person the opportunity to experiment with . . . different selves.[2]

o parental worry and frustration

In our initial meeting, Sue's mother emphasized how different her daughter had become over the past couple of years. She didn't like the new friends Sue had been hanging out with, and she was frustrated and worried about Sue's increased irritability and secretiveness about her friends and about her own comings and goings. Recently her mother had found some marijuana in Sue's purse. When her mother mentioned this during our first session, Sue interrupted emphatically:

> I told you it wasn't mine. I was just holding it for somebody else so they wouldn't get in trouble. I've told you I'll take a urine test to

prove that I haven't been smoking that stuff! It's true that a couple
of my friends smoke weed, but I don't. I just smoke cigarettes and I
don't even do that very often. What's wrong with that? Dad smokes
cigarettes and you used to! You always assume the worst about me
and everybody else!

Her mother turned to me at that point, shrugged, and shook her
head. She said,

You can see the kind of arguments we get stuck in. I just don't
know what to do with her. What I worry most about is that she
seems to be losing interest in her schoolwork, just not caring. She
used to care a lot, and over the past year, her grades have really
been declining a lot!

To emphasize her worry about Sue's declining performance in school,
her mother handed me a copy of Sue's most recent ninth-grade report
card along with copies of her report cards for the sixth, seventh, and eighth
grades. Before looking at these, I asked Sue, "What am I going to see when
I look at these report cards? What should I notice?" Sue responded,

You're going to see that I got almost all A's and just a few B's in
sixth, seventh, and eighth, but this high school report card shows
one B, one C, one C–, and three D's. I got the D's because I failed
my final exams for English, history, and science and then I barely
passed the finals for geometry and French. My parents think I'm so
smart just because I used to suck up to the teachers and they gave
me high grades. Now they can all see the truth—I'm failing all my
major subjects. I'm just not as smart as they think!

○ distinguishing between person and behavior

Her mother then handed me several more papers, disciplinary reports
from the high school, saying,

And it's not just her grades—it's her attitude and her behavior too.
They say she's often late to her classes and sometimes cuts class; she

talks out and sometimes swears out loud in class and often is really disrespectful to the teachers. It's bad enough when she's rude to us at home, but she never did it before in school.

I asked Sue what kind of things she was saying to the teachers or her parents that was getting her in trouble. She said, "I just tell them when they're being stupid—sometimes I get a little carried away with that, and all the kids laugh." With a gloating smile she announced, "They think I'm a real bad-ass." I asked, "And what do you think?" Quietly Sue responded, "Sometimes the teachers really are stupid, but sometimes I'm being pretty stupid myself."

I was again impressed by Sue's ability to recognize and acknowledge her own difficulties, just as I had been impressed by her agenda when we started that conversation, so I spoke up and commented,

> Sounds to me as though you do act pretty stupidly sometimes in school, and maybe at home, but you don't seem to me to be a stupid person. Sounds to me like you're a pretty smart person who's been messing up in school and sometimes in behavior over the past year or so, but I don't think that's because you're stupid. You've been pretty sensible and straightforward here in saying what your problems are; it's just not clear to me why you've been having so much trouble over the past year or so. What else has been happening over the past couple of years?

o undiscussed family stressors

For about a minute, Sue said nothing in response. She mumbled something about high school being harder than middle school. I agreed, but suggested that this wasn't likely to be the primary factor in her difficulties. Then she told me that she and her friends felt that she probably had ADHD. Again, I agreed that she might indeed have ADHD, but asked if there might be something else as well. At that point Sue's eyes filled up, but she didn't speak. I asked if she could tell me what she was thinking about as she looked so sad. She responded simply, "My dad used to be nice to me, but now he's almost always pissed off at me and everybody else." I asked why she thought her dad had changed that way. She said, "He's been getting worse; he can't walk like he used to; his Parkinson's has been getting worse." She wiped some tears from her eyes.

> Clearly Sue was very worried about her dad, but had apparently shown little of this worry to her mother, father, or anyone else except her small group of new friends. Her black attire apparently had more than one meaning.

I had asked Sue and her mother several questions about their family and living situation, but this was the first time I had heard about Sue's father having a diagnosis of Parkinson's disease. As we talked further in that conversation, Sue and her mother explained that her father had been diagnosed seven years earlier with Parkinson's, but had been able to work full-time and move around fairly well until recently, though he got very tired easily. Over the past couple of years, his movements, especially walking, had become stiff and much slower, with a noticeably unsteady shuffle. And his mood had become more irritable. Sue commented that she didn't know how much worse he would be getting. She mentioned that she had read online that there is no real cure for Parkinson's and that people often die from it. Clearly Sue was very worried about her dad, but had apparently shown little of this worry to her mother, father, or anyone else except her small group of new friends. Her black attire apparently had more than one meaning.

After our clinical interview, collecting ADHD rating scale data from Sue and her mother, reviewing school reports, testing Sue's working memory and screening for possible co-occurring disorders, I told Sue and her mother that Sue clearly had been suffering from a rather severe case of ADHD that was complicated by her very understandable anxiety about her father's illness and perhaps some underlying mood problems. I suggested that we ask her physician to prescribe a trial of stimulant medication to see if that might help to alleviate her ADHD symptoms. I also explained that medication alone would not be sufficient to resolve all the difficulties that Sue and her parents were struggling with. I recommended that we continue with additional sessions of individual psychotherapy for Sue, interspersed with some conjoint meetings with both her parents. I asked Sue to invite her father to come with her and her mother for our next meeting. Reluctantly, Sue agreed.

o disappointing response to medication

Two weeks later, we had our first follow-up and conjoint family meeting. Sue reported that she had begun the trial of stimulant medication I had suggested but that it not only did not help but actually made her feel worse. It had produced no improvement in her ability to focus for completing her schoolwork. The physician had started her on a very low dose, as I had suggested; even at that minimal dose, Sue felt very slowed down, but was also very irritable and had more trouble getting to sleep and staying asleep. Her parents agreed and added that even on the starter dose, she "seemed like a zombie." Given this very poor response, I immediately contacted her physician and asked that she discontinue the stimulant and prescribe instead a different, nonstimulant medication that was less likely to produce those adverse effects. The pediatrician quickly agreed, and Sue stopped the stimulant to start the new medication the next day.

o reassurance of love despite frustrations

After sorting out the medication problem, we used the family meeting to discuss openly with Sue's father his impairments from Parkinson's and how he had been having more difficulty over recent months both with his mobility and his moods. He acknowledged that he had been more short-tempered and impatient with Sue and everyone else in the family during this period. He apologized for his moodiness, yet he also told Sue that he had been quite frustrated and annoyed about her persisting rude behavior toward her mother and teachers. He added that he had been worried about Sue's diminished interest in her schoolwork and her declining grades.

In response to her father's comments, Sue cried a bit and mumbled that she felt sorry for adding to his worries when he already had so much to cope with from his Parkinson's. Her dad put his arm around her and said, "I want to see you do better, but you know I still love you."

Three days later, I got a message from Sue's mother reporting that while Sue's father had been helping her with her homework that evening, Sue had set aside her usual guardedness about her feelings and told him, "I feel like a complete failure. I don't do anything right, and I'm not really good at anything anymore." Her father had reassured Sue that he still felt confident that she would be getting her act together and start doing much better, but Sue told him that she really had a lot of doubts about whether she was very smart at all.

o gathering evidence of strengths and difficulties

My response to this report from her mother was to ask her to schedule Sue to come take an IQ test with me the following week. It seemed an opportune time to get some objective data to help Sue and her parents assess how Sue's cognitive abilities stacked up in comparison to other teenagers of the same age. Given my impression that Sue was actually quite bright, I felt confident that the results would help strengthen Sue's self-esteem rather than undermine it.

Sue was a bit tense when she arrived to take the IQ test, but she was also excited, saying, "I'm a little scared about this, but I really do want to know how much I can do compared to other kids." As it turned out, her scores were all in the superior range, in the top 9 percent for her age group. Like that of many people with ADHD, her score for cognitive processing speed was lower than her other cognitive abilities, as was her score on a measure of verbal memory that is not part of the usual IQ test protocol. She was delighted and a bit surprised to learn that she scored better than 91 percent of other students her age. This news seemed to give her an infusion of hope for a better future ahead.

Fortunately, the switch to the new nonstimulant medication was also helpful. Within a few weeks, Sue reported that she felt more calm, less irritable, and a bit more focused for her schoolwork without the unpleas-ant side effects caused by the initial stimulant medication. Sue told me, "My friends say that I'm not as loud and jumpy when I'm taking this medication, and I can see that I'm getting my homework done a lot better without so much hassle at home."

○ reducing parental micromanaging of homework

Another factor that seemed to help with the homework problem was her parents' willingness to try my suggestion that they back off from their ongoing efforts to closely monitor and micromanage Sue's homework. Many students with ADHD need quite a lot of help and support from their parents to organize and manage their homework, but for some of these adolescents, the involvement of parents often creates more problems than it solves. For some teenagers, their parent's involvement in prioritizing assignments can lead to chronic battles between the parent and the student, which undermines the student's sense of ownership of the work and externalizes the student's internal struggle between the wish to get the work done and the wish to put it off to some other time (which may or may not come before it is too late). Sue clearly seemed to be at a point where she needed to take full responsibility for getting her homework done adequately and on time (or not). Fortunately for her, Sue's parents were strong enough that they could resist their urge to put themselves in control of their daughter's work. Sue thus had the chance to take on the responsibility for herself, an opportunity that she was ready for at that time.

○ accommodations in school

Sue's grades did not suddenly and completely improve. During the last couple of months of the term, Sue produced a roller-coaster of improvements followed by some decline, but gradually the overall direction became more positive. Support from staff at her school played a significant role. Shortly after Sue's initial consultation with me, her parents gave my report to the school, where the administration agreed to provide her with support under provisions of a 504 plan. Such plans are named for a federal law stating that schools are obligated to provide accommodations for students with special needs to ensure that they have a fair chance to learn in mainstream classes. Typical examples of such accommodations include allowing the student extended time to complete tests and exams, more frequent monitoring and reporting of student progress, and modified requirements for some assignments, depending on the specific documented needs of the particular student.

Upon receipt of my report, the school agreed to provide Sue with extended time (one-and-a-half times the usual allotment) for taking any tests and exams; to not penalize her for poor handwriting on papers; and to give her a supervised study hall one period each day, during which a trained teacher could assist her with problems in organization of her work and study skills. Sue liked the teacher who was helping her with study skills, and made good use of the supervised study hall sessions each day to get a good start on her homework. With these supports, for the final quarter of her freshman year she was successful in completing most of her assignments and did well enough to bring up to D's the F's she had gotten in all her major subjects at the end of the third quarter.

During that summer after Sue's freshman year, I was going to be traveling quite a lot to teach workshops in several other countries. To support Sue and her parents in the progress they had been making, we arranged for them to work with another psychologist much closer to their home. They had a number of sessions with that therapist over the summer and found them helpful; these were interspersed with a family vacation trip and time visiting with various out-of-town relatives.

o   a shift in appearance and attitude

When Sue returned to see me as school was resuming in September, she was no longer dressed in the Goth style she had adopted during her freshman year. She smiled as she walked in and announced, "I haven't gone over completely to that preppy look, but I'm not so much into the Goth stuff anymore." She reported that she had continued the medication throughout the summer and felt that it had continued to help improve her mood, but she was concerned that it didn't seem to be helping her focus as much as she needed for the more difficult courses she was now taking for her sophomore year. Sue's parents reported that her mood and behavior had been quite improved throughout the summer, with only minor hassles — typical parent-teen problems that settled or blew over within hours or, at most, a day or two. However, they shared Sue's concern about her now facing a challenging set of courses at school and agreed that some adjustment of the medication might be worth a try.

o combining medications for ADHD

After speaking with Sue and her parents, I contacted her pediatrician and asked if we could augment the medication she had been taking with a small dose of stimulant medication to try to improve focus for schoolwork, one dose in the morning and another in late afternoon for homework. The physician agreed, and within a couple of weeks, Sue was reporting that this combination of a nonstimulant and a stimulant medication was working quite well to improve her ability to focus in school and to get her homework done. This time there were no adverse effects from the medication. She also reported that the supervised study hall and the extra help from the study skills teacher were continuing and quite helpful with her heavy course load. Because Sue seemed to be doing quite well and was working well with the psychologist she had been seeing for the summer, we agreed that she and her parents would continue in weekly sessions with that therapist and then check in with me only as needed for follow-up consultations.

o progressive improvement

At the conclusion of the first marking period, Sue came with her parents for a follow-up session. She was beaming as she wordlessly handed me her first-quarter report card. Her grades were all B's with just one C. Teacher comments included, "Has positive attitude toward subject, excellent effort," "Highly motivated and enthusiastic," "Good effort, homework contributes to success," and "Regularly participates in class. Has shown growth in study skills." Her parents were generous in their praise of Sue's efforts, emphasizing that she had made all these improvements with very little input from them. They now helped her with homework only when she asked for help, and those occasions were infrequent.

Sue's next follow-up session was at the end of the second marking period. She came in looking sad as she handed me her report card and then laughed loudly at my surprise when I exclaimed over reading that she had made the honor roll; all of her grades were A's or B's. She then handed me another certificate indicating that she had been selected "Student of the Month." An accompanying letter from her principal said, "Your achievements and contributions are not only personal successes but serve as exemplary standards toward which all students of our school can aspire." This was truly impressive progress over just one year!

"Before you identified the disorder, it was academically and socially debilitating. Since that diagnosis, the medication and therapy have completely changed my life. I do not think I can fully articulate how much this has impacted my life."

The next time I heard from Sue was almost seven years later. Her mother called me first, wanting to let me know that Sue had not only graduated from a competitive college but also applied to graduate school, where she wanted to prepare herself to become a psychologist. Shortly after, I received a letter from Sue telling me that she had been accepted into the psychology program at a very good university. She wrote,

I was a patient of yours almost seven years ago. At that time you diagnosed me with ADHD. Before you identified the disorder, it was academically and socially debilitating. Since that diagnosis, the medication and therapy have completely changed my life. I do not think I can fully articulate how much this has impacted my life and my family's, but I am incredibly thankful for all that you have done. I am now studying to become a psychologist so I can offer that same care and support to others who desperately need it like I did.

○ benefits of identifying strengths and interacting
   problems

In reflecting on this message from Sue, I was struck by the importance
she attached to her receiving the diagnosis of ADHD. It seems that it was
quite helpful for Sue and her parents to learn from our clinical evaluation
that Sue's problematic decline in academic success and her escalating
oppositional behavior at home and school were related to an identifiable
problem that could be treated.

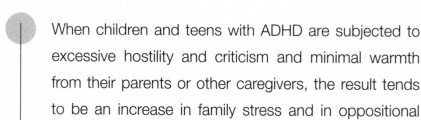

When children and teens with ADHD are subjected to
excessive hostility and criticism and minimal warmth
from their parents or other caregivers, the result tends
to be an increase in family stress and in oppositional
attitudes and defiant behavior in the child.

When we first met, Sue's mother was extremely frustrated, angry,
and worried about her daughter's escalating difficulties; she was bewildered and felt unable to help Sue get her problematic behavior under
better control. She feared that Sue was rapidly heading toward a continuing career of oppositional and defiant behavior that would eventually
lead her to academic and social failure. Much of her interaction with
Sue at that time was confrontational and laden with multiple criticisms,
complaints, and warnings nearly every day. This was all complicated further by the stress the entire family was struggling with in relation to the
father's Parkinson's and his recent decline in functioning that coincided
with Sue's entry into high school.

○ benefits of providing support without excessive
   confrontation

A substantial body of research has demonstrated that when children
and teens with ADHD are subjected to excessive hostility and criticism

and minimal warmth from their parents or other caregivers, the result tends to be an increase in family stress and in oppositional attitudes and defiant behavior in the child. This research has also demonstrated that, completing the vicious circle, parents often react with further expression of negative emotions to the chronic oppositional attitudes and behavior on the part of the child. In contrast, parental warmth and support have been shown to reduce oppositional attitudes and behavior from affected children.[3]

Once they had developed a clear understanding of the nature of ADHD and its impact on Sue, both parents began to back off from their excessively confrontational approach to her and began to provide more support and reassurance; this, in turn, elicited a reduction in Sue's oppositional attitude and behavior. This was vividly illustrated in the father's response to Sue's complaining about his recently increased irritability. He apologized for the irritability, but he also clearly stated to Sue that some of his irritability was the result of her provocative and hostile behavior toward her mother and teachers. He then reassured Sue with his words and with his arm around her, reminding her that he still loved her despite all the difficulties, and that he expected she would be gradually doing better. In the course of our meetings, both of Sue's parents often provided such support to their daughter.

o nurturing hope

Another important way in which Sue's parents helped her treatment was in their offering her realistic hope for her future. As they began more fully to understand Sue's ADHD and its implications, they reduced their repeated warnings to her that she was headed for major failure. Increasingly they spoke of their confidence that eventually she would be able to do better. They did not offer unrealistic "You can do anything you really want to" platitudes. They knew, as Sue did, that she would need to change her approach to school and other people to become more successful, but they also emphasized their confidence that she would eventually make those important changes.

One factor that Sue's parents used to support their expectations for Sue's eventual success was the high ability level she demonstrated on the IQ test. Often, though not constantly, they reminded her that her cognitive abilities were shown on the IQ test to be within the top 9 percent of her age group. They were honest about the fact that a high IQ score does not mean much if the person does not use those abilities to demonstrate serious commitment and effort. Yet they also nurtured her hope for herself—a precious emotion that is essential for sustaining efforts toward achieving success.

What Helped Sue?

- Family therapy including Sue and her parents to recognize her continuing strengths as well as current worrisome difficulties, as well as to acknowledge the impact of parental illness on the whole family
- Tests of IQ and achievement abilities to strengthen the family's awareness of Sue's strong abilities
- Documentation of the need for a 504 plan so that the school would provide accommodations
- Parental reassurance of continuing love and support despite current frustrations
- Adjustments of medication for ADHD to avoid adverse effects and optimize benefits
- Encouraging Sue's parents to avoid micromanaging her homework and to sustain her hope

10

matt

When I was in high school, I had friends. When I got to college, I didn't know anyone and was too shy to make friends. I just kept to myself and almost never left my room except to go to class or get meals. I got pretty depressed, and after a while my sleep got messed up. I've stopped going to some of my classes.

—18-YEAR-OLD COLLEGE STUDENT

As he sat with his mother on the leather couch in my office, Matt described in a very matter-of-fact way his experience of starting college, but it didn't take a lot of imagination to realize that he was telling of a very painful ordeal that had gone on for eight months before he finally gave up on finishing his freshman year at the prestigious college he had looked forward to entering.

○ stresses of transition from high school to college

Contrary to what adolescents usually say to family members and one another, the transition from high school to college is very difficult for many students, especially those with ADHD. For those who move away from home for postsecondary schooling, there is a sudden change not only in where and with whom they live but also in the routine structure of daily life within which they have operated for almost two decades.

185

Many young adults look forward to being liberated from living with parents who are concerned, sometimes excessively and intrusively so, about when they get home, when they go to sleep, when they get up, what they're eating or not eating, whether they're using alcohol or smoking, how they're dressed, whether they're completing their homework, whether they're on time for school and other commitments, friends they're spending time with, what they're viewing on the computer, what grades they're getting, whether they're keeping their room clean and orderly, whether they're sufficiently polite and cooperative with others in the family, and so on.

Upon the freshmen's arrival at the campus, many of the daily burdens of such restrictive expectations and directions are lifted. Students usually welcome this new freedom, and most cope with it quite well. Yet for those who have not yet adequately developed their ability to manage their time, prioritize their tasks, and look after themselves, the sudden, unprecedented absence of familiar family structure may leave a problematic void and multiple problems with managing daily life.

Loss of family structure is not the only challenge these young people face. Often the most painful is the loss of companionship and daily face-to-face interaction with a group of close, familiar friends—those with whom the teen has grown up and with whom countless conversations and adventures, delights and disappointments, hopes and dreams have been shared. During the post–high school diaspora, such relationships may continue via texting, emails, phone calls, Skyping, and holiday visits home, but the closeness is never quite the same as it was when those close friends shared so much of daily life in the same school and community.

This sudden loss of daily direct contact with family and friends leaves some freshmen quite vulnerable to fears and frustrations caused by the many unknowns during first year on campus. For some, that vulnerability can be incapacitating.

This sudden loss of daily direct contact with family and friends leaves some freshmen quite vulnerable to fears and frustrations caused by the many unknowns during their first year on campus. *Will I be able to find new friends I want to hang out with? Will people I meet like me and want to spend time with me? Will I be able to keep up with the work? Will I be better or worse than others in my attractiveness, in my athletic skills, in my academic abilities?* For some, especially those who tend to feel quite uncertain about how they are seen by others, that vulnerability can be incapacitating.

o   o   o

As he spoke about having to withdraw from the college, Matt emphasized his academic problems—difficulties in staying focused during classes, problems in keeping up with the large volume of assigned reading, and struggles in trying to write papers. He said that he had experienced these same difficulties in high school, "but with my mother nagging me, I usually managed to get things done and was able to graduate from high school with honors, just like most of my friends." I commented that when he arrived at college, all that unwanted but needed support was gone, and his good friends were all gone too. He readily agreed.

I asked Matt what he liked to do for fun. He said, "I play piano every day. I've been taking lessons since I was eight. I enjoy it, and it helps me relax. At college, I kept up my playing with private lessons. That's one thing I did keep attending right up until I left the college." He explained that he also enjoyed reading, especially fantasy and science fiction, and that since coming to college he had spent many hours every day playing such video games as World of Warcraft and Call of Duty. On most nights, he stayed up until four or five in the morning playing these games online; his contacts with fellow gamers during those hours on the Internet were almost his only interactions with other people.

o   inadequate sleep

Maintaining healthy sleep patterns is very difficult for many adolescents and adults with ADHD, especially those who do not have a structure of activities requiring them to get up in the morning, to be active during the day, and to rest during the night so they can get up in the morning to continue their daily routine. When Matt began his freshman year, he was initially getting up to attend classes in the morning, but as he became increasingly lonely and depressed, he was unable to keep up with his reading and other assignments. He then began to skip classes so he would not have to take a quiz he wasn't prepared for or to face a professor who might ask him about a paper that was overdue. He then worried excessively about going back to subsequent sessions of those classes because he feared being confronted about his excessive absences. Soon he had given up on attending any of his morning classes and felt no reason to get up before noon. This, in turn, left him with sufficient energy to stay up to play his video games almost until sunrise. With his fellow gamers, he did not feel so alone.

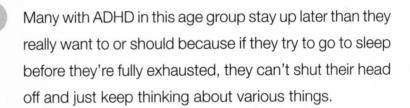

Many with ADHD in this age group stay up later than they really want to or should because if they try to go to sleep before they're fully exhausted, they can't shut their head off and just keep thinking about various things.

Studies of sleep patterns in adolescents and adults have demonstrated that those with ADHD report more than twice the incidence (26 percent versus 12 percent) of difficulty in falling asleep than is reported by a comparison sample of those without ADHD matched for age.[1] Many of those with ADHD in this age group report that they often stay up later than they really want to or should because they've found that if they try to go to sleep before they're fully exhausted, they can't shut their head off and just keep thinking about various things. Once they fall asleep, many of these young people sleep very soundly, often so much so that they are unable to respond to an alarm clock regardless of how many hours of sleep they have had. Often they find themselves late or unable to get up at all for morning commitments. Regulation of sleep and alertness is a significant problem for many adolescents and young adults, but such difficulties are often more troublesome for those with ADHD.

In my initial three-hour consultation with Matt, I took a careful history of his strengths and difficulties, tested his working memory, gathered information from him and his mother using a normed ADHD rating scale, and described our new understanding of ADHD, asking them about how each piece of the new model fit or did not fit him. On the basis of those data, I told him and his mother that he clearly was suffering not just from severe ADHD but also from severe social anxiety and moderately severe depression. They readily agreed with the ADHD and depression diagnoses, but they were puzzled by the social anxiety diagnosis, explaining that Matt had never seen himself as especially anxious. He had, in fact, gotten up in front of large audiences many times to play piano recitals, and he was generally seen as "laid back," rarely feeling or acting nervous. He recognized that he was a bit shy, but didn't see that as an anxiety problem.

○ covert social anxiety

I explained that social anxiety is a type of phobia, a super-intense form of shyness. The person may not feel worried about many other things, but feels intense anxiety about having to interact with unfamiliar people and tries to avoid such interaction as much as possible. Typically those with social anxiety suffer with intense worry that they will appear awkward or foolish or stupid to others. They try to avoid such interactions as much as possible so that they can escape the embarrassment that they assume is inevitable. When they are not forced to enter into the social situations they dread, they show no more anxiety than a person with a phobia of dogs shows when he or she is not anywhere near a dog and does not expect to encounter one.

Hearing this explanation, Matt quickly agreed that he generally felt comfortable when with friends and family, but had lived at college with an intense fear of stepping out of his room; he did so only when necessary to go to classes, use the bathroom, and get meals. He explained that he did not feel comfortable asking to join others in his dorm when they went together to eat lunch or dinner, so he generally went alone to the dining room, ate at a table by himself, and left as quickly as possible to return to his room, where he was alone with his computer and video games. Matt's mother was shocked to hear how isolated he had been for so many months. Until the middle of the second semester, Matt had been telling her in emails and telephone calls that he was doing OK and had made a number of friends.

○ combined medications for ADHD, anxiety, and depression

To address these difficulties, I recommended that Matt begin a course of psychotherapy with me so we could better understand his social anxiety and try to develop better strategies for him to deal with it. I also recommended a trial of stimulant medication to address his ADHD impairments. In addition, I suggested that we start a serotonin reuptake inhibitor (SSRI) after the ADHD medication dosing was adjusted and stabilized; the SSRI was to address his depressive and anxiety symptoms.

I asked Matt what he was planning to do for the coming summer and the next fall. He told me that he planned to take a couple of summer courses at a local university while living at home and hanging out with his friends, and intended to return to his college in September. He said that he was willing to try the medication and also wanted to meet with me to do the psychotherapy work that I was recommending. In my own mind, I wondered whether Matt would really be ready in just a few months to return to his college where he had suffered so much misery, but I chose not to challenge his hopefulness at that time. We agreed to start our work together in the following week.

In our first psychotherapy session, I asked Matt to tell me about what had been happening with his friends and what he had done about the summer courses he was planning to take. He said he had not yet looked at the listing of summer courses and did not know exactly when the courses would begin. During that session, I had him get on the computer and print out the list of courses with details about registration requirements and deadlines. We then talked about his lack of enthusiasm for taking summer courses, even though he knew that doing so would be a good way to challenge his fears of interacting with new people and would also give him a chance to make up some of the credits he had lost when he took his medical withdrawal.

o efforts to hide shame

I also asked Matt about what he had heard from and had said to his friends as they were comparing notes about what they felt about the first year at their various colleges. He said that most of them spoke of liking their school and having a good time, even though the work was tougher than they had expected. When I inquired about what he had told his friends about his first year, he mumbled embarrassedly that he had just said it was tough for him too, but had not told them that he had taken a medical withdrawal and had lost all credits for his second semester. This led us to a discussion about what he thought his friends would be likely to say and what they would be likely to think about him when they found out that he had failed to complete his second semester. Matt was feeling a strong sense of shame over his failure.

After sorting with me through several layers of rationalizations for his keeping his failure a secret, Matt concluded that his friends probably would be surprised that he had to take a medical withdrawal, but would not really be likely to think less of him or be critical of him for it; he said that they would probably be supportive and then just go on with interacting together as they always did. Yet he also said that he still did not want to tell them; he preferred just to say that it was a hard second semester.

I challenged Matt's avoidance by urging him to text one of his friends right then from my office, asking the friend to remind Matt that there is something he wanted to mention to him that he kept forgetting to bring up. Reluctantly Matt agreed, wrote the text, showed it to me, and then sent it. In our next session, he reported that he had in fact told his friends about his problems during the second semester and that, as he had predicted, they expressed some concern, but then went on interacting with him in the same ways they always had.

Matt enrolled in two summer school courses, but reported that it was difficult for him to initiate any conversation with any of the other students in his classes. We role-played possible gambits he might use in chatting with another student before class or during class breaks. He tried these with modest success and learned the names of two other students and a bit about them over several weeks. Initiating even just superficial contact and making brief small talk with unfamiliar people were clearly very hard for him.

o   failure as an unwitting avoidance strategy

Matt's academic work in the two summer courses he was taking was not easy for him either. He reported that he was enjoying one of his courses because the topics were interesting and the professor was an exceptionally good lecturer and discussion leader. However, he had soon fallen behind in completing brief writing assignments due each week in his other course. He had less interest in the topic and found the professor quite boring. He said that the ADHD medication he was taking seemed somewhat helpful, but did not improve his ability to make himself get to work on completing the reading and the brief weekly essays for the class he disliked. In the following week, Matt skipped that class on a day when he was scheduled to give an oral presentation for which he was not adequately prepared. He was then afraid to return.

Matt's parents were quite aware that he was not keeping up with his work for that one course. His mother had been trying to remind and encourage him about it daily, a strategy that had usually worked during high school but was clearly counterproductive at this point in Matt's life. For a time, Matt kept complaining that his mother's nagging was causing him to avoid doing his work for the second course, but he relented when I confronted him with the fact that he was headed toward failing that course in a way that seemed to have a different motivation. I reminded him that his parents had told him that they would not be willing to pay for another semester of tuition if he did not successfully complete both of his summer courses. I suggested that his failing one course might be his way of avoiding returning to college as soon as he had planned, without having to acknowledge that he did not yet feel ready to return.

I asked Matt what percentages would best represent his mixed feelings about returning to college at the start of the fall term as he had planned. He speculated that he felt about 45 percent favorable toward returning in September as planned, and 55 percent toward waiting to return for the spring term instead. Exploring the pros and cons of returning for the coming fall term versus deferring his return for a year led him to describe more fully how profoundly unhappy and ashamed he had felt during his abortive freshman year. This led to his revealing more of the fear and self-loathing he had felt but had not been able fully to share earlier.

Matt and I talked quite a bit about what his options might be if he did not return to his college in the coming fall. He emphasized that he very much liked the school and wanted to go back, but was struggling intensely with fear that the same social anxiety and shame would cause him to fail again, both academically and socially. Yet as he spoke about what it might be like for him to continue to live at home and take more courses at the local university, he emphasized that all his friends would be away at their respective colleges while he would be once again alone without anyone he really knew and felt comfortable hanging out with. Neither option was appealing to him.

After further discussion, Matt decided that he simply did not feel ready to go back as planned and that he still had quite a lot of work to do in his psychotherapy; he suggested that we might increase the frequency of our meetings from two-hour sessions on alternate weeks to one hour every week. We had a meeting with his parents, who readily agreed that Matt should remain at home for the coming academic year and take more courses at the local university, with the aim of returning one year later to the college at which he had started.

Matt did not want to aim for returning at the end of the first semester because he thought it would be more difficult for him to get involved in campus life in midyear when everything was fully under way. Matt's parents accepted this, but told him that they thought he should try to get a job so that he could gain some part-time work experience while continuing to take college courses. They also stated their condition for writing a tuition check for him to return to his original college in the following year: they agreed to pay for another year if, and only if, Matt successfully completed at least four courses at the local university during the coming academic year. Matt agreed that their offer was reasonable.

After the first couple of sessions with his two fall courses at the local university, Matt came in enthusiastic about the interesting professor teaching one course; he complained about the instructor for the other course, saying that he was a boring lecturer whose three-hour weekly class session was a sure cure for insomnia. He also reported that he had met an acquaintance from high school who was enrolled in one of his classes and that, together with that friend, he had begun to attend a campus club for college students interested in history.

o   fragile efforts to overcome social anxiety

A week later, Matt mentioned with a smile that he had noticed an attractive girl named Joanne in one of his classes. He said he was trying to get up his courage to try to talk with her during the fifteen-minute break in the middle of the class session. I asked about his previous experience in getting acquainted with and dating girls. He responded that neither he nor any of his friends were into that when they were in high school. "We were all interested, and none of us is gay, but not one of us is confident enough to try to ask a girl out. We're just a bunch of shy geeks. We never went to parties, and none of us can dance." I asked if he had ever considered taking dance lessons. His response was an emphatic "Never!"

After a couple of weeks, Matt arrived for his session looking dejected. He slumped into the couch and announced that he had finally gotten up the courage to ask Joanne if she'd like to meet for lunch and then study together for an exam that was coming up in their class. She had said she just didn't have time that week. I asked whether he tried to suggest a different time. He was quite certain that she felt no interest in meeting him outside of class at any time, that she could undoubtedly see that he was "pathetic," and that she would never want to go out with him ever, even just for lunch and studying. This led him to say, "I do want eventually to have a relationship with a girl, but that will be a long time from now. I'm too awkward socially." This crushing defeat had exposed another layer of Matt's intensely painful feelings of shame and inadequacy about his body and his personality.

At about the same time, Matt asked his mother if she would try to refrain from nagging him so much about his schoolwork and about getting a job, telling her that her nagging made him feel even less like doing those tasks. She told him that she would try to back off from her daily reminders, but that she found it very difficult to say nothing to him when she saw him wasting a lot of time playing video games while doing very little studying or preparation for his classes and not even trying to get a job, even though she had been presenting him each week with a list of potential openings she thought he might visit.

○ more and less intimidating settings

A day or two later, Matt did make one attempt to find a job. He walked into a local café and asked if they could use any help. They told him that they didn't need anyone now, but invited him to fill out a form so that they could contact him if anything opened up. With a smile, he told me, "So that completes my job search." Despite this, in response to an announcement asking for help in canvassing for a political campaign, he volunteered and began to spend a couple of days each week working in the campaign office and going with another volunteer to canvass potential voters. When I asked Matt why he got so nervous about applying for a job and did not seem nervous about doing volunteer work for the political campaign, he explained that in the campaign there were very specific tasks to do and very specific comments they were told to use in canvassing; it was more structured and felt less awkward.

○ resistance to making changes in behavior

Matt's academic work during the fall semester continued to be just as mixed as in the summer session. He reported that he frequently participated in class discussion during the one class he enjoyed and that he had earned an A– on the midterm. He also told me that he rarely spoke in his other class and had skipped several class meetings. He also reported that he had gotten considerably behind in his reading and in writing several short papers required for that course. Moreover, there was a research paper required for the course. He had selected a topic for his paper, but had done little work to prepare for it, even when he was just a few weeks from the deadline at the end of the term.

I suggested to Matt that if he brought his notes and computer to our next session, I would be willing to try to help him organize his thoughts so he could get a start on the paper. He thanked me politely, but told me that he would prefer to do it completely by himself. In our next meeting, he announced that he had read some of the material assigned for the paper, but still had not managed to write anything. He told me,

> Every day I sit down in front of the computer and say to myself, "OK, I'm going to get started on this now. I really need to get going on it." Then I just open up another Web page and start doing something else until it's too late to do anything. And then I just go to bed and say, maybe tomorrow.

I asked him once again why he felt so opposed to bringing the material into our session so that we could try to get a better idea of what was blocking him from getting started on this paper, which was to be only five pages long. After just a moment's thought he blurted out, "I just don't want you to see how little I know about this stuff I've read and how stupid I am about organizing my ideas." My response: "So you'd rather save yourself being embarrassed in front of me and avoid this task until you end up being embarrassed in front of your parents and others because you couldn't write a five-page paper and failed the course."

My goal at that point was to try to help Matt overcome his fear of the immediate situation — the embarrassment of showing me how little he had thus far mastered the material. To do that, I was confronting him with the idea that the failure likely to come from continuing to refuse help on the paper would probably cause him to fail the course and thus bring an even greater embarrassment upon himself.

My goal at that point was to try to help Matt overcome his fear of the immediate situation — the embarrassment of showing me how little he had thus far mastered the material he was trying to write about. To do that, I was confronting him with the idea that the failure likely to come from continuing to refuse help on the paper would probably cause him to fail the course and thus bring an even greater embarrassment upon himself. I was trying to help him manage his immediate fear by calling attention to his likely fears of the more distant stressor — failure of the course. Matt and others with social phobia repeatedly avoid fearful situations — a strategy that is very difficult to overcome because it is so effective in reducing current anxiety. Sometimes it takes intensification of one fear to overcome another.

change of ineffective medication

At that point, I also mentioned to Matt that I was concerned about how little benefit he seemed to be getting from the SSRI he had been taking to alleviate his anxiety and dysthymic symptoms. He said that although his meds had caused him no adverse effects and helped him feel a bit less depressed, they did not seem to be helping his anxiety at all. We agreed that I would contact Matt's physician and ask for discontinuation of the present medication and a trial of a different one that might be more effective. I reminded Matt that we could not rely on medication to fix his difficulties. He responded that he was not looking for a miracle, but was hoping for the medication to take some of the edge off his tendency to be excessively worried about what others might think of him.

Matt arrived for our next session with his computer and the materials he was planning to use to write his paper. After some fumbling around, he came up with a thesis statement and then showed me five articles he had downloaded to use for development and support of his thesis. Those articles all came from a list the professor had recommended. I asked him to extract from each paper a few direct quotes that he thought might be helpful.

When he had these, I suggested that he add a sentence or two after each one to explain in his own words what he thought that quote added to his argument. I was impressed by how quickly Matt was able to identify important ideas in those sources and then elaborate on each one in his own words. Within two of our one-hour sessions, he had more than enough material to put together the five-page paper he needed to hand in. He estimated, probably correctly, that it would take only about four hours of work to transform the materials he now had prepared into a finished paper.

o   failure repeated

Despite that preparation, Matt made no further progress in pulling the paper together during the next week, and thus missed the deadline for handing it in. He mustered his courage to request an extension; his professor was kind enough to grant him an extra week, but made it clear that failure to submit the completed paper at that time would bring a failing grade for the course. Matt was unable to bring himself to complete the paper by that extended deadline and thus finished the fall semester with an A – in one course and an F in the other.

Matt was clearly disappointed in himself as he reported that he had been unable to complete that paper, despite the extension, but he did not appear demoralized. He reported that he had registered for three courses for the following semester and fully intended to pass all three so that he would be able to meet the condition his parents had set for his return to his college (four courses satisfactorily completed over the academic year). When I asked how he expected to accomplish this goal, he handed me the syllabi for his three new courses and told me that he was now ready to start working more closely with me on getting his work done each week. He said,

> I've decided I need your help not just at the end of the semester for the final paper, but to help me stay on top of my work week by week throughout the semester. I don't like needing so much help, but I think that's the only way I can do what I need to do this semester and also learn how to take care of my own stuff when I go back. I wasn't ready before, but I think I am now.

I responded by telling him,

> Sounds good, but what matters is whether you follow through or not. We have to figure that your balance between wanting to return to the college and wanting not to return may now have shifted a bit more toward wanting to go back, but it will still be a struggle. You aren't likely to forget that you were pretty miserable when you were there; fears like that don't just suddenly disappear. They can be sneaky and get in your way.

o structure and monitoring for behavior change

"I know that all too well," Matt said, "but let's get started." We then put our heads together to develop a plan for Matt to switch from trying to do all of his schoolwork in the evening to doing three hours of work during daylight hours and three hours in the evening on each of the four days he was not scheduled to be attending classes. He suggested that he move his bedtime up from 4 a.m. to 2 a.m. and that he plan to get up at 9 a.m. every day. I proposed that he go to the university on at least three of the days he did not have any classes and work in the university library for his three daylight hours in that environment, where he was less likely to get involved in playing video games. He agreed to this and said that he would hold off from any Web surfing or gaming until he had put in the total six hours of study he had scheduled for those four days without classes.

Matt agreed that he would underline key passages in all assigned readings so that he could show me that he had done the reading and also could more easily review what he had read. He also suggested that he would develop a form on which he would log each day how much time he actually put in on studying and how much time on avoidance; his plan was to bring this weekly sheet to each of his sessions so that we could monitor his progress together. We agreed that we would take some of our time together each week to review his progress and to identify what factors were presenting obstacles to his implementing his plans.

In addition to these plans to strive for academic success, Matt also wanted to improve his ability to interact with people he did not already know. He recognized that improving his social interaction skills would be essential to his making a success of his next year of college. We agreed that he would try to initiate at least brief conversations with at least two other students in each of his three classes. He also agreed to work toward finding a study partner in each of his classes to prepare together for the midterm exams. Matt thought that these social tasks would be far more difficult for him than the academic reforms he had planned.

Matt's implementation of these social and academic plans over the course of that semester was far from perfect. There were some occasions when he worked considerably less than he had scheduled, and there were some times when he fell a bit behind in his reading. There were also a number of times when he totally avoided interacting with other students in his classes. Yet overall, from that point onward, Matt was much more collaborative with me and much more successful in getting his work done and in reaching out for casual interactions with other students in his classes. He completed two of his courses that semester with A's; he earned a B in the other. He returned to his original college the following fall and found that he actually enjoyed it and sustained a solid B+ average.

What Helped Matt?

- Talk therapy to reduce denial and acknowledge the misery of his social as well as academic experience during freshman year of college, encouraging candid sharing with friends
- Education for Matt and his parents about the severity of his social anxiety and depressive symptoms
- Medications to alleviate depressive symptoms and social anxiety concurrent with ADHD medication; switching to alternative medication when one proved ineffective
- Parents' requiring successful completion of courses locally before return to his previous college
- One-on-one coaching to address writer's block and improve paper-writing skills
- Talk therapy to address failure as fear-based avoidance; direct confrontation to increase fear of potential longer-term problems if shorter-term fears were not challenged

11

lois

I teach special education, so I've taught a lot of kids with ADHD, but never realized I have it. I have trouble organizing my stuff and finishing paperwork on time, and sometimes I'm forgetful. I got through college and I've been teaching for ten years, but over the past year I've had a harder time, and those ADHD problems are getting worse—especially since difficulties at home began.

—37-YEAR-OLD SCHOOL TEACHER

Although Lois had been a special education teacher for ten years and had taught many children with ADHD, she had not realized that she suffered from ADHD herself until she heard me describe symptoms of the disorder in a lecture at a professional conference. She said that all through her years of schooling and throughout her years of teaching, she always had experienced difficulty in staying focused on task, in completing paperwork on time, in organizing her stuff, and in remembering what she had read or been told. I asked how recently those problems had been getting worse for her. She responded that they always had been difficult, but had gotten much worse over the past couple of years as she had experienced some troubles at home.

○ persistent grief and continuing disappointment

I asked Lois what sort of troubles she had been having at home, and she
suddenly burst into tears and sobbed as she explained that while she was
with him one day five months ago, her father had suffered a heart attack
and died as she tried frantically to perform CPR. She said,

> I know I should be getting over it by now, but I've kept crying a
> lot every day since it happened, and I can't get that picture of him
> lying there out of my mind. I miss him so much! He was the one
> who had been helping me the most since my husband got hurt a
> year before that.

I asked what kind of injury her husband had suffered. She explained
that he had been in a car crash without a seatbelt, hit his head on the
windshield, and suffered a traumatic brain injury that left him still seriously impaired after more than six months in the hospital. Treatment
had restored his ability to walk and talk, but he was still quite moody, no
longer himself; he was able to work only an unskilled job and was not
expected ever to be the same again. Quietly I commented that she had
suffered two massive losses in a very short time and that nobody would
be able to get over such things quickly or easily.

Although it is true that anyone would suffer immensely from either
of the losses Lois had experienced, especially when the events occurred
so close together, it is also true that many people with ADHD have an
especially hard time coping with loss and stress because they tend to have
greater difficulty in modulating and coping with intense emotions. As a
result, their painful life situations often become more intense and tend to
be more disruptive than for many others in comparable circumstances.

Although most individuals in stressful situations and painful
circumstances are able gradually to "put the lid" on their intense hurt
and worry for much of the time by remembering and focusing on other
aspects of their life, those with ADHD often get stuck in single-minded
preoccupation with experiences of worry and pain. Several studies
have shown that people with ADHD tend to have impairments of
working memory that make it difficult for them to keep multiple facts

or concerns in mind simultaneously.[1] Their more limited working memory capacity may make it more difficult for them to keep in mind more hopeful memories and facts that may help modulate or counter anxious or depressing thoughts.

> Those with ADHD tend to have less capacity to physio-
> logically "gate" intense emotions in synaptic connections
> within the brain

Research has shown that individuals with greater working memory capacity tend to be more effective in dealing with unpleasant emotional situations without getting too caught up in them.[2] Additional research has suggested that those with ADHD tend to have less capacity to physiologically "gate" intense emotions in synaptic connections within the brain.[3] Regardless of the causes, Lois had remained persistently and intensely caught up in her painful emotions about both the death of her father and the ongoing struggles related to her husband's traumatic brain injury.

o depression co-occurring with ADHD

From our initial consultation, it was clear that Lois certainly suffered from ADHD as she had expected, but it was also clear that she was severely depressed and had continued to be flooded daily with intensely painful memories and feelings of hopelessness since the unexpected death of her father. She also had seriously diminished appetite and much difficulty in getting to sleep most nights. To address her severe depressive symptoms, I arranged with her physician for Lois to begin a course of antidepressant medication and agreed with Lois to begin an ongoing course of psychotherapy. I suggested that we could get her started on medication for her ADHD after she had become stabilized for at least six weeks on the antidepressant medication.

Within a couple of months of starting the medication and some psychotherapy focused on her complicated feelings of guilt over not being able to save her father with CPR, her anger with him for abandoning her by his death, and her profound grief over the severe impairments of her husband's brain injury, Lois began to eat and sleep more adequately and experienced fewer days when she was constantly preoccupied with her losses.

In our psychotherapy sessions, Lois explained to me that there were only two activities that provided her any distraction from the misery of her grief: her relationships with the students she was teaching and her shopping for various materials she planned to use in her classroom or for items she could use in her home. Lois had always wanted to become a mother, but her husband's severe brain injury made the couple feel that they could not take on the responsibilities of becoming parents. She suggested that her shopping was a way of giving herself something to make up for the loss of her husband's health and the continuing disappointment of her persistent longing to have a child of her own. Despite these losses in their relationship, Lois had demonstrated intense, persisting commitment to caring for and supporting her husband in the six months of his hospitalization and after.

Lois had always enjoyed her teaching, but after she realized that she would probably never have children of her own, she intensified her already great interest and effort in providing for the needs of her elementary school–age special education students. She learned the names of all their siblings and often held lengthy conversations with their parents after school hours, sometimes involving herself in family matters in ways that seemed a bit excessive.

Lois's enthusiasm for teaching and working with her students was matched only by her great enthusiasm for shopping. She often spoke of how much she enjoyed roaming from one tag sale or flea market to another on weekends, searching for books or toys that might interest her students or wandering in shopping malls to take advantage of any sale that might offer a good price on something that she needed, wanted, or might need or want for them or herself sometime in the future.

o compulsive buying and hoarding

One day Lois came in for her therapy session and lamented that she had been spending too much money shopping. I asked about how severe the problem was. I was surprised to learn that Lois had forty pairs of blue jeans, over a hundred sets of underwear, and twenty-five frying pans in addition to comparable quantities of many other items she had acquired over recent years. She told me that her house was filled with stacks of large boxes and plastic containers that took up so much space that there were only narrow pathways to walk from room to room and just a couple of spaces where she and her husband could sit to watch TV. They had to eat each meal on snack trays because their dining room and kitchen tables were both piled too high with stuff for which they could find no other place. When I asked whether she and her husband were able to move or get rid of any of this stuff, Lois looked panicked at the mere thought. She exclaimed, "I could never do that; it makes me too nervous to get rid of any of these things."

> Those with hoarding problems seem to suffer from exaggerated difficulty with the executive functions that allow most people to organize and prioritize their possessions.

At that point it became clear to me that Lois's great interest in shopping and gathering materials for her students and her home were aspects of a compulsive hoarding disorder. Until recently, hoarding was considered to be an aspect of OCD. However, the most recent version of the psychiatric diagnostic manual has reclassified hoarding as a discrete disorder in itself. Hoarding Disorder, as it is now conceptualized, involves a person's persistently accumulating and saving large quantities of possessions that he does not need or use. Typically these possessions clutter or congest his living space, but he feels much distress if he tries to discard them. Often his collections of these possessions intermingle valuable items with other items that most other people would regard as trash.[4]

Those with such hoarding problems seem to suffer from exaggerated difficulty with the executive functions that allow most people to organize and prioritize their possessions. Studies have demonstrated that more than half of people with Hoarding Disorder also suffer from Major Depressive Disorder, and about 40 percent also have ADHD. Lois reported that her mother tended to buy and hang on to a lot of stuff that she didn't actually use or need, but Lois also noted that her own problems with hoarding had become much more severe than those of her mother over the past two years since her husband's accident and her recognition that she was not likely to be able to become a mother herself. It almost seemed that Lois was behaving as though buying and saving all this stuff would somehow help her feel less emptiness in her grief over the loss of the healthy husband she had started with and the baby she had hoped and expected someday to carry and raise. We touched briefly on these issues in a few therapy sessions, but Lois was not ready to deal with them further at that time.

After two months of treatment with antidepressant medication and psychotherapy, Lois reported that she was feeling considerably less depressed and wanted to address her ADHD impairments, the problem for which she originally sought treatment. She was concerned about her problems with staying focused on tasks, organizing her paperwork, avoiding excessive distractions, and effectively using her working memory to keep track of things she needed to be doing.

o adding ADHD medication to the antidepressant medication

After I reported my diagnosis of ADHD, Lois's physician agreed to start her on a trial of stimulant medication while continuing her antidepressant. Her physician also agreed to collaborate with me in fine-tuning the dosing regimen for the stimulant so that we could determine what dose and timing would work best for Lois. Within a few weeks, Lois was reporting that she felt that the medication was helping her improve most of her ADHD difficulties, at least for that portion of her day during which the medication was active.

At that point, Lois felt that she was functioning much better than when she had begun treatment with me. She proposed to take a break from psychotherapy for a while with the understanding that she would continue her medication regimen. She told me that she was planning to resume psychotherapy eventually, but was not sure when that would be. I agreed, but encouraged her to continue taking the medications, to meet with me at least every six weeks to monitor them, and to get in touch with me promptly if she began to feel very depressed again.

About six months later, Lois called to report that she was, once again, feeling very depressed, and needed to come in soon. When we met, she explained that she had stopped taking her medication, that her husband's father had died suddenly, and that his death had been very upsetting to her and her husband. She had not felt very close to her father-in-law, but attending the wake and funeral had stirred up vivid memories of her own father's funeral a year earlier, bringing back the intensely painful feelings of sadness and hopelessness that she had experienced many months earlier.

○ rekindling grief

Lois's sadness was complicated further by two additional deaths that occurred within the next month. First, she learned from the TV news that one of her former students and a sibling had been burned to death in a tragic fire. Lois wept over this for many hours each day for several weeks. Then she got word that the principal of the school where she had been working had lost his wife to cancer. Lois told me of how this principal had been "like a father to me, helping me when my father died." She felt very upset when she saw his wife in the casket. "When it was time to go, I didn't want to leave him alone in the funeral home." Lois's concern for the principal's feeling lonely probably was intensified by her own loneliness at that time because her mother had recently moved to Florida to spend the winter and would not return until spring. This combination of new losses and their rekindling of her earlier losses was overwhelming to Lois, flooding her thoughts and immobilizing her.

At my urging, Lois agreed to resume taking the medications that had been helpful to her earlier and to resume psychotherapy. One month later, Lois was notified that her school was no longer going to have the self-contained special education class she had been teaching and that she was being transferred to another school where she would not have her own class or classroom. She would be taking small groups of students out of their regular classes for brief periods to provide tutorial-style assistance to improve their reading skills. For Lois, this was equivalent to having her own family of children suddenly snatched away. She would no longer have a group of students for whom she was the primary teacher; she did not even have her own classroom to decorate. She was being forced to leave the familiar building and group of colleagues with whom she had been working for five years.

○   exacerbation of depression by additional life stresses

Lois had suffered egregious multiple losses in just a few months: the death of her father-in-law, the death of her principal's wife, the tragic death of her former student, and the anticipated losses involved in being transferred to a new school where she would no longer have her own class and classroom. None of these adversities were her doing or under her control; yet this cascade of painful losses, direct and indirect, seriously exacerbated Lois's depression and her ADHD. Lois had reported that prior to the death of her father-in-law, the medications she was taking were helpful in improving both her mood and her ability to focus and do her work. She was not experiencing any adverse effects, but she had not refilled the prescriptions when they ran out and had not come back to her physician or to me to monitor and reinstate the medications once she had run out. That very day, we reactivated her prescriptions, and she agreed to take them.

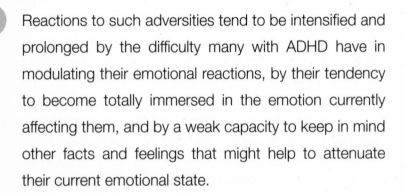

Reactions to such adversities tend to be intensified and prolonged by the difficulty many with ADHD have in modulating their emotional reactions, by their tendency to become totally immersed in the emotion currently affecting them, and by a weak capacity to keep in mind other facts and feelings that might help to attenuate their current emotional state.

There is not much research on the effect of adversity on ADHD. A couple of studies have looked at the impact of stressors such as poverty, mental illness of a parent, severe marital discord, and the like on children with ADHD,[5] but virtually no published research has addressed these issues in adults with ADHD. It is not possible to know how Lois would have fared had she experienced a much longer period of stability in her work and family life before she had to cope with additional deaths or a substantial change in the nature or setting of her job. Yet it seems likely that, as for the children already studied, no particular form of adversity worsens ADHD, but the cumulative subjective weight of multiple stressors is likely to cause significant exacerbation of ADHD impairments in adults.

Reactions to such adversities tend to be intensified and prolonged by the difficulty many with ADHD have in modulating their emotional reactions, by their tendency to become totally immersed in the emotion currently affecting them, and by a weak capacity to keep in mind other facts and feelings that might help to attenuate their current emotional state. Not only do those with ADHD often have difficulty in shifting their attention away from the worry, frustration, sadness, hopelessness, or anger that currently troubles them; many also tend to suffer from "attentional bias," a tendency to recall and tilt their attention toward memories of other examples of times when they have felt similarly worried, frustrated, disappointed, and so on, often neglecting to recall contrasting facts or experiences. Some studies have documented this attentional bias problem in people with chronic anxiety or depression, but clinical work with those who have ADHD indicates that similar attentional bias often occurs not only with anxiety and depression but with a variety of other emotions as well.[6] Lois's tendency to focus on and become immersed in memories of loss and disappointment is an example of this problem common among many with ADHD.

In response to Lois's recurrence of depression, we agreed to talk with her physician to arrange an increase in her antidepressant medication and to resume meeting for psychotherapy. During therapy sessions over the next few months, it became clear that Lois's husband was having great difficulty in coping with the death of his father. He became increasingly depressed and was often extremely hostile and verbally abusive to Lois in ways that were totally uncharacteristic of him before his brain injury.

He attempted a course of psychotherapy and some medication, but this seemed to make little difference in his interactions with her. Lois and her husband attempted some conjoint marital counseling, but this did not work out.

○ shattered dreams and ending a marriage

Six months later, Lois reluctantly decided to see an attorney and told her husband that she was filing for divorce. He reacted with desperate rage and depression, threatening to kill himself or her (or both). He was voluntarily placed in a psychiatric hospital for a few weeks, after which the couple remained separated and subsequently divorced. Because she earned significantly more income than her husband, Lois was required by the court to pay him alimony. Lois continued to be preoccupied with feelings of depression over the shattering of her dreams and hopes for her marriage, guilt over abandoning her husband, and hopelessness about life ever getting any better for her.

○ gradual decline in functioning

Lois had increasing difficulty in her work in the ensuing months. She made the transition to the new school, but, despite her use of ADHD medications and adjustments of dose and timing, she struggled to fulfill her responsibilities, which now included far more paperwork, a task with which she had always had considerable difficulty. She was required to document the specific programs, interventions, and progress of each of the increased number of children she was now tutoring individually or in small group sessions, but often she had not documented her interventions adequately and had great difficulty in sorting her papers and prioritizing her tasks. Her ADHD symptoms increasingly intensified under the impact of her depression and anxiety. The new principal and her departmental supervisor began a series of monitoring meetings with her in an effort to help her get her paperwork up-to-date.

For months in this new setting, Lois was working frantically three or more hours after school most days trying to complete her documentation and sort her records, but she was unable to work efficiently. Despite these extended hours, she often arrived at the supervisory meetings with an armload of papers, and was unable to find the information about specific students that her principal and supervisors were asking her to provide. Each meeting was followed up by a formal written report. This increased supervision and assessment further intensified Lois's already consuming worry about herself and her own adequacy. She assumed (correctly) that they were not only trying to provide her with assistance but also laying a paper trail that could easily lead to termination.

○ intensive day treatment and efforts to rescue someone else

Lois's depressive symptoms and anxiety intensified over the next few months to the point that it was clear that she was no longer able to fulfill her teaching responsibilities. Her employment as a teacher was terminated by the school system. Two weeks later, she had become so depressed and agitated that I had to refer her to an intensive day treatment program for psychiatric patients at a local hospital.

Lois found considerable support in the intensive outpatient treatment program, where she was engaged in group sessions with other patients who were also struggling with difficult life situations. She reported that in those group sessions, she often took on the role of a particularly empathetic and supportive participant. When one patient, a depressed woman about ten years older than Lois, complained that she had been evicted from her rented apartment and had no place to go, Lois impulsively volunteered to have the woman come and live temporarily with her in the home she had once shared with her husband. Staff at the outpatient program recommended against this, but Lois insisted, and the woman moved in.

Soon Lois was complaining that this new housemate was insisting on Lois's cooking dinner for her every night and wanted Lois by her side constantly; one month, she ran up Lois's telephone bill to over $1,000. Moreover, this woman did nothing to help with household chores. After two months of frustration in trying to care for this woman, Lois enlisted the support of her own sister to force her to move out; at about the same time, Lois's participation in the intensive outpatient program was concluded because her insurance would no longer cover it.

o impulsive efforts to find stability

Meanwhile, even before that woman moved out, Lois had found a boyfriend to whom she immediately felt a strong attraction. He had been divorced for seven years, but had a continuing interaction with his wife due to court-mandated visits with their two children. Lois liked the apparent strength she saw in this man and reported that he was very nice to her; Lois also told me, however, that "at times, he says really mean things to me." I cautioned her about the need to take some time to assess this relationship before getting further involved. Lois responded to this by avoiding any further contact with me for the next few months.

Three months later, Lois returned to resume psychotherapy, shortly after she had married this new boyfriend "on relatively short notice." Subsequent to their marriage, Lois had paid off a $1,200 prior debt for her new husband. She reported that he had two motor vehicle accidents while driving her car without any insurance coverage, and, without her knowledge or consent, moved much of the stuff Lois treasured out of what was now their house and into a couple of metal tool sheds he had put up in their yard. After she discovered that her husband had quit his job, was dealing marijuana, and had run up her gas station credit card to over $500, she told him that she needed to get a divorce so that she would not be burdened with any further debts created by him. He balked, but agreed to the divorce when she threatened to go to the police to file a complaint against him.

In reflecting on her decisions to take the woman into her home and to marry this man whom she scarcely knew, Lois soon realized that these impulsive actions were poorly considered attempts on her part to solve a major life problem. She took on the role of caretaker for people who were needy, in the desperate hope that they would return her kindnesses with affection such as she had once gotten from her father until his death, from her husband until his brain injury, and from her students until she lost her job.

After these difficulties, Lois remained unemployed and was not a good prospect for further employment. She filed for disability retirement under the contract of her teachers' union. Initially the union board declined her request, but after recommendations from a doctor they selected and from me, they reconsidered and granted her request. Lois then moved out of state to live with some other relatives whom she liked and who agreed to take her in.

o   o   o

Lois's story illustrates how adult patients with severe ADHD, even very bright ones, may experience a long series of adversities, some of which, like Lois's father's death and her husband's brain injury, are due simply to misfortune or bad breaks. Others may be due to co-occurring disorders such as depression or anxiety; some are primarily due to the ADHD impairments themselves. This was demonstrated in a recent study involving over two hundred men and women with ADHD, which provided clear evidence that severity of ADHD inattention and/or hyperactivity, independent of co-occurring psychiatric disorders, was associated with negative life events, such as being fired from a job, marital separation or divorce, major change or loss of financial status, major change in living conditions, and so on.[7]

o   difficulties in sustaining treatment

Lois had no control over the death of her father or the severe brain injury of her husband, but her inability to keep up with her work, which led eventually to the loss of her job, was clearly related to her inadequately treated ADHD. Her ADHD impairments of inattention to details, disorganization, and poor working memory also contributed to Lois's frequent difficulty in keeping her prescriptions filled and taking her medications regularly. Those ADHD impairments also caused her to miss therapy sessions often, despite reminder calls, and sometimes to avoid treatment, often for many weeks at a time. Unlike some patients, she was unfortunately without someone else involved enough with her to help her do what was needed to sustain the treatment of her ADHD, depression, and anxiety.

If Lois had been able to sustain treatment for her ADHD and depression, it is likely, though not certain, that she would have been able to do her job well enough to remain employed and to derive some satisfaction from her work, as she had for the previous ten years. Unfortunately, the severity of her symptoms, her loss of sufficient social support, and her inability to sustain treatment caused a cascade of adversity that eventually overwhelmed Lois's desire and ability to sustain herself.

o   o   o

Fortunately, Lois's disability pension gave her at least minimal financial stability. Her situation improved substantially more when she received an invitation from a recently widowed maternal aunt in a distant state. This aunt was hoping that Lois might come to live with her and help her provide day care and baby-sitting assistance for two of her young grandchildren, who lived nearby. Lois happily accepted that invitation and subsequently reported that it was working out well. That new setting with an extended family member offered Lois a chance to provide support for her aunt in daily life and in helping care for children, two roles in which she would probably be successful.

What Helped Lois?

- Talk therapy to address grief and guilt over her father's death, her inability to have a child, and her husband's injury with persisting disability
- Medication for disabling major depression
- Assessment, diagnosis, and medication treatment of long-standing ADHD impairments
- Recognition of excessive buying and hoarding problem

- Resumption of talk therapy to deal with divorce, rekindled grief, and added stressors
- Referral for intensive day hospital treatment when she was unable to function
- Therapeutic support for acquiring disability payments and achieving residential stability

12

james

If I don't finish four papers this month, I'm going to be put on probation at school. I just can't get myself to finish. I've had this problem for a long time, but now it's worse than ever before. I've done the research for most of my papers, but I can't get myself past the first paragraph in any one of them. I'm stuck!

—20-YEAR-OLD COLLEGE STUDENT

James's parents stepped up quickly to introduce themselves when I first met them and their son in my waiting room. James stood behind them. He looked several years younger than his age and seemed a bit shy as he stepped forward and introduced himself with a very formal handshake but little eye contact. When the four of us sat down in my office, I asked James directly about his understanding of why we were meeting; his mother immediately began explaining why they had come. I had to interrupt her to redirect my question to James. His response was, "to help me write the four papers I owe so I can go back to college a month from now and do better for my junior year."

I asked James how he thought I would be able to help him finish in the next four weeks these papers that he had not been able to finish during the spring semester or in the almost two months that had passed since he began summer break. "I don't know if you can," he responded.

"I had to drop out of a summer school course I was taking earlier this summer, and I may have to take a semester or two off from college. My situation has been looking a bit hopeless." Quickly his parents jumped in to reassure James with their confident expectation that he would be able to complete the papers before the deadline so that he could get started on his junior year. His father added, "I don't think your problems are that serious." Meanwhile, James reached over and took his mother's hand as a young child might, continuing to hold it during much of our conversation.

In the ensuing three-hour consultation, James spoke of his getting stuck in writing term papers, even though he had done a lot of research to prepare them. His father reported that he had tried to assist with writing some of these papers, but had not been able to help much. James told his parents and me that he had been increasingly worried and unhappy during the spring semester, isolating himself in his room for many hours most days to play video games when he intended to work on his papers. He also reassured us that he had not been drinking alcohol or using marijuana or any other drugs.

His parents recalled a period in fifth grade when James had been bullied a lot by other students who felt he was being a snob because his grades in most subjects were so much higher than those of all the other students in his class. Although that recollection was intended to emphasize James's academic strengths, it also alerted me to his history of social vulnerability and his parents' difficulty in recognizing the seriousness of their son's impairments, which clearly extended far beyond having trouble completing term papers.

At the conclusion of the consultation, I told James and his parents that he seemed to be struggling not only with a problem in writing papers but also with a much broader range of difficulties with executive functions (EFs) that fit the diagnosis of ADHD. His difficulties with prioritizing, organizing, holding focus, sustaining effort, and using working memory were affecting many aspects of his life, most obviously his ability to write papers. I added that what he had told me also suggested that he had been struggling for some time with a lot of anxiety, particularly about social relationships and self-esteem, and that, over recent months, he seemed to be having increasing difficulty with depression.

James and his parents were surprised to hear that someone so bright who had been quite successful in school for many years could have ADHD, but they acknowledged that my description of ADHD and these related impairments certainly fit his experience. They asked for my suggestions about what might be done. Because his parents lived much too far away for James to commute to my office regularly, I proposed, as I sometimes do, that if he wanted to be in treatment with me and to try to get those papers completed within the next month, he could arrange to rent a nearby apartment for the month and plan to meet with me five times each week while also trying some medication to alleviate his symptoms. My suggestion was that this month of intensive treatment could serve as a time not only for him to try to complete those papers but also for both of us to evaluate whether he really was ready to return to college in September as he had planned.

On the next morning, James and his parents returned to make the necessary arrangements for the plan I had proposed. His parents helped him sublet a furnished apartment near my office and then began their trip home, leaving James with encouraging words about their confidence that he would be able to get all this worked out within the month and would be ready to return to college in September. After they left, James told me that he was not as confident about getting everything worked out so quickly as his parents were, that he had not really told them how bad things had been for him throughout his last semester. We agreed that we would divide our time: some blocks would be devoted to therapeutic discussion of a broad range of personal emotional issues, others would focus exclusively on the writing tasks that were his originally stated reason to seek consultation.

○ struggling to translate oral fluency into written text

James arrived on time for our appointment the next morning. As I had requested, he brought with him his computer and the books and note-books needed for the first of the papers he had been trying to write.

He showed me the course syllabus and instructions the professor had given for the paper; he then described in great detail the information he had gathered from doing his readings. I was impressed by how much he had learned about the material and how fluent he was in explaining the information. But I also saw that he had not marked the pertinent sections of books he planned to use, nor had he made any notes from his reading. He had been trying to do the whole thing in his head.

I asked James to show me what he had been able to write for his outline and rough draft of this paper thus far. He opened the file on his computer and showed me three sentences he had written for the opening paragraph. He explained that he never did any outline and had never been able to write a rough draft and then go back to expand and edit it. He always had to write the whole paper as a final draft, struggling to get each sentence "just right" before he could go on to write the next sentence. The contrast between his impressive fluency in explaining the material to me, incorporating many specific facts and dates, and his seriously diminished ability to put these thoughts into sentences and paragraphs on paper was quite striking.

> Problems with written expression are very common among people with ADHD. A large population-based study found that 64 percent of boys and 57 percent of girls diagnosed with ADHD had what is known as disorder of written expression.

Problems with written expression are very common among people with ADHD. A large population-based study found that 64 percent of boys and 57 percent of girls diagnosed with ADHD had what is known as disorder of written expression, whereas only 17 percent and 9 percent, respectively, of those without ADHD had such a disorder.[1] One clinical study compared achievement test scores for reading, math, and written expression in a sample of children and adolescents with ADHD;

for 70 percent of those students, scores for written expression were the lowest of their three achievement test scores. Other studies have shown that 46 to 65 percent of children diagnosed with ADHD also meet criteria for a specific learning disorder in written expression, whereas a sample of children without ADHD included only 10 percent who had serious enough difficulty to qualify for diagnosis with a specific learning disorder in written expression.[2]

○ impact of impaired executive functions on written expression

It is not surprising that many with ADHD suffer from impairments in written expression. The task of generating and organizing words into sentences and then sequencing those sentences into paragraphs on a blank page is one that places much greater demands on EFs than do reading and math. In reading, one needs to decode the words and ascertain their meaning in context by using working memory to keep in mind what one has just read, drawing on relevant memories, and integrating those meanings to understand what has been written. For the reader, the stimuli to be processed are already on the page, as are the numbers for math problems. The writer is faced with the blank page and must generate the words, organize them to convey a specific message, and edit the output so that it will convey in an understandable way his or her thoughts and feelings. For most people, written expression is more challenging than reading or math. For those who suffer from ADHD-related impairments of EFs such as working memory, organizing and prioritizing, and sustaining and shifting focus, written expression is even more challenging.

Because of the critical role of EFs in written expression, I considered it important for James to get started immediately with a prescription of stimulant medication to try to alleviate his ADHD symptoms, particularly to help him with the writing tasks he was facing. It took about a week to fine-tune the dose and timing to establish an effective regimen for James. Soon thereafter, he reported that the medication was helping him get started on his writing tasks and sustain effort on those tasks.

This is consistent with clinical reports from other patients who indicate that stimulant medication has been helpful for improving their attention and effort for writing tasks. Few controlled studies have addressed the effects of stimulant medication for problems of written expression in college students with ADHD, but one pilot study found that medication improved both writing mechanics and writing composition in college students with ADHD to the point that they performed similarly to matched controls without ADHD.[3]

 Sometimes emotions become entangled in both the learning of skills and the deployment of those skills.

Although James was better at focusing while taking the medication, the pills did not give him the skills he needed to translate his ideas into text. Nor did the medication alleviate his emotional problems with writing, his feeling that each sentence had to sound "just right" before he could go on to write the next sentence. Sometimes emotions become entangled in both the learning of skills and the deployment of those skills.

One of the problems impeding James's ability to write his paper was difficulty with organizing and prioritizing his thoughts. He had a vast store of information about the topic he was trying to write about. He had done that portion of his homework quite well, but he had all this information piled up in his head with very little sense of which were the more important facts and concepts and which were more subordinate, to be used for examples and elaboration. When I asked him questions about the material, he responded with very good answers, but he had great difficulty in generating the organizing and follow-up questions for himself.

The emotional problems James was struggling with as he tried to write included not only his excessive perfectionism in composing each sentence but also his accumulated anxiety and feelings of inadequacy about being able to write. His protracted struggles to perform writing tasks had left him with strong feelings of helplessness in the face of any lengthy writing assignment.

○ using a graphic organizer as preparation for writing

To address his organizing problem, I asked James to read sections of a short book on organizing academic papers.[4] I also introduced him to WebspirationPRO, a graphic organizer software program designed for college students and businesspeople. This program allowed him to put down in small, separate ovals a few words for each of the many ideas and facts he had already gathered in his head. I coached him then to move these ovals around on the computer screen, identifying the most important items and then using the tools on-screen to link these to one another to form examples and supporting points at several different levels of abstraction. He then gradually began to arrange these in hierarchical clumps. Once that task was completed, James clicked an icon that caused the software to organize what he had created graphically into a preliminary traditional outline that he could then modify, expand, and elaborate.

○ excessive perfectionism as an impediment to writing

Although the software was useful to James, it did not remove his emotional difficulties with written expression. At several points in this process, James became impatient and wanted to turn immediately to the task of trying to write sentences and paragraphs as he was accustomed to doing. As I inquired into the inflexibility of James's usual approach, he explained:

> I always feel that I need to get the first sentence of the first paragraph worded so it sounds just right before I go on to write the next sentence. I then have to get that sentence worded so it sounds good before I can move on to write the next sentence, etc., etc. That's the way I have to do it for every paper. Often this takes a really long time because it may take me a while to find the right words for a sentence. Until I've got that sentence worded just so, I feel I can't go on to write anything more. The professors usually like what I've written, but often my grade gets lowered because I'm late in getting the paper in; sometimes I can't get it done at all and then I fail the assignment.

This anxiety-laden, perfectionistic approach to writing is not peculiar to James. I have encountered similar difficulties in a number of patients with ADHD. This "first sentence has to be perfect before I can write the next one" approach is actually a variant of OCD that involves a "sticky perseveration" on mental set and task orientation; that is, the person feels unable to let go and move on from one aspect of a task until that aspect is performed to a standard that feels "just right."[5] Someone who feels compelled to write papers in this tediously slow manner is bound to feel overwhelmed by the task of preparing any long academic paper. Anticipating such a long and intensive struggle, the person is likely to procrastinate or totally avoid the task.[6]

I asked James to fight his repeated impulse to move directly to writing sentences and paragraphs. Instead, I urged him to try to experiment with this alternative approach, which involves taking time to organize the ideas and facts before trying to write any text of the paper. James took the program back to his apartment to work on it by himself, announcing that he would have a rough draft of the paper ready to show me at our writing tutorial two days later.

On the next day, our meeting was scheduled as a psychotherapy session. James arrived on time, but looked quite tired. He explained that he had been trying to work on his paper, but had gotten sidetracked with other activities "the same way I always do when I'm trying to write." Soon after starting work on his paper, James had decided to take a study break "for just half an hour" to play one of the several video games he had on his laptop. One thing led to another, and he continued to play the game until 3:30 a.m., at which time he decided he needed to go to sleep so that he could work on the paper in the morning. He then slept until almost noon, getting up just in time to get himself to our appointment.

o "booster doses" of medication

I asked James whether he had taken his ADHD medication before attempting to work on his paper. He hadn't! I suggested that he was wasting his time in trying to work on his paper without medication. We discussed how he could take a booster dose of his stimulant medication when he needed to extend coverage past the hours covered by his dose taken in the morning. Over the coming days, he found that booster dose quite useful. Without it, he was unable to engage productively in the late afternoon or evening when his sustained-release medication taken in the morning had worn off. After the coverage with stimulant medication was stabilized, I arranged for James to begin a trial of a selective serotonin reuptake inhibitor (SSRI) to try to address his chronic anxiety, his perseverative worries, his rigidity, and his underlying depression.

○ "addiction" to playing video games

Because I was curious about the specific appeal of those video games for James, I asked him to tell me a bit about the game he had been playing. He described it as a warfare strategy game in which there is a lot of bombing and shooting. With a smile that seemed both embarrassed and a bit smug, James commented, "In these games and on YouTube, I have a ghoulish interest in watching people get shot or blown up." James explained that, for him, the games served to take him out of a chronic state of boredom and also to calm and soothe him. I asked James to estimate how many hours he spent playing these games on most days during the last couple of months when he was at college. He said it varied between four and eight hours most days, sometimes much more, and that once he started, he found it almost impossible to stop himself from continuing to play. Although he rarely missed classes to play, James reported that his many hours of Internet gaming often prevented him from working on his reading assignments, studying, or preparing academic papers.

There has been increasing interest in "Internet addiction." The term *addiction* is defined in various ways, but essentially it is used to refer to a habitual compulsion to engage in a certain activity or to use a substance, despite significant negative consequences.

Over recent years, there has been increasing interest in "Internet addiction." The term *addiction* is defined in various ways, but essentially it is used to refer to a habitual compulsion to engage in a certain activity or to use a substance, despite significant negative consequences that follow from persistence in that activity or substance use. Addictive use of the Internet has been assessed in several studies of samples of individuals from the United States, Korea, China, India, and several other cultures. Differences in the definitions and methodologies used in these studies are problematic, but across studies, the incidence of "Internet addiction" has been estimated to be about 6 to 15 percent of the general population and 13 to 18 percent of college students.[7]

My interest in James's excessive use of Internet gaming was focused around his motivations, the emotional appeal that those games had for him. What did that gaming provide for him that drew him into it so much, so often, for so long? The games that interested James most were of the type referred to as massively multiplayer online role-playing games (MMORPGs); one of the most popular is World of Warcraft, which was reported to have over eleven million players in 2010.

These games are played online in complex virtual worlds where the player creates a virtual personality called an avatar, which the player then directs to undertake various tasks, advance its capabilities, and interact with other avatars in positive and negative ways within the ever-changing virtual world of the game, which continues to evolve even while any given player is not participating. Concurrent with game play, players can and often do engage in chat with other players, known or unknown, regarding the game itself and/or many other aspects of their personal lives.

Research on motivations for playing MMORPGs has identified several dimensions of interest described by players of these games. One dimension is achievement. A player can direct his or her avatar to garner improved equipment, which increases the avatar's capacity to undertake challenging tasks that may confer increased status. A second dimension is social interaction: players may gather into online groups or guilds as well as carry on social conversations with other players, some of whom may actually become familiar friends. A third dimension is emotional intensity of participation, the level of immersion in the fantasy world of the game.

Because the game is complex and highly varied and can be totally anonymous, it offers players opportunity to take on new roles, some of which they may never be willing or able to take on in the real social world. Within the game, they can immerse themselves in the role of an intensely fierce competitor or a powerfully violent aggressor, even if such roles are widely discrepant from their real-life persona, without exposing such aspects of themselves to others in their actual social environment, where they may fear negative reactions. For some, such games are simply a pleasant pastime; but for others, immersion in the game may become so intense that it provides for them an alternative and perhaps more satisfying self in what may become an important concurrent life.[8]

For many, these MMORPGs provide an alternative world that offers them emotional satisfactions that are similar to those obtained by others who sustain active participation in friendships, athletic teams, clubs, fraternities, sororities, military service, academic studies, employment, dating, marriage, or other relationships that involve face-to-face interactions with other people. For some people at some times in their lives, such virtual world experiences may appear as the most appealing or perhaps the only options available to obtain such satisfactions.

○ ○ ○

I asked James to estimate his time spent playing video games in comparison with his time spent doing things with classmates, other than in class. He responded, "Much more time on video games. Doing stuff with other people is a chore for me. I think I give off the vibe that I don't want to hang out with other people. Like, for me, going to dinner is a time for food intake, not a time for socializing." I queried about what kind of "vibe" he was talking about. He responded with examples of several times that other students had told him that he often seemed aloof and standoffish. When I asked if he recognized what they were talking about, he said he didn't know. This led to a discussion of how James often felt socially awkward with peers, even though he was quite confident in his ability to relate to adults. He said he was particularly uncomfortable trying to socialize with girls, even though he wanted very much to have a girlfriend.

○ social anxiety and avoidance

James sounded quite discouraged as he told me, "This stuff is part of what makes me think my situation is pretty hopeless. It's not just writing the papers. College is supposed to be a time when you have fun with other people, but I just haven't learned how to do that yet." We agreed that we would consider his feelings of social awkwardness and social anxiety as an important part of the work we were setting out to do.

Over the next few weeks, James gradually caught on to the need to organize his thoughts and research data before trying to write papers, though he continued to have considerable difficulty in implementing the process. He continued to struggle with his tendency to distract himself with video games and YouTube anytime he worked alone. I had him go to the local public library to work for specific hours and then come back to show me each day what he had or hadn't been able to accomplish. With this structure and intensive support, he was able to complete the writing of the four papers just prior to the deadline.

○ conflicting feelings about continuing with
    intensive treatment

In the course of the last week of that month, James and I spent several hours discussing the decision he had to make as to whether to return to college to start the fall term or to stay and continue his treatment with me. He found the stimulant medication for his ADHD to be quite helpful and had begun to feel some benefit from his antidepressant medication, but he recognized that he was very dependent on the structure being provided in his work with me, and he did not feel confident that he was yet ready to manage by himself his social anxieties and his difficulties in getting written work done. He told me, "I feel like a still have a lot of stuff to work out here, but I know my parents are going to pressure me to go back to school right away." We talked about how it was not just his parents who wanted him to return immediately to his college. James himself felt torn between his wish to take a year off from his college so that he could continue his therapy and his own wish to pack up and return to his campus to continue with his junior year without delay, figuring that somehow things would just work out for him.

When we met together with his parents, James told them that he was having trouble deciding what he should do. He and his parents asked me for my recommendation. I told them that I was impressed that James had been able to complete his four papers, but I also recognized that he had done this only with a lot of very intensive support, far more than was likely to be available to him at his college, and without the demands of other courses being taken concurrently.

My recommendation was that James take at least one semester off from his college to continue intensive treatment for the coming academic year, while attending a local university and taking a full load of courses where he could address both his social and academic problems in a real-life setting with others his age. I explained that I would not be willing to provide further treatment for James unless he was enrolled in a substantial load of college courses taken for transfer credit. That setting was necessary, I thought, to structure his time and to provide a realistic laboratory in which he and I could learn more about his strengths and difficulties in both academic and social situations—a setting where he could practice making some needed changes.

Following that meeting, James spent an evening with his parents. They returned the next day having decided that they would go forward with the plan for James to take at least the first semester off from his college to continue intensive treatment with me while taking courses at a local university. Near the end of the first semester, James would make the decision to go back to his university for the spring semester or to continue his treatment for the full academic year.

We all agreed that it would be important for James to wrap up his treatment with me and return to his university after no more than two semesters, possibly after just one. James's parents suggested that during this time, James might also benefit from taking driving lessons and get his driver's license, a task he had been avoiding for several years. James agreed with that goal and with the overall plan, though he also acknowledged honestly that he was scared and continued to have mixed feelings about doing it.

○ revising priorities in treatment

Together James and his parents went to a local university, where he was able to enroll as a nonboarding student taking a full load of academic courses, several of which would help him meet requirements for his major at his home university. A few days later, after the necessary arrangements were in place, James had a tearful good-bye with his parents, and they left. His courses began a few days later.

As he prepared to start his classes, I asked James to talk with me about what he was hoping we would be able to accomplish from our work together over the coming semester. I found it interesting that the first goals he stated were mostly related to social and emotional concerns—for example, "to make friends more easily," "to feel or display emotion more readily so I don't feel so out of it," "to cut down on my negative thinking about myself and my situation," and "to not be so passive, just letting life happen to me." He also added academic concerns: "to improve my ability to organize and write papers" and "to plan my work more effectively and start my assignments earlier, not at the last minute." When I asked about what James thought the first step in this should be, he answered, "To cut down on the amount of time I waste on my laptop."

James's listing of his priorities highlighted his strong wish to feel more successful in interacting with peers, a wish that was closely linked to his wish for gaining more mastery of his academic work. Yet he also pointed to his excessive time spent on computer gaming as a primary impediment that he would need to overcome in order to make progress on his social and academic goals. It was already clear that his excessive gaming was an entrenched escape from the anxiety he felt in social interactions and the frustration he experienced when faced with the need to prepare academic papers. Reducing his gaming would be likely to intensify his anxiety and frustration due to excessive perfectionism, even as it made more time for him to socialize and prepare his papers.

○ gradual progress

Our work together went on throughout the first semester, after which James chose to continue treatment with me for the second semester as well. Throughout those months, we met several times each week to explore James's insecurities in social relationships, his feelings of inadequacy despite his many strengths, and his efforts to change his complicated relationship with his parents, who tended to be overprotective in some ways while also minimizing or ignoring many of his persisting social and intrapersonal difficulties.

During that academic year, James continued to struggle a great deal with meeting deadlines and controlling his continuing urge to immerse himself in online gaming. Yet he made significant progress in each of these areas and was able to achieve high grades in his courses.

During his second semester of treatment, after much avoidance and great struggle with himself and his fears, James was able to take driving lessons and earn his driver's license. He asked me to accompany him for some practice driving prior to his exam and to his driver's license test. I was able to witness both his fear of taking on the responsibility of driving a car and his great pride in overcoming that fear, not only by getting his license but also by repeatedly driving himself to and from the university and eventually also to various errands in the community. This was a major accomplishment for James, which significantly boosted his sense of himself as an adult.

Over the course of those months, James also gained a clearer sense of how he tended to put off others, especially his peers, with his overly formal style of speech, his tendency to be excessively critical of others' efforts and opinions, his unrecognized sarcasm, and his avoidance of the small talk that serves to lubricate much social interaction. Much of this increased self-awareness came from his reporting in therapy sessions various interactions with other students that were puzzling or uncomfortable for him; often we would role-play alternative ways he could have responded. As we were concluding his year of treatment, we both agreed that James still had much work to do in developing his empathy and social skills, but he was hoping to make further growth in this area while living in the dormitory at his university, where he would have more opportunity for casual interactions with others of his age in a group living situation.

After completing his year of treatment, James returned as planned to his original university. He was apprehensive, but he seemed ready to address his difficulties more directly rather than to continue his previous pattern, which he had described as "just letting life happen to me as though I could do nothing to make it better."

What Helped James?

- Change of context to separate from parents and engage in intensive psychotherapy to address anxiety, video game addiction, emotional immaturity, and needed social coaching
- One-on-one coaching to improve organization and writing of papers for college while taking a full-time load of courses
- Prescription and fine-tuning of stimulant medication to alleviate ADHD impairments
- Recognition of the impact of excessive perfectionism in slowing written expression
- Confronting Internet gaming addiction and its role in social and academic avoidance
- Support for challenging and mastering his long-standing fear of becoming a licensed driver

13

getting unstuck

Understanding emotional aspects of ADHD is essential for helping those who struggle with this disorder. It's important to remember that multiple emotions played a critical role in the difficulties of the teens and adults described in this book. Getting stuck in their schooling, family life, social relationships, and jobs was inextricably linked not only to the emotional aspects of their ADHD impairments but also to their frustration, shame, discouragement, guilt, and worry as they struggled to cope with their ADHD and the emotional reactions of those around them.

○ strategies that help now but hurt later

In some instances, the people in these stories suffered not from a lack of awareness of important emotions but from an inability to tolerate those emotions enough to deal effectively with them. They became caught up in patterns of behavior designed to avoid painful emotions that seemed to them overwhelming. Faced with stressors—looming deadlines for school papers or business projects; a need to face parents, teachers, or employers disappointed in their performance; peers who repeatedly teased or bullied them; getting acquainted with an unfamiliar group of classmates in a new school setting and living situation; a parent with serious depression or medical illness; collapse of a dating relationship or marriage; getting laid off or fired from a job; or loss of a parent to death—they locked up in patterns of self-defeating avoidance and denial.

Within many of these stories are examples of strategies my patients employed to try to help themselves avoid embarrassment and shield themselves from fear, at least temporarily. Karen sat on the steps outside rather than walking into the class she needed to resume her studies so she could complete her degree. She also repeatedly lied to her parents to put off their inevitable discovery of what she had been unable to do. Matt remained in his room rather than going out to meet and get to know some of his fellow freshman as he started in college. Martin anesthetized himself with excessive use of marijuana, and Lisa distracted herself from emotional pain by cutting to inflict physical pain on her body. James immersed himself in compulsive use of Internet role-playing games to engage in fantasy violence. For many, these strategies to avoid embarrassment, shame, and fear brought temporary relief, but also created additional burdens and escalating problems.

o works in progress

As discussed, these teenagers and adults did not sign up for ADHD, and they cannot get rid of it by dint of "willpower." However, it is also important for those with ADHD not to get caught up in identifying themselves as victims in life. They need to be supported in recognizing that having ADHD doesn't mean that they're destined for inevitable frustration, helplessness, and failure. Many with ADHD are able to benefit considerably from treatment that enables them to work effectively to fulfill their potential. Many also have impressive abilities and personality strengths that allow them, with or without treatment, to achieve significant success in various aspects of education, work, social relationships, and family life.

Many stories in this book demonstrate that some with ADHD who get quite stuck at one or several points in life are able eventually to get unstuck and move on. Eric, Martin, Mike, Lisa, Sue, Matt, and James eventually found significant success in their schooling and went on to continue to build their futures. Karen left full-time schooling, but went on to find satisfaction in full-time employment while continuing her education part-time. Steve was not successful in marriage, but continued to be quite successful in his work and in relationships with friends. Sarah was quite successful in marriage and parenting; eventually she was also successful in returning to full-time work in her chosen field. Lois suffered many tragic losses and defeats, but was finally able to establish a new life situation that worked for her. Although it is certainly true that not every life has a happy ending, it is also true that some individuals are able to win amazing victories after a great many frustrations and defeats. Each of us continues to be a work in progress.

o   variety in levels of difficulties, resources, and strengths

ADHD comes in small, medium, and large sizes. For some affected individuals, their level of severity is mild to moderate, and they respond promptly and quite well to medication treatment with appropriate education about the disorder. They pretty much know what they ought to be doing, and, with the help of medication and brief treatment, they can do it reasonably well. Others need more intensive and sustained treatment because their ADHD symptoms are much more severe and may be complicated by a number of additional co-occurring disorders. Moreover, they may suffer problematic bodily reactions to medications, or their emotions related to their life situation and treatment may be quite mixed, tangled, and complex. These can present difficult obstacles to treatment, and bringing about a successful outcome then requires much more time and effort.

Patients described in this book vary widely in the severity of their ADHD impairments and related problems, as well as in the intensity and length of their treatment with me. Most had been evaluated and treated by at least one other clinician previously, but were not satisfied with the outcome and were hoping that a different approach might be more helpful. Many of those whose stories are included here were suffering from rather complex difficulties that required many months — in a few cases, years — to resolve. Although their symptoms were more difficult and complex than those of most others treated for ADHD, their more intensive and sustained treatment allowed greater opportunity for us to explore and gradually understand the complexity of their struggles, and, in some cases, help them get unstuck and move on.

○ getting unstuck

When someone is stuck due to difficulties that may include ADHD, there are three important steps to take.

Step 1: Evaluation and Thorough Explanation

First, the person should receive an adequate diagnostic evaluation for ADHD done by a clinician familiar with ADHD who can use clinical interviews and rating scales to elicit information about that person's strengths and difficulties in managing activities and tasks of daily life. This evaluation needs to take into account the person's educational and personal family history and current living situation. It needs to assess relevant cognitive abilities and to consider health history as well as past and current stressors. The evaluation also needs to consider any substance use and any additional psychiatric or medical problems that might better explain the person's difficulties or that are complicating the ADHD.

If the evaluation indicates ADHD, it should be followed with science-based education of the patient and relevant family members about what ADHD is and how it's treated. Explanation should include specific examples of the range of ADHD symptoms and should clarify that this disorder is not due to lack of willpower and is not likely to be overcome adequately without appropriate support and treatment. The clinician should also discuss various options for treatment, helping inform the patient and family about advantages and potential disadvantages of each option. This discussion should include careful attention to any specific worries or misunderstandings the patient or family have about any of these options. The story about Mike in this book illustrates how parental attitudes and misunderstanding can be problematic but also may be changed by appropriate education of the parents and patient.

Step 2: Consider Options for Treatment and/or Accommodations

After adequate evaluation, diagnosis, and education about the disorder, the clinician should help the patient obtain whatever treatment and/or accommodations (at work, school, or both) are appropriate and agreed to by the patient and, in the case of minors, his or her parents. If the evaluating clinician is licensed to prescribe appropriate ADHD medications and has the relevant training, he or she can give or arrange an appropriate medical exam and then provide needed prescriptions.

If the clinician evaluating the patient is not licensed to prescribe, that clinician should collaborate with the patient to communicate the results of the evaluation to the patient's primary care provider or another appropriate prescriber to make the necessary arrangements for a preliminary physical examination of the patient and prescription of appropriate medications to help in improving focus and working memory so that the patient can deal more adequately with the emotions that complicate life with ADHD.

A Note About Medications   Regardless of who is prescribing, for any patient beginning or continuing medication treatment for ADHD, it is critically important that arrangements be put in place for monitoring of the medication's effectiveness and potential side effects. Follow-up often requires a number of visits to assess how a patient is responding to the medication and whether the dose or timing of doses should be fine-tuned. Often doses need to be increased or decreased or given at different times in order to optimize response. Several of the patients described in this book needed many changes of medication before we could establish an effective treatment regimen.

Accommodations   In addition to medication, some patients also need accommodations or additional services to alleviate or compensate for their ADHD-related impairments of executive function. Some, though not all, students with ADHD need extended time for taking tests and examinations.[1] Karen and Sue were students who needed and benefited from such an accommodation. Arranging this accommodation usually requires a comprehensive battery of standardized tests to establish eligibility, particularly for students taking the SAT, ACT, GRE, MCAT, LSAT, GMAT, or other examinations required for admission to colleges and universities or for licensure or board certification in certain professions.

Some other individuals with ADHD need specialized tutoring for academic skills or personalized coaching to help with improving their ways of coping with specific tasks or stressors in schooling, employment, or social relationships. Some need to change their life situation, seeking work in a different field than they had planned or taking an alternative route to education and employment. And some need specialized psychological or psychiatric treatment for additional problems co-occurring with their ADHD.

Step 3: Find Supportive Counseling or Psychotherapy

The third critical component for helping those with ADHD who are seriously stuck is supportive counseling or psychotherapy to identify the specific emotional and cognitive difficulties that are currently blocking them from dealing effectively with their life situation. For some, this might be provided by just a few sessions from time to time with a supportive clinician who understands the complexities of ADHD and is skilled in helping patients develop increased understanding of themselves and of their specific difficulties, while working to develop more effective strategies for addressing those difficulties.

For others who are more severely stuck, more intensive treatment for the patient and, perhaps, the family such as has been described in this book may be needed to help them find more effective ways of coping with their ADHD and related emotional difficulties. Usually the first step in intensive treatment of those seriously stuck is for the therapist to try to learn with the patient about emotional conflicts that may be complicating the person's efforts to resolve his or her difficulties. Often those who are seriously stuck are caught up in unrecognized emotional conflicts that sabotage their efforts to get unstuck. Examples include Lois, who repeatedly interrupted her treatment; Mike, who only dimly recognized his fear of leaving home after his mother's serious depression; and Matt, who was torn between his conscious wish to return to his college and his less conscious wish to fail in some of his courses so that he could delay his return and avoid his fear of failing again.

Because ADHD impairments often become more noticeable or problematic as the person is faced with new challenges that arise as he or she progresses in schooling, employment, and other developmental tasks that emerge over the course of adolescence and adulthood, he or she may intermittently need treatment across the life span. For some, just the initial evaluation and treatment may be sufficient; but, for many, there is need for additional support and interventions from time to time for assistance in meeting new challenges as they emerge.

It is also important for people with ADHD and for their families to realize that the course of treatment usually is not like a steady escalator ride of ongoing progress. Stories in this book show that often there are repeated disappointments and failures that frustrate and worry the patient and all those involved in trying to provide help and support. Each failure renders those involved more vulnerable to being overcome with discouragement and tempted to give up on efforts to improve their situation. For some, that burden is too great to bear. For many, however, persistence in sustaining effective treatment yields benefits that enable them to develop their strengths and talents in ways not previously imagined or possible.

o cultivating realistic hope

Regardless of the mode, intensity, or duration of treatment, an important aim for such intervention is to help the person with ADHD and his or her family to develop a particularly important emotion: realistic hope. Hope is essential to sustain patients' efforts to get themselves unstuck so they can develop their strengths and cope more effectively with stressors. Realistic hope is not Pollyannaish. Realistic hope is not blind to the person's limitations and constraints; realistic hope does not convey a "You can do anything you want to do, if only you try hard enough" message while ignoring true obstacles. Realistic hope recognizes and sustains awareness of potential constraints and obstacles while working to help the person develop ways to cope with his or her life situation as it really is and to work to make it better. Getting unstuck is a process that involves thoughtful assessment and effective treatment, usually with medication. In many cases, getting unstuck also requires an ongoing supportive counseling or psychotherapy relationship to address complex and often hidden emotions. With the right supports in place, many of those stuck by ADHD can develop realistic and sustainable hope and learn to survive—and even to thrive.

questions for discussion

The following questions may help to facilitate your reflections on *Smart but Stuck*. They may also be used to stimulate discussion of *Smart but Stuck* among parents, families, students, and clinicians.

Chapter 1: ADHD and the Emotional Brain

1. Brown says, "Emotions guide what we notice and what we ignore, what we focus on intently and what we carefully avoid. Conflicting emotions can cause us to disrupt engagement with a task we want to accomplish, or lead us repeatedly to do what we consciously intend never to do again." What are some examples of this in your own life or in the lives of those with ADHD whom you know?

2. How and why do those with ADHD experience and deal with emotions differently from those who do not have ADHD? How does this affect their performance in day-to-day tasks?

3. What does it mean to say that, as neuroscientist Antonio Damasio puts it, "the emotional signal can operate entirely under the radar of consciousness"?

4. How are emotions and memory linked? What functions does this linkage serve for all people, not just those with ADHD?

5. What are the two primary ways in which emotions play a critical role in the chronic difficulties of those with ADHD? How are impairments of working memory involved in each?

6.   What does it mean to say that people with ADHD often experience life as though they were watching a basketball game through a telescope?

7.   How do emotions associated with ADHD create stress in families and other relationships of those with ADHD? What can be done to reduce such stress?

Chapter 2: Eric

1.   What emotional factors contributed to Eric's having so much difficulty in getting himself motivated to do his college coursework? How did the change of context from home to college affect this?

2.   How did Eric's social anxiety show up, and how did he try to avoid it?

3.   Did it make sense to use a "harm reduction" approach rather than a "total abstinence" approach to deal with Eric's excessive use of marijuana? Why or why not?

4.   How does Eric's experience illustrate the concept of "delay aversion"? What strategies can be used to deal with such a problem in someone this age?

Chapter 3: Karen

1.   How did Karen's role in her family and her family's attitude about shame contribute to her various avoidance strategies? Why did her avoidance persist so long, and what could have been done to reduce it?

2.   How did Karen's ADHD impairments affect her ability to complete the heavy reading requirements of her college studies and her ability to do well on exams? What interventions can be helpful for these problems, and how can they be arranged?

3.   What does the smoke detector example illustrate about brain function and emotion in people with ADHD? To what other emotions in those with ADHD might this apply?

4.   Were there any advantages to Karen in the way things turned out for her at college? What are the risks and benefits to various struggling students with ADHD if they drop out of full-time college

studies and switch to part-time schooling while working full-time or part-time?

Chapter 4: Martin

1. What emotional effects are likely to occur in high-IQ students with ADHD if their impairments are not correctly diagnosed and adequately treated? Why are exceptionally bright students with ADHD often not recognized as having ADHD until relatively late in their educational career?

2. What conflicting emotions are illustrated in Martin's running away from his friends at the club and his signing up for the dance class at the gym the next day? How was this similar to and different from his experience in dealing with his therapist and with the professor who employed him?

3. In what ways did Martin's use of marijuana impair him and in what ways did it help him at various times in his life before and during treatment? How did it help and/or hinder his schoolwork, his relationships with peers, and his relationship with his therapist?

4. What helped Martin overcome his feelings of hopelessness when he realized he would need to take an extra year to complete his degree? How does the fact that Martin and his father both began to be much more productive at about the same age fit with research on delayed brain maturation in those with ADHD? What else may have contributed to his successfully seeking and completing his master's degree immediately after his protracted struggle to complete his B.A.?

Chapter 5: Sarah

1. Although Sarah apparently did not have ADHD during childhood or adolescence, what symptoms of executive function impairments characteristic of ADHD emerged during her late forties? Which of her specific symptoms seemed more like ADHD than just depression?

2. How might the estrogen decline of perimenopause/menopause cause some women with no previous history of ADHD to develop

ADHD-like cognitive impairments? How is this similar to "chemofog"?

3. Why are neuropsychological "tests of executive function" not likely to be effective in assessing executive function impairments associated with ADHD? What measures are more effective in assessing ADHD-associated impairments of executive functions in adolescents and adults?

4. What have preliminary studies shown regarding effective treatment for late-onset cognitive impairments related to ADHD in adult women at midlife who were without any history of ADHD during childhood or adolescence?

Chapter 6: Mike

1. How does Mike's description of his problems at college illustrate the situationally specific nature of ADHD impairments? What are the similarities and differences in how this variability of symptoms from one task to another affected Mike and his parents?

2. Many students report that they have tried an ADHD medication given to them by a friend. What are their reasons for doing this? What are the potential risks and benefits of such experimentation? Why would this not be an adequate test of whether the person has ADHD?

3. Describe the "possible self" images Mike had of himself. Where did each of these come from? What emotions are attached to each? How do you think they affected his performance?

4. How did medication and psychotherapy help Mike deal with his social anxiety about dating, his worries about his parents, and his conflicting feelings about changing his major in college? Why did these issues not come up in the initial evaluation?

Chapter 7: Lisa

1. How did medication "rebound" affect Lisa and her family? How was this problem alleviated?

2. What does it mean to say that Lisa's parents were "polarized," and how does the concept of "triangulation" describe this family's pattern of interaction? What emotions were involved? How can such difficulties be alleviated?

3. Which of Lisa's problems with peers were typical of children with ADHD, and which were more similar to those of teenagers with autism spectrum disorders? How did her delayed pubescent development add to her emotional and social difficulties?

4. What factors helped increase Lisa's hope for her future despite the disappointment, shame, and anger she was coping with and that she demonstrated in her self-cutting? How did her parents help her? How did her teachers and coaches help her? How did her psychotherapy help her? How did her medication help her? What were her strengths?

Chapter 8: Steve

1. Give examples of how Steve's inability to "switch gears" and his difficulty in accurately sizing up the emotions of others caused him to get fired in spite of the high quality of his work.

2. Why did Steve need an SSRI in addition to his ADHD medication? Was it helpful? What happened that made it necessary to switch to a different type of medication for his OCD impairments?

3. Which of the problems that led to Steve's wife's divorcing him are probably attributable to his ADHD, and which ones are more likely to be due to his autism spectrum impairments?

4. How does Steve's statement, "I'm good at programming computers, but I'm not good at programming myself" both describe and illustrate his difficulties with emotions? How would you explain his frustration and annoyance with his previous doctor, his wife, and his boss?

5. Do you agree that it made sense to refrain from challenging Steve's decision to avoid any more intimate relationships after the breakup of his marriage? What is the relevance of the statement that "there are many different ways to live a life"?

Chapter 9: Sue

1. Why was Sue's transition into middle school so difficult for her and for her mother? What specific factors made it more difficult for her than for many of her peers? What emotions do you think Sue and her parents felt when they first heard that she was being diagnosed with ADHD?

2. Sue's father apologized to Sue after she complained to him about his being more moody recently, but he also told Sue of his worries and frustration about her being rude to her teachers and to her mother. He also told Sue that he was worried about her diminished interest in her schoolwork. What did he do along with this that was probably quite helpful to Sue? How do you think the father's comments and the willingness of both parents to back off from micromanaging Sue's homework affected her attitude toward her work? Would this approach be effective for all students who have ADHD?

3. What emotions were probably evoked in Sue and her parents when the first medication Sue tried was not only ineffective but also problematic? How can patients and their families be helped to avoid overreacting to such problems?

4. How did taking and hearing the results of the IQ test affect Sue and her parents? What emotions did that intervention address in the family? Would that intervention be equally good for any student with ADHD? Why or why not?

Chapter 10: Matt

1. Matt initially explained his struggles in starting college in terms of his academic difficulties. In addition to his ADHD problems, what emotional difficulties eventually led to his having to withdraw? How did he try to protect himself from his misery in the new setting? Why did he wait so long before letting his parents know how immobilized and depressed he had become?

2. Why was it important for Matt to tell some of his friends the truth about his problems at college without delay? How did doing that help him test the accuracy of his fearful assumptions?

3. Matt's avoidance strategies were powerfully entrenched and continued as he was taking summer courses. Why was it essential for him to be engaged in supportive yet confrontational psychotherapy as he did this? Would medication alone or with less confrontational counseling have been likely to help him change his established patterns of dealing with his social phobia?

4. Why did Matt continue to be so resistant to bringing his coursework with him for discussion in psychotherapy sessions? What helped him recognize that his fearful avoidance of current threats was setting him up for even more embarrassing problems in the not-too-distant future?

Chapter 11: Lois

1. Lois suffered several severe stresses and major losses prior to seeking treatment and after, but her reactions to these were extreme in intensity and duration. How does her excessive difficulty in controlling her reactions illustrate impairments of "top-down" controls, insufficient working memory, and inadequate gating of emotion that occurs in many with ADHD?

2. How does Lois's hoarding behavior reflect impairments of executive functions such as the ability to inhibit, organize, and prioritize that are seen in many with ADHD who do not hoard? What emotions intensified her difficulties with these functions?

3. What new stressors and adversities intensified the struggles Lois was having with anxiety, depression, and grief? What was the role of "attentional bias"?

4. What emotional factors led Lois to act in ways that sabotaged her treatment? What advantages did the opportunity to live with her aunt in a distant state offer for Lois?

Chapter 12: James

1. How did the attitude of James's parents make it difficult for him to acknowledge the severity of his emotional and social problems to them and to himself? What emotions did he need to keep under wraps in dealing with them?

2. James had studied the material needed for each of his overdue papers and was able to talk fluently about the facts and events in response to his therapist's questions. However, he had great difficulty in organizing and prioritizing that information in written form. What executive functions associated with ADHD does this difficulty illustrate? How did his excessive perfectionism complicate these difficulties?

3. What was the emotional appeal of multiplayer role-playing video games to James? What functions did his gaming serve for him?

4. What significance do you see in James's delaying seeking his driver's license and his eventually fighting successfully to overcome his avoidance so that he could get his license and then actually drive himself? What emotions were involved?

Chapter 13: Getting Unstuck

1. How does the "willpower assumption" tend to intensify feelings of hopelessness, inadequacy, and/or victimhood in many individuals with ADHD? What are some indirect ways in which family or friends might unwittingly afflict a patient with that assumption?

2. What are the benefits of including education of family members about the modern understanding of ADHD early in a course of treatment for ADHD?

3. What are some obstacles that prevent many with ADHD from seeking, finding, and sustaining adequate assessment and treatment?

4. How is realistic hope different from unrealistic hope?

notes and additional reading

Introduction

1   LeDoux, J. E. (1996). *The emotional brain: The mysterious underpinnings of emotional life.* New York, NY: Simon & Schuster.

2   Dodge, K. A. (1991). Emotion and social information processing. In J. Garber & K. A. Dodge (Eds.), *Development of emotion regulation and dysregulation* (pp. 159–181). New York, NY: Cambridge University Press.

Chapter 1: ADHD and the Emotional Brain

1   Shechner, T., Britton, J. C., Perez-Edgar, K., Bar-Haim, Y., Ernst, M., Fox, N. A., … Pine, D. S. (2012). Attention biases, anxiety, and development: Toward or away from threats or rewards? *Depression and Anxiety, 29,* 282–294; Seymour, K. E., Chronis-Tuscano, A., Halldorsdottir, T., Stupica, B., Owens, K., & Sacks, T. (2012). Emotion regulation mediates the relationship between ADHD and depressive symptoms in youth. *Journal of Abnormal Child Psychology, 40,* 595–606; Schmeichel, B. J., Volokhov, R. N., & Demaree, H. A. (2008). Working memory capacity and the self-regulation of emotional expression and experience. *Journal of Personality and Social Psychology, 95,* 1526–1540.

2   Sobanski, E., Banaschewski, T., Asherson, P., Buitelaar, J., Chen, W., Franke, B., … Faraone, S. V. (2010). Emotional lability in children and adolescents with attention deficit/hyperactivity disorder (ADHD): Clinical correlates and familial prevalence. *Journal of Child Psychology and Psychiatry, 51,* 915–923.

3   Barkley, R. A., & Fischer, M. (2010). The unique contribution of emotional impulsiveness to impairment in major life activities in hyperactive children as adults. *Journal of the American Academy of Child and Adolescent Psychiatry, 49,* 503–513; Surman, C.B.H., Biederman, J., Spencer, T., Yorks, D., Miller, C. A., Petty, C. R,

Faraone, S. V. (2011). Deficient emotional self-regulation and adult attention deficit hyperactivity disorder: A family risk analysis. *American Journal of Psychiatry, 168,* 617–623.

4 Barkley, R. A. (2010). Deficient emotional self-regulation: A core component of attention-deficit/hyperactivity disorder. *Journal of ADHD and Related Disorders, 1*(2), 5–37.

5 Brown, T. E. (2005). *Attention deficit disorder: The unfocused mind in children and adults.* New Haven, CT: Yale University Press; Castellanos, F. X., Sonuga-Barke, E. J., Scheres, A., Martino, A. D., Hyde, C., & Walters, J. R. (2005). Varieties of attention-deficit/hyperactivity disorder-related intra-individual variability. *Biological Psychiatry, 57,* 1416–1423; Perry, G. M., Sagvolden, T., & Faraone, S. V. (2010). Intra-individual variability in genetic and environmental models of attention-deficit/hyperactivity disorder. *American Journal of Medical Genetics. Part B, Neuropsychiatric Genetics, 153B,* 1094–1101; Sonuga-Barke, E. J., Wiersema, J. R., van der Meere, J. J., & Roeyers, H. (2010). Context-dependent dynamic processes in attention deficit/hyperactivity disorder: Differentiating common and unique effects of state regulation deficits and delay aversion. *Neuropsychology Review, 20*(1), 86–102; Uebel, H., Albrecht, B., Asherson, P., Börger, N. A., Butler, L., Chen, W., … Banaschewski, T. (2010). Performance variability, impulsivity errors and the impact of incentives as gender-independent endophenotypes for ADHD. *Journal of Child Psychology and Psychiatry, 51,* 210–218.

6 Gross, J. J., & Thompson, R. A. (2007). Emotion regulation: Conceptual foundations. In J. J. Gross (Ed.), *Handbook of emotion regulation* (pp. 3–24). New York, NY: Guilford Press.

7 Volkow, N. D., Wang, G., Newcorn, J. H., Kollins, S. H., Wigal, T. L., Telang, F., … Swanson, J. M. (2010). Motivation deficit in ADHD is associated with dysfunction of the dopamine reward pathway. *Molecular Psychiatry, 302,* 1084–1091; Volkow, N. D., Wang, G., Kollins, S. H., Wigal, T. L., Newcorn, J. H., Telang, F., … Swanson, J. M. (2009). Evaluating dopamine reward pathway in ADHD: Clinical implications. *Journal of the American Medical Association, 302,* 1084–1091.

8 Brown, *Attention deficit disorder*; Brown, T. E. (2013). *A new understanding of ADHD in children and adults: Executive function impairments.* New York, NY: Routledge.

9 LeDoux, J. E. (1996). *The emotional brain: The mysterious underpinnings of emotional life.* New York, NY: Simon & Schuster; LeDoux, J. E., & Schiller, D. (2009). The human amygdala: Insights from other animals. In P. J. Whalen & E. Phelps (Eds.), *The human amygdala* (pp. 43–60). New York, NY: Guilford Press; Vuilleumier, P. (2009). The role of the human amygdala in perception and attention. In P. J. Whalen & E. Phelps (Eds.), *The human amygdala* (pp. 220–249). New York, NY: Guilford Press; Buchanan, T. W., Tranel, D., & Adolphs, R. (2009). The human amygdala in social function. In P. J. Whalen & E. Phelps (Eds.), *The human amygdala* (pp. 289–318). New York, NY: Guilford Press.

10   Castellanos, F. X., Sonuga-Barke, E. J., Milham, M. P., & Tannock, R. (2006). Characterizing cognition in ADHD: Beyond executive dysfunction. *Trends in Cognitive Sciences, 10*, 117–123; Kerr, A., & Zelazo, P. D. (2004). Development of "hot" executive function: The children's gambling task. *Brain and Cognition, 55*, 148–157.

11   Dodge, K. A. (1991). Emotion and social information processing. In J. Garber & K. A. Dodge (Eds.), *Development of emotion regulation and dysregulation* (pp. 159–181). New York, NY: Cambridge University Press.

12   Kagan, J. (2010). *The temperamental thread: How genes, culture, time and luck make us who we are*. New York, NY: Dana Press, p. 60; see also Kagan, J. (2007). *What is emotion? History, measures, and meanings*. New Haven, CT: Yale University Press.

13   Ochsner, K. N., & Gross, J. J. (2007). Neural architecture of emotion regulation. In J. J. Gross (Ed.), *Handbook of emotional regulation* (pp. 87–109). New York, NY: Guilford Press.

14   Damasio, A. R. (2003). *Looking for Spinoza: Joy, sorrow, and the feeling brain*. Orlando, FL: Harcourt.

15   Dodge, Emotion and social information processing.

16   Damasio, *Looking for Spinoza*, p. 148.

17   LeDoux, *Emotional brain*, p. 65.

18   Bargh, J. A., Chen, M., & Burrows, L. (1996). Automaticity of social behavior: Direct effects of trait construct and stereotype activation on action. *Journal of Personality and Social Psychology, 71*, 230–244.

19   Bargh, J. A. (2005). Bypassing the will: Toward demystifying the nonconscious control of social behavior. In R. Hassin, J. Uleman, & J. A. Bargh (Eds.), *The new unconscious* (pp. 19–36). New York, NY: Oxford University Press; Wegner, D. M. (2005). Who is the controller of controlled processes? In R. Hassin, J. Uleman, & J. A. Bargh (Eds.), *The new unconscious* (pp. 19–36). New York, NY: Oxford University Press; Bargh, J. A. (2007). Introduction. In J. A. Bargh (Ed.), *Social psychology and the unconscious: The automaticity of higher mental processes* (pp. 1–9). New York, NY: Psychology Press; Bargh, J. A., & Barndollar, K. (1996). Automaticity in action: The unconscious as repository of chronic goals and motives. In P. M. Gollwitzer & J. A. Bargh (Eds.), *Psychology of action: Linking cognition and motivation to behavior* (pp. 457–481). New York, NY: Guilford Press; Bargh, J. A., & Williams, L. E. (2007). Nonconscious regulation of emotion. In J. J. Gross (Ed.), *Handbook of emotion regulation* (pp. 429–445). New York, NY: Guilford Press; Moors, A., & De Houwer, J. (2007). What is automaticity? An analysis of its component features and their interrelations. In J. A. Bargh (Ed.), *Social psychology and the unconscious: The automaticity of higher mental processes* (pp. 11–50). New York, NY: Psychology Press.

20   Schafer, R. (1976). *A new language for psychoanalysis*. New Haven, CT: Yale University Press.

21   Cortese, S., Kelly, C., Chabernaud, C., Proal, E., Di Martino, A., Milham, M. P., & Castellanos, F. X. (2012). Toward systems neuroscience of ADHD: A meta-analysis of 55 fMRI studies. *American Journal of Psychiatry, 169*, 1038–1055; Castellanos,

F. X., & Proal, E. (2012). Large-scale brain systems in ADHD: Beyond the prefrontal-striatal model. *Trends in Cognitive Sciences, 16*, 17–26.

22   Marner, L., Nyengaard, J. R., Tang, Y., & Pakkenberg, B. (2003). Marked loss of myelinated nerve fibers in the human brain with age. *Journal of Comparative Neurology, 462*, 144–152.

23   Nagel, B. J., Bathula, D., Herting, M., Schmitt, C., Kroenke, C. D., Fair, D., & Nigg, J. T. (2011). Altered white matter microstructure in children with attention-deficit/hyperactivity disorder. *Journal of the American Academy of Child and Adolescent Psychiatry, 50*, 283–292; Cortese, S., Imperati, D., Zhou, J., Proal, E., Klein, R. G., Mannuzza, S., ... Castellanos, F. X. (2013). White matter alterations at 33-year follow-up in adults with childhood attention-deficit/hyperactivity disorder. *Biological Psychiatry, 74*, 591–598.

24   Rubia, K., Halari, R., Cubillo, A., Mohammad, A. M., Brammer, M., & Taylor, E. (2009). Methylphenidate normalises activation and functional connectivity deficits in attention and motivation networks in medication-naïve children with ADHD during a rewarded continuous performance task. *Neuropharmacology, 57*, 640–652.

25   Zuo, X. N., Di Martino, A., Kelly, C., Shehzad, Z. E., Gee, D. G., Klein, D. F., ... Milham, M. P. (2010). The oscillating brain: Complex and reliable. *NeuroImage, 49*, 1432–1445.

26   Fassbender, C., Zhang, H., Buzy, W. M., Cortes, C. R., Mizuiri, D., Beckett, L., & Schweitzer, J. B. (2009). A lack of default network suppression is linked to increased distractibility in ADHD. *Brain Research, 1273*, 114–128.

27   Peterson, B. S., Potenza, M. N., Wang, Z., Zhu, H., Martin, A., Marsh, R., ... Yu, S. (2009). An fMRI study of the effects of stimulants on default-mode processing during stroop task performance in youths with ADHD. *American Journal of Psychiatry, 166*, 1286–1294.

28   Shaw, P., Eckstrand, K., Sharp, W., Blumenthal, J., Lerch, J. P., Greenstein, D., ... Rapoport, J. L. (2007). Attention-deficit/hyperactivity disorder is characterized by a delay in cortical maturation. *Proceedings of the National Academy of Sciences, 104*, 19649–19654.

29   Swanson, J., Baler, R. D., & Volkow, N. D. (2010). Understanding the effects of stimulant medications on cognition in individuals with attention-deficit hyperactivity disorder: A decade of progress. *Neuropsychopharmacology, 36*, 207–226.

30   Prince, J. B., & Wilens, T. E. (2009). Pharmacotherapy of ADHD and comorbidities. In Brown (Ed.), *ADHD comorbidities* (pp. 339–384).

31   Bedard, A. C., Jain, U., Johnson, S. H., & Tannock, R. (2007). Effects of methylphenidate on working memory components: Influence of measurement. *Journal of Child Psychology and Psychiatry, 48*, 872–880; Chelonis, J. J., Johnson, T. A., Ferguson, S. A., Berry, K. J., Kubacak, B., Edwards, M. C., & Paule, M. G. (2011). Effect of methylphenidate on motivation in children with attention-deficit/hyperactivity disorder. *Experimental and Clinical Psychopharmacology, 19*, 145–153; Metha, M. A., Goodyer, I. M., & Sahakian, B. J. (2004).

Methylphenidate improves working memory and set-shifting in AD/HD: Relationships to baseline memory capacity. *Journal of Child Psychology and Psychiatry*, *45*, 293–305; Shields, K., Hawk, L. W., Reynolds, B., Mazullo, R., Rhodes, J., Pelham, J. D., ... Gangloff, B. P. (2009). Effects of methylphenidate on discounting of delayed rewards in attention deficit/hyperactivity disorder. *Experimental and Clinical Psychopharmacology*, *17*, 291–301.

32 Brown, T. E., Holdnack, J., Saylor, K., Adler, L., Spencer, T., Williams, D. W., ... Kelsey, D. (2011). Effect of atomoxetine on executive function impairments in adults with ADHD. *Journal of Attention Disorders*, *15*, 130–138; Spencer, T. J., Adler, L. A., Weisler, R. H., & Youcha, S. H. (2008). Triple-bead mixed amphetamine salts (SPD465), a novel, enhanced extended release amphetamine formulation for the treatment of adults with ADHD: A randomized, double-blind, multicenter, placebo-controlled study. *Journal of Clinical Psychiatry*, *69*, 1437–1448.

33 Manos, M. J., Brams, M., Childress, A. C., Findling, R. L., López, F. A., & Jensen, P. S. (2010). Changes in emotions related to medications used to treat ADHD. *Journal of Attention Disorders*, *15*, 101–112. doi:10.1177/1870054710381230

34 Groom, M. J., Scerif, G., Liddle, P. F., Batty, M. J., Liddle, E. B., Roberts, K. L., ... Hollis, C. (2010). Effects of motivation and medication on electrophysiological markers of response inhibition in children with attention-deficit/hyperactivity disorder. *Biological Psychiatry*, *67*, 624–631.

35 Solanto, M. V., Wender, E. H., & Bartell, S. S. (1997). Effects of methylphenidate and behavioral contingencies on sustained attention in attention-deficit hyperactivity disorder: A test of the reward dysfunction hypothesis. *Journal of Child and Adolescent Psychopharmacology*, *7*, 123–136.

36 Kohls, G., Herpertz-Dahlmann, B., & Konrad, K. (2009). Hyperresponsiveness to social rewards in children and adolescents with attention-deficit/ hyperactivity disorder (ADHD). *Behavioral and Brain Functions*, *5*. doi: 10.1186/1744-9081-5-20

37 Brown, T. E. (2009). *ADHD comorbidities: Handbook for ADHD complications in children and adults*. Washington, DC: American Psychiatric Publishing; Brown, *Attention deficit disorder*; Brown, *A new understanding of ADHD*.

38 Safer, J. (2002). *The normal one: Life with a difficult or damaged sibling*. New York, NY: Free Press.

39 Wilford, J. N. (2008). How epidemics shaped the modern metropolis. *New York Times*, April 15, 2008. http://www.nytimes.com/2008/04/15/science/15chol.html?pagewanted=all&_r=0.

Chapter 2: Eric

1 Kessler, R. C., Adler, L., Barkley, R., Biederman, J., Conners, C. K., Demler, O., ... Zaslavsky, A. M. (2006). The prevalence and correlates of adult ADHD in the United States: Results from the National Comorbidity Survey Replication. *American Journal of Psychiatry*, *163*, 716–723; Kessler, R. C., Adler, L. A., Barkley, R., Biederman, J., Conners, C. K., Faraone, S. V., ... Zaslavsky, A. M. (2005). Patterns and predictors of attention-deficit/hyperactivity disorder persistence into

adulthood: Results from the National Comorbidity Survey Replication. *Biological Psychiatry, 57,* 1442–1452.

2 Brown, T. E., & McMullen, W. J., Jr. (2001, June). Attention deficit disorders and sleep/arousal disturbance. *Annals of New York Academy of Sciences, 931,* 271–286.

3 Marlatt, G. A., & Witkiewitz, K. (2010). Update on harm-reduction policy and intervention research. *Annual Review of Clinical Psychology, 6,* 591–606.

4 Barkley, R., & Cox, D. (2007). A review of driving risks and impairments associated with attention-deficit/hyperactivity disorder and the effects of stimulant medication on driving performance. *Journal of Safety Research, 38,* 113–128; Reimer, B., Mehler, B., D'Ambrosio, L. A., & Fried, R. (2010). The impact of distractions on young adult drivers with attention deficit hyperactivity disorder (ADHD). *Accident Analysis and Prevention, 42,* 842–851; Thompson, A. L., Molina, B. S., Pelham, W., & Gnagy, E. M. (2007). Risky driving in adolescents and young adults with childhood ADHD. *Journal of Pediatric Psychology, 32,* 745–759; Fried, R., Monuteaux, M. C., Hughes, S., Jakubowski, A., & Biederman, J. (2009). Driving deficits in young adults with attention-deficit/hyperactivity disorder. *Journal of ADHD and Related Disorders, 1*(1), 49–57.

5 Torrente, F., Lischinsky, A., Torralva, T., Lopez, P., Roca, M., & Manes, F. (2010, March 5). Not always hyperactive? Elevated apathy scores in adolescents and adults with ADHD. *Journal of Attention Disorders.* doi:10.1177/1087054709359887

6 Campbell, S. B., & Stauffenberg, C. v. (2009). Delay and inhibition as early predictors of ADHD symptoms in third grade. *Journal of Abnormal Child Psychology, 37,* 1–15.

7 Luman, M., Oosterlaan, J., & Sergeant, J. A. (2005). The impact of reinforcement contingencies on AD/HD: A review and theoretical appraisal. *Clinical Psychology Review, 25,* 183–213; Luman, M., Tripp, G., & Scheres, A. (2010). Identifying the neurobiology of altered reinforcement sensitivity in ADHD: A review and research agenda. *Neuroscience and Biobehavioral Reviews, 34,* 744–754; Marco, R., Miranda, A., Schlotz, W., Melia, A., Mulligan, A., Müller, U., … Sonuga-Barke, E. J. (2009). Delay and reward choice in ADHD: An experimental test of the role of delay aversion. *Neuropsychology, 23,* 367–380; Sonuga-Barke, E. J. (2002). Psychological heterogeneity in AD/HD: A dual pathway model of behaviour and cognition. *Behavioural Brain Research, 130*(1–2), 29–36; Sonuga-Barke, E. J. (2003). The dual pathway model of AD/HD: An elaboration of neuro-developmental characteristics. *Neuroscience and Biobehavioral Reviews, 27,* 593–604; Strohle, A., Stoy, M., Wrase, J., Schwarzer, S., Schlagenhauf, F., Huss, M., … Heinz, A. (2008). Reward anticipation and outcomes in adult males with attention-deficit/hyperactivity disorder. *NeuroImage, 39,* 966–972; Toplak, M. E., Jain, U., & Tannock, R. (2005, June 27). Executive and motivational processes in adolescents with attention-deficit-hyperactivity disorder (ADHD). *Behavioral and Brain Functions, 1*(8). doi: 10.1186/1744-9081-1-8

8 Volkow, N. D., Wang, G., Newcorn, J. H., Kollins, S. H., Wigal, T. L., Telang, F., … Swanson, J. M. (2010). Motivation deficit in ADHD is associated with

dysfunction of the dopamine reward pathway. *Molecular Psychiatry, 302,* 1084–1091; Volkow, N. D., Wang, G., Kollins, S. H., Wigal, T. L., Newcorn, J. H., Telang, F., ... Swanson, J. M. (2009). Evaluating dopamine reward pathway in ADHD: Clinical implications. *Journal of the American Medical Association, 302,* 1084–1091.

9   Plichta, M. M., Vasic, N., Wolf, R. C., Lesch, K. P., Brummer, D., Jacob, C., ... Grön, G. (2009). Neural hyporesponsiveness and hyperresponsiveness during immediate and delayed reward processing in adult attention-deficit/hyperactivity disorder. *Biological Psychiatry, 65,* 7–14; Scheres, A., Milham, M. P., Knutson, B., & Castellanos, F. X. (2008). Ventral striatal hyporesponsiveness during reward anticipation in attention-deficit/hyperactivity disorder. *Biological Psychiatry, 61,* 720–724; Tripp, G., & Wickens, J. R. (2008). Research review: Dopamine transfer deficit; A neurobiological theory of altered reinforcement mechanisms in ADHD. *Journal of Child Psychology and Psychiatry, 49,* 691–704.

Chapter 3: Karen

1   Locascio, G., Mahone, E. M., Eason, S. H., & Cutting, L. E. (2010). Executive dysfunction among children with reading comprehension deficits. *Journal of Learning Disabilities, 43,* 441–454; Sesma, H. W., Mahone, E. M., Levine, T., Eason, S. H., & Cutting, L. E. (2009). The contribution of executive skills to reading comprehension. *Child Neuropsychology, 15,* 232–246; Shaywitz, S. E., & Shaywitz, B. A. (2008). Paying attention to reading: The neurobiology of reading and dyslexia. *Development and Psychopathology, 20,* 1329–1349; Swanson, H. L., Zheng, X., & Jerman, O. (2009). Working memory, short-term memory, and reading disabilities: A selective meta-analysis of the literature. *Journal of Learning Disabilities, 43,* 260–287.

2   Brown, T. E., Reichel, P. C., & Quinlan, D. M. (2011). Extended time improves reading comprehension for adolescents with ADHD. *Open Journal of Psychiatry, 1,* 79–87.

3   Pomerantz, E. M., Grolnick, W. S., & Price, C. E. (2005). Role of parents in how children approach achievement: A dynamic process perspective. In A. J. Elliot & C. S. Dweck (Eds.), *Handbook of competence and motivation* (pp. 259–278). New York, NY: Guilford Press.

4   Boszormenyi-Nagy, I., & Spark, G. M. (1973). *Invisible loyalties: Reciprocity in intergenerational family therapy.* New York, NY: Harper & Row; Safer, J. (2002). *The normal one: Life with a difficult or damaged sibling.* New York, NY: Simon & Schuster; Stierlin, H. (1974). *Separating parents and adolescents: A perspective on running away, schizophrenia and waywardness.* New York, NY: Quadrangle; Winnicott, D. W. (1965). *The family and individual development.* New York, NY: Tavistock.

5   Levy, F. (2004). Synaptic gating and ADHD: A biological theory of comorbidity of ADHD and anxiety. *Neuropsychopharmacology, 29,* 1589–1596.

Chapter 4: Martin

1 Mangels, J. A., Butterfield, B., Lamb, J., Good, C., & Dweck, C. S. (2006). Why do beliefs about intelligence influence learning success? A social cognitive neuroscience model. *Social Cognitive and Affective Neuroscience, 2,* 75–86; Dweck, C. S., & Molden, D. C. (2005). Self-theories: Their impact on competence motivation and acquisition. In A. J. Elliot & C. S. Dweck (Eds.), *Handbook of competence and motivation* (pp. 122–140). New York, NY: Guilford Press.

2 Antshel, K. M., Faraone, S. V., Stallone, K., Nave, A., Kaufmann, F. A., Doyle, A., ... Biederman, J. (2007). Is attention deficit hyperactivity disorder a valid diagnosis in the presence of high IQ? Results from the MGH Longitudinal Family Studies of ADHD. *Journal of Child Psychology and Psychiatry, 48,* 687–694; Antshel, K. M., Faraone, S. V., Maglione, K., Doyle, A., Fried, R., Seidman, L., & Biederman, J. (2008). Temporal stability of ADHD in the high-IQ population: Results from the MGH Longitudinal Family Studies of ADHD. *Journal of the American Academy of Child and Adolescent Psychiatry, 47,* 817–825; Brown, T. E., Reichel, P. C., & Quinlan, D. M. (2009). Executive function impairments in high IQ adults with ADHD. *Journal of Attention Disorders, 13,* 161–167; Brown, T. E., Reichel, P. C., & Quinlan, D. M. (2011). Executive function impairments in high IQ children and adolescents with ADHD. *Open Journal of Psychiatry, 1,* 56–65; Kaplan, B. J., Crawford, S. G., Dewey, D. M., & Fisher, G. C. (2000). IQs of children with ADHD are normally distributed. *Journal of Learning Disabilities, 33,* 425–432; Schuck, S. E., & Crinella, F. M. (2005). Why children with ADHD do not have low IQs. *Journal of Learning Disabilities, 38,* 262–280.

3 Ardila, A., Pineda, D., & Rosselli, M. (2000). Correlation between intelligence test scores and executive function measures. *Archives of Clinical Neuropsychology, 15*(1), 31–36; Brown, T. E. (2005). *Attention deficit disorder: The unfocused mind in children and adults.* New Haven, CT: Yale University Press; Delis, D. C., Lansing, A., Houston, W. S., Wetter, S., Han, S. D., Jacobson, M., ... Kramer, J. (2007). Creativity lost: The importance of testing higher-level executive functions in school-age children and adolescents. *Journal of Psychoeducational Assessment, 25*(1), 29–40; Rommelse, N. N., Altink, M. E., Oosterlaan, J., Buschgens, C. J., Buitelaar, J., & Sergeant, J. A. (2008). Support for an independent familial segregation of executive and intelligence endophenotypes in ADHD families. *Psychological Medicine, 38,* 1595–1606.

4 Aronson, J., & Steele, C. M. (2005). Stereotypes and the fragility of academic competence, motivation, and self-concept. In A. J. Elliot & C. S. Dweck (Eds.), *Handbook of competence and motivation* (pp. 436–456). New York, NY: Guilford Press.

5 Shafran, R., & Mansell, W. (2001). Perfectionism and psychopathology: A review of research and treatment. *Clinical Psychology Review, 21,* 878–906.

6 Bowlby, J. (1978). Attachment theory and its therapeutic implications. In S. Feinstein & P. L. Giovacchini (Eds.), *Adolescent psychiatry: Developmental and clinical studies* (pp. 5–33). Chicago: University of Chicago; Chen, S., Fitzsimons, G. M., & Andersen, S. M. (2007). Automaticity in close relationships. In J. A. Bargh (Ed.),

Social psychology and the unconscious: The automaticity of higher mental processes (pp. 133–172). New York, NY: Psychology Press.

7 Sullivan, H. S. (1953). *The interpersonal theory of psychiatry.* New York, NY: Norton.

8 Woodward, L. J., & Ferguson, D. M. (2000). Childhood peer relationship problems and later risks of educational under-achievement and unemployment. *Journal of Child Psychology and Psychiatry, 41,* 191–201.

9 Cherek, D. R., Lane, S. D., & Dougherty, D. M. (2002). Possible amotivational effects following marijuana smoking under laboratory conditions. *Experimental and Clinical Psychopharmacology, 10*(1), 26–38; Lane, S. D., Cherek, D. R., Pietras, C. J., & Steinberg, J. L. (2005). Performance of heavy marijuana-smoking adolescents on a laboratory measure of motivation. *Addictive Behaviours, 30,* 815–828; Medina, K. L., Hanson, K. L., Schweinsburg, A. D., Cohen-Zion, M., Nagel, B. J., & Tapert, S. F. (2007). Neuropsychological functioning in adolescent marijuana users: Subtle deficits detectable after a month of abstinence. *Journal of the International Neuropsychological Society, 13,* 807–820.

10 Weinstein, A., Brickner, O., Lerman, H., Greemland, M., Bloch, M., Lester, H., … Even-Sapir, E. (2008). A study investigating the acute dose-response effects of 13 mg and 17 mg Delta 9- tetrahydrocannabinol on cognitive-motor skills, subjective and autonomic measures in regular users of marijuana. *Journal of Psychopharmacology, 22,* 441–451.

11 Rhodewalt, F., & Vohs, K. D. (2005). Defensive strategies, motivation, and the self: A self-regulatory process view. In A. J. Elliot and C. S. Dweck (Eds.), *Handbook of competence and motivation* (pp. 548–565). New York, NY: Guilford Press.

12 Shaw, P., Eckstrand, K., Sharp, W., Blumenthal, J., Lerch, J. P., Greenstein, D., … Rapoport, J. L. (2007). Attention-deficit/hyperactivity disorder is characterized by a delay in cortical maturation. *Proceedings of the National Academy of Sciences, 104,* 19649–19654.

Chapter 5: Sarah

1 Brown, T. E. (1996). *Brown Attention Deficit Disorder Scale for Adults.* San Antonio, TX: Psychological Corporation.

2 Quinlan, D. M., & Brown, T. E. (2003). Assessment of short-term verbal memory impairments in adolescents and adults with ADHD. *Journal of Attention Disorders, 6,* 143–152.

3 American Psychiatric Association. (2000). *Diagnostic and statistical manual of mental disorders* (4th ed., text rev.). Washington, DC: Author; American Psychiatric Association. (2013). *Diagnostic and statistical manual of mental disorders* (5th ed.). Washington, DC: Author.

4 Faraone, S. V., Biederman, J., Spencer, T., Mick, E., Murray, K., … Monuteaux, M. C. (2006). Diagnosing adult attention deficit hyperactivity disorder: Are late onset and subthreshold diagnoses valid? *American Journal of Psychiatry, 163,* 1720–1729.

5 Faraone, S. V., Kunwar, A., Adamson, J., & Biederman, J. (2009). Personality traits among ADHD adults: Implications of late-onset and sub-threshold diagnoses. *Psychological Medicine, 39,* 685–693.

6   Akiskal, H., & Cassano, G. B. (Eds.). (1997). *Dysthymia and the spectrum of chronic depressions.* New York, NY: Guilford Press; Subodh, B. N., Avashi, A., & Chakrabarti, S. (2008). Psychosocial impact of dysthymia: A study among married patients. *Journal of Affective Disorders, 109,* 199–204; Sansone, R. A., & Sansone, L. A. (2009). Dysthymic disorder: Forlorn and overlooked? *Psychiatry, 6*(5), 46–50.

7   Hammen, C. L. (1995). Stress and the course of unipolar and bipolar disorders. Does stress cause psychiatric illness? In C. M. Mazure (Ed.), *Does stress cause psychiatric illness?* (pp. 87–110). Washington, DC: American Psychiatric Press.

8   Brown, T. E. (2000). Emerging understandings of attention-deficit disorders and comorbidities. In T. E. Brown (Ed.), *Attention deficit disorders and comorbidities in children, adolescents and adults* (pp. 3–55). Washington, DC: American Psychiatric Publishing.

9   McEwen, B. S., & Parsons, B. (1982). Gonadal steroid action on the brain: Neurochemistry and neuropharmacology. *Annual Review of Pharmacology and Toxicology, 22,* 555–598; McEwen, B. S. (1991). Non-genomic and genomic effects of steroids on neural activity. *Trends in Pharmacological Sciences, 4,* 141–147; Thompson, T. L., & Moss, R. L. (1994). Estrogen regulation of dopamine release in the nucleus accumbens: Genomic and non-genomic-mediated effects. *Journal of Neurochemistry, 62,* 1750–1756.

10 Sherwin, B. B. (1998). Estrogen and cognitive functioning in women. *Proceedings of the Society for Experimental Biology and Medicine, 217*(1), 17–22; Phillips, S. M., & Sherwin, B. B. (1992). Effects of estrogen on memory function in surgically menopausal women. *Psychoneuroendocrinology, 17,* 485–495.

11 Shaywitz, S. E., Shaywitz, B. A., Pugh, K. B., Fullbright, R. K., Skudlarski, P., Mencl, W. E., … Gore, J. C. (1999). Effect of estrogen on brain activation patterns in postmenopausal women during working memory tasks. *Journal of the American Medical Association, 281,* 1197–1202.

12 Sherwin, B. B., & Henry, J. F. (2008). Brain aging modulates the neuroprotective effects of estrogen on selective aspects of cognition in women: A critical review. *Frontiers in Neuroendocrinology, 29*(1), 88–113; Greendale, G. A., Huang, M. H., Wright, R. G. Seeman, T., Luetters, C., Avis, N. E., … Karlamangla, A. S. (2009). Effects of the menopause transition and hormone use on cognitive performance of midlife women. *Neurology, 72,* 1850–1857; Duff, S. J., & Hampson, E. (2000). A beneficial effect of estrogen on working memory in postmenopausal women taking hormone replacement therapy. *Hormones and Behavior, 38,* 222–276; Elsabagh, S., Hartley, D. E., & File, S. E. (2007). Cognitive function in late versus early postmenopausal stage. *Maturitas, 56,* 84–93.

13 Ahles, T. A., Saykin, A. J., Furstenberg, B. C., Cole, B., Mott, L. A., Skalla, K., … Silberfarb, P. M. (2002). Neurologic impact of standard-dose systemic chemotherapy in long-term survivors of breast cancer and lymphoma. *Journal of Clinical Oncology, 20,* 485–493; Reid-Arndt, S. A., Yee, A., Perry, M. C., & Hsieh, C. (2009). Cognitive and psychological factors associated with early post-treatment

functional outcomes in breast cancer survivors. *Journal of Psychosocial Oncology,* *27,* 415–434.

14 Ahles, T. A., & Saykin, A. J. (2007). Candidate mechanisms for chemotherapy-induced cognitive changes. *Nature Reviews. Cancer, 7,* 192–201; Correa, D. D., & Ahles, T. A. (2007). Cognitive adverse effects of chemotherapy in breast cancer patients. *Current Opinion in Supportive and Palliative Care, 1*(1), 57–62.

15 National Cancer Institute. (2005). Dexmethylphenidate reduces some symptoms of chemobrain. Retrieved from http://www.cancer.gov/clinical trials/results/chemobrain0605. (Link may no longer be available.)

16 Epperson, C. N., Pittman, B., Czarkowski, K. A., Bradley, J., Quinlan, D. M., & Brown, T. E. (2011). Impact of atomoxetine on subjective attention and memory difficulties in perimenopausal and postmenopausal women. *Menopause: Journal of the North American Menopause Society, 18*(5), 1–7.

17 Barkley, R. A. (2011). *Barkley Deficits in Executive Functioning Scale (BDEFS).* New York, NY: Guilford Press; Brown, T. E. (2006). Executive functions and attention deficit hyperactivity disorder: Implications of two conflicting views. *International Journal of Disability, Development and Education, 53*(1), 35–46.

18 Brown, T. E. (2005). *Attention deficit disorders: The unfocused mind in children and adults.* New Haven, CT: Yale University Press.

Chapter 6: Mike

1 Rommelse, N. N., Altink, M. E., Oosterlaan, J., Buschgens, C. J., Buitelaar, J. K., & Sergeant, J. (2008). Support for an independent familial segregation of executive and intelligence endophenotypes in ADHD families. *Psychological Medicine, 38,* 1595–1606. doi: 10.1017/S0033291708002869

2 Ardila, A., Pineda, D., & Rosselli, M. (2000). Correlation between intelligence test scores and executive function measures. *Archives of Clinical Neuropsychology, 15*(1), 31–36; Delis, D. C., Houston, W. S., Wetter, S., Han, S. D., Jacobson, M., Holdnack, J., Kramer, J. (2007). Creativity lost: The importance of testing higher-level executive functions in school-age children and adolescents. *Journal of Psychoeducational Assessment, 25,* 29–40; Brown, T. E., Reichel, P. C., & Quinlan, D. M. (2009). Executive function impairments in high IQ adults with ADHD. *Journal of Attention Disorders, 13,* 161–171; Brown, T. E., Reichel, P. C., & Quinlan, D. M. (2011). Executive function impairments in high IQ children and adolescents with ADHD. *Open Journal of Psychiatry, 1,* 56–65.

3 Smith, M. E., & Farah, M. J. (2011). Are prescription stimulants "smart pills"? The epidemiology and cognitive neuroscience of prescription stimulant use by normal healthy individuals. *Psychological Bulletin, 137,* 717–741; Rabiner, D. L., Anastopoulos, A. D., Costello, E. J., Hoyle, R. H., McCabe, S. E., & Scott, H. (2009). Motives and perceived consequences of nonmedical ADHD medication use by college students: Are students treating themselves for attention problems? *Journal*

of Attention Disorders, 13, 259–270; Swanson, J. M., Wigal, T. L., & Volkow, N. D. (2011). Contrast of medical and nonmedical use of stimulant drugs, basis for the distinction, and risk of addiction: Comment on Smith and Farah. *Psychological Bulletin, 137*, 742–748; Rabiner, D. L., Anastopoulos, A. D., Costello, E. J., Hoyle, R. H., & Swartzwelder, H. S. (2010). Predictors of nonmedical ADHD medication use by college students. *Journal of Attention Disorders, 13*, 640–648; Peterkin, A. L., Crone, C. C., Sheridan, M. J., & Wise, T. N. (2010, April 21). Cognitive performance enhancement: Misuse or self-treatment? *Journal of Attention Disorders*, pp. 1–6. doi: 10.1177/1087054710365980; Arria, A. M., Garnier-Dykstra, L. M., Caldeira, K. M., Vincent, K. B., O'Grady, K. E., & Wish, E. D. (2011). Persistent nonmedical use of prescription stimulants among college students: Possible association with ADHD symptoms. *Journal of Attention Disorder, 15*, 347–356.

4 Markus, H., & Nurius, P. (1986). Possible selves. *American Psychologist, 41*, 954–969.

5 Brown, M. A., & Stopa, L. (2007). The spotlight effect and the illusion of transparency in social anxiety. *Journal of Anxiety Disorders, 21*, 804–819; Gilovich, T., Medvec, V. H., & Savitsky, K. (1998). The illusion of transparency: Biased assessments of others' ability to read one's emotional states. *Journal of Personality and Social Psychology, 75*, 332–346.

6 Kessler, R. C., McGonagle, K. A., Zhao, S., Nelson, C. B., Hughes, M., Eshleman, S., … Kendler, K. S. (1994). Lifetime and 12-month prevalence of DSM-III-R psychiatric disorders in the United States: Results from the National Comorbidity Survey. *Archives of General Psychiatry, 51*, 8–19; Kessler, R. C., Adler, L., Barkley, R., Biederman, J., Conners, C. K., Demler, O., … Zaslavsky, A. M. (2006). The prevalence and correlates of adult ADHD in the United States: Results from the National Comorbidity Survey Replication. *American Journal of Psychiatry, 163*, 716–723.

7 Stierlin, H. (1974). *Separating parents and adolescents*. New York, NY: Quadrangle; Boszormenyi-Nagy, I., & Spark, G. M. (1973). *Invisible loyalties: Reciprocity in intergenerational therapy*. New York, NY: Harper & Row.

Chapter 7: Lisa

1 Brown, T. E. (2005). *Attention deficit disorder: The unfocused mind in children and adults*. New Haven, CT: Yale University Press.

2 Ibid.

3 Erhardt, D., & Hinshaw, S. P. (1994). Initial sociometric impressions of attention-deficit hyperactivity disorder and comparison boys: Predictions from social behaviors and from nonbehavioral variables. *Journal of Consulting and Clinical Psychology, 62*, 833–842; Melnick, S. M., & Hinshaw, S. P. (1996). What they want and what they get: The social goals of boys with ADHD and comparison boys. *Journal of Abnormal Child Psychology, 24*, 169–185; Blachman, D. R., & Hinshaw, S. P. (2002). Patterns of friendship among girls with and without attention-deficit/hyperactivity disorder. *Journal of Abnormal Child Psychology, 30*, 625–640; Hoza, B. (2007). Peer functioning in children with ADHD. *Journal*

of Pediatric Psychology, 32, 655–663; Miller, M., & Hinshaw, S. P. (2010). Does childhood executive function predict adolescent functional outcomes in girls with ADHD? *Journal of Abnormal Child Psychology, 38,* 315–326; Miller, M., Nevado-Montenegro, A. J., & Hinshaw, S. P. (2012). Childhood executive function to predict outcomes in young adult females with and without childhood diagnosed ADHD. *Journal of Abnormal Child Psychology, 40,* 657–668. doi: 10.1007/s10802-011-9599-y; Miller, M., Sheridan, M., Cardoos, S. L., & Hinshaw, S. P. (2013). Impaired decision-making as a young adult outcome of girls diagnosed with attention-deficit/hyperactivity disorder in childhood. *Journal of the International Neuropsychological Society, 19*(1), 110–114. doi: 10.101/S1355617712000975

4   Reiersen, A. M., Constantino, J. N., Volk, H. E., & Todd, R. D. (2007). Autistic traits in a population-based ADHD twin sample. *Journal of Child Psychology and Psychiatry, 48,* 464–472; Rommelse, N. N., Franke, B., Geurts, H. M., Hartman, C. A., & Buitelaar, J. K. (2010). Shared heritability of attention-deficit/hyperactivity disorder and autism spectrum disorder. *European Child & Adolescent Psychiatry, 19,* 281–295.

5   Brown, T. E., Reichel, P. C., & Quinlan, D. M. (2011). Executive function impairments in high IQ children and adolescents with ADHD. *Open Journal of Psychiatry, 1,* 56–65; Brown, T. E., Reichel, P. C., & Quinlan, D.M. (2009). Executive function impairments in high IQ adults with ADHD. *Journal of Attention Disorders, 13,* 161–167.

6   Croyle, K. L., & Waltz, J. (2007). Subclinical self-harm: Range of behaviors, extent, and associated characteristics. *American Journal of Orthopsychiatry, 77,* 332–342; Nixon, M. K., Cloutier, P., & Jansson, S. M. (2008). Nonsuicidal self-harm in youth: A population-based survey. *Canadian Medical Association Journal, 178,* 306–312.

7   Klonsky, E. D., & Olino, T. M. (2008). Identifying clinically distinct subgroups of self-injurers among young adults: A latent class analysis. *Journal of Consulting and Clinical Psychology, 76,* 22–27.

Chapter 8: Steve

1   Biederman, J., Petty, C. R., Fried, R., Kaiser, R., Dolan, C. R., Schoenfeld, S., … Faraone, S. V. (2008). Educational and occupational underattainment in adults with attention-deficit/hyperactivity disorder: A controlled study. *Journal of Clinical Psychiatry, 69,* 1217–1222; Biederman, J., Faraone, S. V., Spencer, T. J., Mick, E., Monuteaux, M. C., & Aleardi, M. (2006). Functional impairments in adults with self-reports of diagnosed ADHD: A controlled study of 1001 adults in the community. *Journal of Clinical Psychiatry, 67,* 524–540; de Graaf, R., Kessler, R. C., Fayyad, J., ten Have, M., Alonso, J., Angermeyer, M., … Posada-Villa, J. (2008). The prevalence and effects of adult attention-deficit/hyperactivity disorder (ADHD) on the performance of workers: Results from the WHO World Mental Health Survey Initiative. *Occupational and Environmental Medicine, 65,* 835–842; Barkley, R. A., & Murphy, K. R. (2010). Impairment in occupational functioning

and adult ADHD: The predictive utility of executive function (EF) ratings versus EF tests. *Clinical Neuropsychology, 25,* 157–173.

2 Britton, J. C., Rauch, S. L., Rosso, I. M., Killgore, W.D.S., Price, L. M., Ragan, J., … Stewart, S. E. (2010). Cognitive inflexibility and frontal-cortical activation in pediatric obsessive-compulsive disorder. *Journal of the American Academy of Child and Adolescent Psychiatry, 49,* 944–953.

3 Biederman, J., Faraone, S. V., Spencer, T. J., Mick, E., Monuteaux, M. C., & Aleardi, M. (2006). Functional impairments in adults with self-reports of diagnosed ADHD: A controlled study of 1001 adults in the community. *Journal of Clinical Psychiatry, 67,* 524–540.

4 Minde, K., Eakin, L., Hechtman, L., Ochs, E., Bouffard, R., Greenfield, B., & Looper, K. (2003). The psychosocial functioning of children and spouses of adults with ADHD. *Journal of Child Psychology and Psychiatry, 44,* 637–646.

5 Eakin, L., Minde, K., Hechtman, L., Ochs, E., Krane, E., Bouffard, R., Greenfield, B., & Looper, K. (2004). The marital and family functioning of adults with ADHD and their spouses. *Journal of Attention Disorders, 8,* 1–10.

6 Grzadzinski, R., Di Martino, A., Brady, E., Mairena, M. A., O'Neale, M., Petkova, E., … Castellanos, F. X. (2010). Examining autistic traits in children with ADHD: Does the autism spectrum extend to ADHD? *Journal of Autism and Developmental Disorders, 41,* 1178–1191; Nijmeijer, J. S., Minderaa, R. B., Buitelaar, J. K., Mulligan, A., Hartment, C. A., & Hoekstra, P. J. (2008). Attention-deficit/hyperactivity disorder and social dysfunctioning. *Clinical Psychology Review, 28,* 692–708; St. Pourcain, B. S., Mandy, W. P., Heron J., Golding, J., Smith, G. D., & Skuse, D. H. (2011). Links between co-occurring social-communication and hyperactive-inattentive trait trajectories. *Journal of the American Academy of Child and Adolescent Psychiatry, 50,* 892–902; van der Meer, J. M., Oerlemans, A. M., van Steijn, D. J., Lappenschaar, M. G., de Sonneville, L. M., Buitelaar, J. K., & Rommelse, N. N. (2012). Are autism spectrum disorder and attention-deficit/hyperactivity disorder different manifestations of one overarching disorder? Cognitive and symptom evidence from a clinical and population-based sample. *Journal of the American Academy of Child and Adolescent Psychiatry, 51,* 1160–1172.

7 Nijmeijer, J. S., Hoekstra, P. J., Minderaa, R. B., Buitclaar, J. K., Altink, M. E., Buschgens, C. J., … Hartman, C. A. (2009). PDD symptoms in ADHD, an independent familial trait? *Journal of Abnormal Child Psychology, 37,* 443–453; Ronald, A., Simonoff, E., Kuntsi, J., Asherson, P., & Plomin, R. (2008). Evidence for overlapping genetic influences on autistic and ADHD behaviours in a community twin sample. *Journal of Child Psychology and Psychiatry, 49,* 535–542.

8 Page, T. (2009). *Parallel play: Growing up with undiagnosed Asperger's.* New York, NY: Doubleday, pp. 182, 185.

9 Ibid., p. 178.

10 Ibid., p. 6.

Chapter 9: Sue

1   Langberg, J. M., Epstein, J. N., Altaye, M., Molina, B. S., Arnold, L. E., & Vitiello, B. (2008). The transition to middle school is associated with changes in the developmental trajectory of ADHD symptomatology in young adolescents with ADHD. *Journal of Clinical Child and Adolescent Psychology, 37*, 651–663.
2   Csikszentmihalyi, M., & Larson, R. (1984). *Being adolescent*. New York Basic Books, p. xiii.
3   Christiansen, H., Oades, R. D., Psychogiou, L., Hauffa, B. P., & Sonuga-Barke, E. J. (2010). Does the cortisol response to stress mediate the link between expressed emotion and oppositional behavior in attention-deficit/hyperactivity-disorder (ADHD)? *Behavioral and Brain Functions, 6*(45). doi: 10.1166/1744-9001

Chapter 10: Matt

1   Gau, S. S.-F., & Chiang, H. L. (2009). Sleep problems and disorders among adolescents with persistent and subthreshold attention-deficit/hyperactivity disorders. *Sleep, 32*, 671–679.

Chapter 11: Lois

1   Quinlan, D. M., & Brown, T. E. (2003). Assessment of short-term verbal memory impairments in adolescents and adults with ADHD. *Journal of Attention Disorders, 6*, 143–152; Martinussen, R., Hayden, J., Hogg-Johnson, S., & Tannock, R. (2005). A meta-analysis of working memory impairments in children with attention-deficit/hyperactivity disorder. *Journal of the American Academy of Child and Adolescent Psychiatry, 44*, 377–384.
2   Schmeichel, B. J., Volokhov, R. N., & Demaree, H. A. (2008). Working memory capacity and the self-regulation of emotional expression and experience. *Journal of Personality and Social Psychology, 95*, 1526–1540.
3   Levy, F. (2004). Synaptic gating and ADHD: A biological theory of comorbidity of ADHD and anxiety. *Neuropsychopharmacology, 29*, 1589–1596.
4   Timpano, K. R., Exner, C., Glaesmer, H., Rief, W., Keshaviah, A., Brähler, E., & Wilhelm, S. (2011). The epidemiology of the proposed DSM-5 hoarding disorder: Exploration of the acquisition specifier, associated features, and distress. *Journal of Clinical Psychiatry, 72*, 780–786; Frost, R. O., Steketee, G., & Tolin, D. F. (2011). Comorbidity in hoarding disorder. *Depression and Anxiety, 28*, 876–884; Hartl, T. L., Duffany, S. R., Allen, G. J., Steketee, G., & Frost, R. O. (2005). Relationships among compulsive hoarding, trauma, and attention-deficit/hyperactivity disorder. *Behaviour Research and Therapy, 43*, 269–276.
5   Biederman, J., Milberger, S., Faraone, S. V., Kiely, K., Guite, J., Mick, E., … Reed, E. (1995). Family-environment risk factors for attention-deficit hyperactivity disorder. *Archives of General Psychiatry, 52*, 464–470.

6   Shechner, T., Britton, J. C., Pérez-Edgar, K., Bar-Haim, Y., Ernst, M., Fox, N. A., … Pine, D. S. (2012). Attention biases, anxiety, and development: Toward or away from threats or rewards? *Depression and Anxiety, 29,* 282–294; Seymour, K. E., Chronis-Tuscano, A., Halldorsdottir, T., Stupica, B., Owens, K., & Sacks, T. (2012). Emotion regulation mediates the relationship between ADHD and depressive symptoms in youth. *Journal of Abnormal Child Psychology, 40,* 595–606.

7   Garcia, C. R., Bau, C. H., Silva, K. L., Callegari-Jacques, S. M., Salgado, C. A., Fischer, A. G., Grevet, E. H. (2012). The burdened life of adults with ADHD: Impairment beyond comorbidity. *European Psychiatry, 27,* 309–313.

Chapter 12: James

1   Yoshimasu, K., Barbaresi, W. J., Colligan, R. C., Killian, J. M., Voigt, R. G., Weaver, A. L., & Katusic, S. K. (2011). Written-language disorder among children with and without ADHD in a population-based birth cohort. *Pediatrics, 128,* 605–612.

2   Mayes, S., & Calhoun, S. (2006). Frequency of reading, math, and writing disabilities in children with clinical disorders. *Learning and Individual Differences, 16,* 145–157.

3   Brown, T. E., Reichel, P. C., & Quinlan, D. M. (August 2010). Impairments of written expression in 13–25 year old students with ADHD. Poster session presented at annual meeting of the American Psychological Association, San Diego, CA; Semrud-Clikeman, M., & Harder, L. (2011). Neuropsychological correlates of written expression in college students with ADHD. *Journal of Attention Disorders, 15,* 215–223.

4   Graff, G., & Birkenstein, C. (2006). *They say, I say: The moves that matter in academic writing.* New York, NY: Norton.

5   Geller, D. A., & Brown, T. E. (2009). ADHD with obsessive-compulsive disorder. In T. E. Brown (Ed.), *ADHD comorbidities: Handbook for ADHD complications in children and adults* (pp. 177–187). Washington, DC: American Psychiatric Publishing.

6   Shafran, R., & Mansell, W. (2001). Perfectionism and psychopathology: A review of research and treatment. *Clinical Psychology Review, 21,* 879–906.

7   Young, K. S., Yue, Y. D., & Ying, L. (2011). Prevalence estimates and etiologic models of Internet addiction. In C. S. Young & C. N. de Abreu (Eds.), *Internet addiction: A handbook and guide to evaluation and treatment* (pp. 3–17). Hoboken, NJ: Wiley.

8   Blinka, L., & Smahel, D. (2011). Addiction to online role-playing games. In C. S. Young & C. N. de Abreu (Eds.), *Internet addiction: A handbook and guide to evaluation and treatment* (pp. 73–90). Hoboken, NJ: Wiley.

Chapter 13: Getting Unstuck

1   Brown, T. E., Reichel, P. C., & Quinlan, D. M. (2011). Extended time improves reading comprehension test scores for adolescents with ADHD. *Open Journal of Psychiatry, 1,* 79–87.

index

Page references followed by *fig* indicates an illustrated figure.

Coaching strategy, 201, 240

Cognitive functioning: how THC in marijuana affects, 96–97; role of emotions in, 2. *See also* Executive functions (EFs)

Cognitive impairments: caused by THC, 96–97; "chemofog" and, 113; declining estrogen level during menopause and, 110–113; OCD and cognitive inflexibility, 158–159; treatment for midlife-onset, 114–117

Cognitive inflexibility, 158–159

College difficulties: Eric's story on decline during college, 43–49; James' story on being placed on probation, 219–221; Karen's story on her rapid decline in college, 65–75; Matt's story on loss of family structure and having, 185–192. *See also* Homework assignments; School work

Compulsive buying, 206–208

Context: "the fundamental attribution error" assumption on behavior and, 49; how behavior is impacted by, 47–49; importance for people with ADHD, 49; Martin's story on making a new start in a new, 86–87. *See also* Behaviors; Change of context strategy

Contradictory emotional responses, 28

Counseling, 240–241

Counseling strategy, Karen's story on revising goals and plans, 80

Cultivating realistic hope, 241–242

D

Daily assistance strategy, Eric's story on using awakening through, 64

Damasio, Antonio, 27

Dating anxiety, 129–131

Day hospital treatment, 213–214, 217

Decision making: amygdala role in reasoning and, 26–27; automaticity of interpersonal situation in, 27–28

Default brain pattern, 31

"Delay aversion" research, 59–61

Delayed pubescent development: growth hormone treatments for, 145, 153; social problems related to, 144–146

Denial. *See* Avoidance and denial

Depression: co-occurring with ADHD, 205–206; dysthymia (low-grade chronic depression), 109–110; Lois' losses and persistent grief and, 204–206, 209–212; Major Depressive Disorder, 207; Mike's caretaker role during mother's, 133–135; SSRI medication to treat, 118, 190

Dexedrine, 56

Dexmethylphenidate, 113, 115

Digit-span test, 38

Diagnostic "pigeonholes," 5

Divorce: common complaints about adults with ADHD during, 163; Lois' marital difficulties and, 212; Lois' second marriage and, 214;

Steve's story on wife's initiation of, 159–160; study comparing adults with and without ADHD and, 162. *See also* Marriage

Dodge, Kenneth, 1, 3, 25

Dopamine, 111–112

Driver's license, 233, 234

Driving accidents, 55–56

DUI violations, 56

Dyslexia, role of attention in reading comprehension and, 68–69

Dysthymia, 109–110

E

Education. *See* ADHD education

Effort, impaired in ADHD, 17*fig*, 18

Embarrassment: Eric's feelings of rejection and, 46, 50–52; Eric's story on fear of being, 50–52; Karen's worry over being, 70, 75; Lisa's anger over her, 149; Martin's denial due to, 35, 91, 97, 104–105; Matt's covert social anxiety and, 189–190; Matt's fear of the immediate situation and, 196–197; memories of, 25; Mike on his feelings of, 128; strategies that help now but hurt later for avoiding, 235–236. *See also* Shame

Emotional attachment research, 93

The Emotional Brain (LeDoux), 2

Emotional intelligence, 92

Emotional problems: blaming the victim, 41–42; chronic stress and "willpower assumption" burden, 39–41, 236; extreme reactions, 34–35; family stresses and, 38–39; ignoring emotional information and impaired working memory, 35–38

Emotional responses: ADHD research on less capacity to "gate" emotions during, 205; automaticity of, 27–28; avoidant behavior and immobilizing, 94–95; contradictory and unrecognized, 28; difficulties people with ADHD have with, 8–9; how ADHD impairments affect processing of, 29; ignition problem, 12; impaired in ADHD, 17*fig*, 18; role of unconscious emotions in, 25–28; shaped by "bottom-up" experiences and temperament, 23–24; situational influences on the, 22–24; strategies that help now but hurt later, 235–236. *See also* Stress

Emotional self-regulation: ADHD and related problems with, 3–4; ADHD research on less capacity to "gate" emotions, 205; of conflicting or unrecognized emotions, 28, 90–94; inability to distinguish between serious threats and minor problems, 76; inadequate modulation of anxiety, 75–78; support for diagnostic criteria for ADHD to include, 11

Emotions: attentional bias due to, 9; the brain as source of all, 8; daily role played by, 7; entangled in learning and deployment of skills,